Under Discussion **The Encyclopedic Museum**

Under Discussion

The Encyclopedic Museum

Edited by
Donatien Grau

Getty Research Institute Los Angeles

CONTENTS

PREFACE AND ACKNOWLEDGMENTS

Every book is a journey. This has definitely been one. From my initial conversation on the top of the hill with former Getty Research Institute director Thomas Gaehtgens, to the times of these many conversations, six years have lapsed. They have been occupied by writing and by interviews in person and on the phone in many places across Europe, Asia, Africa, and the Americas. It has been a marvelous experience and a privilege to gather the views of such distinguished thinkers and practitioners. From a personal standpoint, what it has brought me is invaluable.

This journey began six years ago, when Thomas Gaehtgens sent me on a mission: to question and assess the meaning of the encyclopedic museum. Its concept, its realities were at stake. At that point, James Cuno's book *Museums Matter: In Praise of the Encyclopedic Museum* (Chicago: University of Chicago Press, 2013) was only a few years old, and the encyclopedic museum had become a motto of sorts. Over the course of the realization of this book, the Louvre Abu Dhabi opened and the topic of restitutions returned to the center of the discussion. The conversations in this book, which have been edited all the way to the present, gather words by specialists whose institutions and positions have sometimes changed in the span of these years. Yet, they present viewpoints that are still so relevant for today.

At this point, seeing the book realized, and the product of my travels and conversations materialized, I would like to express my heartfelt gratitude to all the participants who have given their time addressing a theme they knew to be of the utmost relevance for our worlds: the world of museums, the world of ideas, the world of culture, our human world. I would like to thank Thomas Gaehtgens, who truly initiated this process, and Mary E. Miller, who embraced it at the GRI, as well as Andrew Perchuk, Gail Feigenbaum, and Michele Ciaccio, who have supported it and followed it all the way. Conversations with many colleagues have also proven of great importance, chief among them Laurence des Cars and Sébastien Allard. Peter Behrman de Sinéty has been an important contributor in making these conversations into a text. Mary Christian made this text into a book.

This book is, in many ways, a collective and collaborative endeavor. It would not have been possible without the work of scholars, thinkers, and museum staffers who every day serve the public and provide new, more complete ways of experiencing our world. It is dedicated to all of them.

Donatien Grau

INTRODUCTION

The Encyclopedic Museum: A Catchphrase, a Concept, a History

Donatien Grau

The encyclopedic museum primarily is defined as a museum in which the works of a broad expanse of cultures coexist. The description of certain museums as encyclopedic itself has a history and problems. The model appears to be of particular significance and requires questioning especially today, when, on the one hand, many of the world's cultures tend to disappear as an effect of globalization and when, on the other, those cultures struggle to live on the same planet, as summarized already in the 1990s by Samuel Huntington's prediction of a coming "clash of civilization."[1] There is a tendency to all remain in our borders, while the knowledge of the Other, the acceptance of Otherness, as well as the recognition of the commonality among all human beings are far from being real in many parts of the world—some would argue, in any part of the world. We are, today, far from the "end of history" that was predicted, after Hegel, by Francis Fukuyama.[2]

The encyclopedic museum has been considered the remedy against such inability to sense the possible coexistence of differences and commonalities. Its definition, however, is quite difficult, as so many possible answers have been offered. At first, it can be seen as a museum model in which objects from all cultures exist under the same roof, where the identities of these cultures are not wiped out but preserved, and where the specificity of each is to be cherished, studied, and displayed to the public. In Europe, encyclopedic museums are the heirs of imperial nations such as Germany, France, and the United Kingdom. They were born in the eighteenth century—the Louvre, the British Museum—and developed through the nineteenth. Most of the time, their collections are centuries older, as they stem from kingly holdings. Yet "encyclopedic" is rarely used as a museum descriptor in Europe, and this type follows very different models in the United States and in other parts of the world, such as India and the Persian Gulf, where new forms of it are being developed.

In the United States encyclopedic museums were created with the holdings of American collectors and donors from just before the third quarter of the nineteenth century onward. The Metropolitan Museum of Art, the United States' quintessential encyclopedic museum, opened in 1870; its collections evolved and expanded through gifts and acquisitions, but it was mostly built ex nihilo. As of today, these museums with distinct histories connect and confront similar interrogations.

Recent events in the world's cultural heritage—the destruction in 2001 of the Bamiyan Buddhas in the land of Afghanistan, the destruction of the Nabataean temples in Palmyra in 2015—have shed a cruel light on the necessity to empower such institutions, where the legacy of humankind could find itself in relative safety. For reasons both theoretical and practical, the encyclopedic museum has become a tipping point where the debate on museums—for a long time limited to the world of curators, conservators, scholars, collectors, and connoisseurs—is now deeply embedded in contemporary world politics and philosophy, in the issue of how we are to live together, and, eventually, in who we are. It is therefore not surprising that the opening of the Louvre Abu Dhabi in 2017 has been accompanied by considerable debate, both for[3] and against.[4]

And yet, the encyclopedic model is under considerable pressure, as since the 1970s it has been tied into the debates on restitutions. It was recently brought to the forefront by Senegalese economist Felwine Sarr and art historian Bénédicte Savoy in their *Rapport sur la restitution du patrimoine culturel africain: Vers une nouvelle éthique relationnelle* (Report on the restitution of African cultural heritage: toward new relational ethics), delivered to the French government in June 2018. They held museums accountable for the conditions in which African works in French collections were acquired and suggested new ways of bringing stolen works back to the African continent, as well as pushed for other strategies of exchange. The report, as well as the powerful responses and debates it provoked, addressed mostly "anthropological" collections that include works of African heritage, but it also more broadly questioned museums that have such holdings, and other objects brought under unclear conditions. Since the encyclopedic museum considers itself a repository for such objects, its status also came under question. Recent political movements have also placed under severe scrutiny the very attempt to offer one narrative for the world—a narrative that could be questioned as coming from forces of domination.

These recent developments have occurred in a world that has changed dramatically over the last two decades. The debate now relates to whether artworks looted over centuries should be given back to the national states from where they were expatriated. The encyclopedic museum was the result of and the answer to different conditions in history, and the need for the accessibility and protection of the world's heritage. The issues at stake are political. How can the encyclopedic museum propose a laboratory for a view of the world at its best, creating a model for a community? If all sorts of objects made by humans can coexist, why should humans not be able to do the same? How can such a museum address its own history, and what should it do with its collections of questionable origins? This approach has been taken in museums in different places of the world, stemming from the traditional institutions of the West—the Louvre, the British Museum, the Met, the Hermitage, Berlin's Museum Island—and is expanding as a methodology throughout many parts of the globe.

The questions are political and theoretical. An encyclopedic museum brings together objects as both testimony and as matrices of contemplation, as documentation and as art. Thus these questions emanate from the nature of art as representation, its relation to the humanity of museum visitors, the role of the inner life, and the relevance of the surrounding world. It is not by chance that science was thrown out of encyclopedic museums in the nineteenth century; even though stones and minerals were very much present in the original British Museum, they are now completely absent from it and from the narratives drawn from it. Encyclopedic museums are considered to be the devices humankind has at its disposal to write its own history—and to experience it with objects.

The encyclopedic museum presents itself as an inclusive museum for humanity in the making—from its historical past to its very present. The current debate makes such a definition more acute, even more relevant. It bridges the gap established over the course of the nineteenth century between the museum and the library, between narrative and contemplation. We would like to argue here that this museum type represents no mere gathering of objects, but in fact a milestone where we question how we relate to one another, how things relate to one another, and how we can learn from things as well as experience them aesthetically. The eighteenth-century genesis of this model of museum precedes the age of Hegelian aesthetics, and therefore it can offer something other than aesthetic contemplation—although that can be enjoyed as well. As more museums are founded in the world, and as museums have become established as repositories for our cultures, it appears fundamental to engage with this model anew—not only as existing institutions, but also considering museums in general, and our contemporary existence.

A Problem of Definition

One needs to draw the line between the "encyclopedic museum," which is a modern phrase used in the English-speaking world to describe such museums as the British Museum and the Metropolitan Museum of Art, and the "universal museum," the "musée universel," which can be related to the phrase used to describe the Louvre from its creation at the beginning of the nineteenth century: Muséum Central des Arts.[5]

These two phrases seem to overlap: the French, and the world influenced by the French, would say "musée universel"—and the Louvre indeed defines itself as such a museum[6]—while the British, the Americans, and the world influenced by them would say "encyclopedic museum"; but essentially they would cover the same reality. The Louvre, the Hermitage, the British Museum, Berlin's Museum Island, and the Metropolitan Museum of Art would all equally be universal museums and encyclopedic museums—which in a sense is accurate.

Nonetheless, there is a fundamental difference in naming those museums, which in fact conveys a substantial discrepancy in their ambition: *encyclopedic* signifies that every entry is a box, which can connect to another entry, another box (there are indications at the end of every entry suggesting another consultation), but which nonetheless is separate. The very idea of universality alludes to the oneness of mankind and its creations. In a sense, the universal museum would be a preface to the contemporary museum and its global approach. As Henri Loyrette argues in these pages, here the term *encyclopedic* is a method, while *universality* is an ambition. There would be a historical oneness of the world that would be correlated to a contemporary oneness. The notion of encyclopedia is much more rooted in a plurality, a multiplicity that would then build this unity.[7]

In the recent past, the word *encyclopedic* seems to have gained ground over *universal*, as if there were, in the whole idea of encyclopedia, more openness to differences and how they can be played out. The use of the phrase *encyclopedic museums* is often traced back to the Enlightenment, in relation to the practice and ideology of encyclopedism; however, the phrase that actually comes from the Enlightenment, and was used then, is *musée universel*. So there is this paradox that the phrase we would consider to be more Enlightenment-oriented in fact does not come from the Enlightenment, while the less category-based one is in fact a recent construct that appeared in discourse only over the past two decades—thus Carol Duncan and Alan Wallach's seminal 1980 essay "The Universal Survey Museum,"[8] using a description that has since then been replaced in public discourse by *encyclopedic museum*.

Today the term *encyclopedic museum* conveys a very specific meaning: it is a museum that includes as many cultures as possible as well as one—and this is the new current—that brings these cultures into a dialogue, and perhaps even includes them in a narrative. Therein lies the major difference between the British Museum in 1753 and the British Museum in the twenty-first century: the British Museum then was an updated and more open version of a *Kunstkammer* and a *Schatzkammer*;[9] it brought objects of different status and origins together—sometimes including books and even natural specimens—but there was no plan for giving a comprehensive insight into the many manifestations of human creativity.

There was no voiced encyclopedic desire—or comprehensive narrative—in what is considered the first encyclopedic museum. Even in previous manifestations, such as the Ashmolean Museum in Oxford,[10] which, too, came from the stream of the *Schatzkammer* and brought it into the public domain of museums, there was no narrative and comprehensive intent built on the evolution of the collection and on the definition of what the public mission of a museum is. The architecture of these early museums was tentative, not self-aware, and it kept shifting. The Louvre famously had a Mexican museum, when such was the trend; Louis-Philippe opened a museum devoted to the navy; there was Chinese art at the Louvre, which then moved to the Musée Guimet. The presences and absences, the moves in and out, were all timely. They followed neither a two-hundred-year rule that would extend for the whole history of the museum, nor a framework.[11]

There are many differences between the "original" museums that are today deemed encyclopedic and today's version of them; the model certainly may come from these very roots of bringing objects of various sorts and origins together, but it is also, and perhaps even more so, a contemporary paradigm, a response to the limitations of the previous paradigms of museums that have appeared and manifested themselves over the last century and a half. As a model, it is the museums' response to their own limitations. The concept of an encyclopedic museum is the combination of two apparently separate orders, those of the museum—objects—and of the library—the encyclopedia. This combination means that the information contained in the library finds itself embodied, and, as a consequence, the artworks are also taken in a narrative that makes them something other than polarized objects—but in fact, the artworks are a network of ideas, containers for information and thought ready to be unveiled.

The institutions currently known as encyclopedic museums are, more than anything, very particular and rooted; they are read from the point of view of encyclopedism. The Louvre, the Hermitage, the British Museum, the institutions of Berlin's Museum Island, and the Metropolitan Museum of Art are tightly connected to the narratives of national identity: the Louvre's location in the palace of the kings, the Hermitage in the palace of the czars, the British Museum bearing "British" even in its name, the Museum Island being a creation of the very young German Empire in the late nineteenth century. Even the Met is clearly tied to its location in the metropolis of New York and the rise of American power. The institutions considered encyclopedic, and therefore open to the world, beyond the limitations of a nation, are in fact equally national, and even local. None of these institutions could be considered a purely, intrinsically, and exclusively encyclopedic one, or exclusively opened to the world and refusing other forms of identity.

Questioning the encyclopedic museum today as a cultural, political, philosophical, and evidently artistic paradigm goes beyond the reality of existing encyclopedic museums, even though their reality is to be taken into consideration and analyzed. But the issues at hand in the encyclopedic museum have much more to do with the definition of what this form of museum signifies in the present—how it can be defined, redefined, and how its challenges are set now, rather than in the examination of the current manifestations of that museum format, which had not been set when those museums were conceived. This questioning can only be done with the understanding that the encyclopedic museum, in its actuality, is always something else—a model challenging every model, including itself; it is open for questioning categories and for investigating the possibilities of humanity.

Debates

Over the last two decades, encyclopedic museums have found themselves more than ever to be in the public debate. The controversy around 2000 over restitutions,[12] reignited in 2018, has led to a questioning of encyclopedic museums as centers for gathering objects acquired under questionable conditions. The debate deals with the guilt inherent in having collected objects that had been taken from their contexts, looted from their civilizations, and brought into Western metropolises. This debate has led to an intense critique of Western and encyclopedic museums as products of empires, whose genesis was inherently culpable, as they did not have the moral right to tell a narrative of the world to the world.

The first response museums formulated implied a critical rethinking of what the encyclopedic museum was and an assertion of its role. It manifested itself in several ways: first, through the "Declaration on the Importance and Value of Universal Museums," signed in December 2002 by the directors of almost twenty leading institutions (many of which were in fact neither encyclopedic museums nor universal museums per se),[13] in which the signing directors stated, "Over time, objects so acquired—whether by purchase, gift, or partage—have become part of the museums that have cared for them, and by extension part of the heritage of the nations which house them. Today we are especially sensitive to the subject of a work's original context, but we should not lose sight of the fact that museums too provide a valid and valuable context for objects that were long ago displaced from their original source." It is very clear in those words that this declaration is a reaction to the claims for restitutions rather than an assertion of a model in itself. At the same moment, the development of the notion of an encyclopedic museum led to the production of critical content.

The debate over encyclopedic museums is intertwined with the debates over museums themselves, and eventually over the status of art objects in a cultural display in and beyond nations. What has stood at the center of that debate was the fact that a nation-state—by its nature modern and which owned objects that had been created on its territory centuries or millennia ago by civilizations often remote from those that occupy the national territory—was antagonistic to the construct of a museum that was designed to set itself free from the borders of nations and provide an extraordinarily open view onto the world.[14] That debate led to claims that works belonged to the nations that had produced them, as opposed to a cosmopolitan view of the world, in which all civilizations were to be treated as individual yet in dialogue with the great human community and that all works could be gathered in one place, beyond the localization of their original cultures. In that regard, the encyclopedic museum offered a way out of both national borders and global culture, of wiping out local identities and their limitations. It is, in fact, a layering of identities.

New Debates

Concurrent with the debate on restitution, the elevation of the encyclopedic museum model has led to more experimentations in theory and practice over the last decade than in the previous hundred years. The British Museum has launched a program of worldwide traveling exhibitions and has produced narratives from all around the world. Non-encyclopedic museums, such as the J. Paul Getty Museum in Los Angeles, the CSMVS (Chhatrapati Shivaji Maharaj Vastu Sangrahalaya, or King Shivaji Museum) in Mumbai, and the Fine Arts Museums of San Francisco are considering ways to place their geographical collections in an encyclopedic framework of sorts, by means of temporary exhibitions and loans. The Louvre has created new platforms to experiment with the structure of the encyclopedic museum: the Louvre-Lens, which opened in 2012, consists of a temporary exhibition center and a space for collection display according to dynamics that are no longer those of the stable geographical order that governs the Paris museum. The Galerie du Temps, in which chronology brings together works from very different origins, emphasizes the varieties of human creativity as well as the similarities.

In 2017 the Louvre Abu Dhabi opened, which is another attempt at building a non-national encyclopedic museum and which has the benefit of not being burdened by the emphases of an ancient collection and its history. The United Arab Emirates had an interest in having such a model established as part of a wider approach at shaping the minds of a cultural elite in the Middle East;[15] critics have been quick to see this development in the Gulf as a succursal of the Louvre,[16] and to look into the will of the UAE to have such an institution as simply a form of tourism. But these are also serious attempts that manifest the desire for the encyclopedic museum as a model. The purpose is therefore not simply to develop within the walls of the first institutions to bear this name but also to expand, in new museums, in developments to museums, and even to shape a new model.

At the time the "Declaration on the Importance and Value of Universal Museums" was released, there was a need for advocacy toward encyclopedic museums—they were under attack and therefore had to assert their relevance. In recent times, however, there has been little question that this-model of museum is relevant, that it matters, and therefore can inspire other realities. The imperial roots of the original of that museum model—and currently the main manifestations—have been questioned and have by now become an object of self-awareness. What matters now is no longer the criticism that museums come from empires—something they cannot change—but how they can deal with such imperial pasts, and engage with the future.

A Museological Interrogation

From a museological point of view, there appears to be more promise in the model of the encyclopedic museum than in the models of the museum of modern art, the traditional art museum, or the ethnographic museum, which are all rooted in Western definitions of modernity in their clear separation of the status of the objects, which is by definition rooted in Western culture. A museum of modern art,[17] for example, is founded to honor the sacredness of each object it contains; in the traditional art museum, the strategies of displaying paintings and sculptures follow the historical narratives of the picture gallery; and in the ethnographic museum, whose structure comes from a methodology of the human sciences defined at the beginning of the twentieth century—from the Musée de l'Homme in Paris, which was the center of anthropological research—objects are seen as documents, not as subjects of contemplation. This model is now undergoing intense scrutiny, as we are now retrieving the circumstances of the acquisition of each of those objects and looking into their histories.

The methodology of the encyclopedic museum is even more promising than the success in the 1990s and 2000s of the contemporary museum, as defined by the Guggenheim: the contemporary museum, by its nature, builds on the reality of global culture. It creates a space above local, regional, and national identities, in which all such definitions of human beings and their creativity are minimalized in order to highlight the existence of all beings and all things in a nomadic world, where there are no actual roots anymore and where the same art can be shown in Shanghai, Abu Dhabi, Delhi, London, Paris, Johannesburg, Helsinki, Bilbao, New York, and São Paulo.[18] It is global.

By its conservative structure, the encyclopedic museum engages much more deeply with the past and with the legacies of humankind than the contemporary museum does. At the same time, as it aims to gather all of humankind's creations—just as the encyclopedia can collect diverse realities in the same book. Even in the case of the word *universal*, which is primarily used for the Louvre, the structure of the museum still highlights the diversity of the schools, time periods, and locations: the universality manifests itself in encyclopedism. The encyclopedic museum, going into the past, carries within itself the depth of humankind. It uses the past to give depth to the present and it increasingly allows itself to engage with the contemporary world, which it can do with a methodology that is consistently different from the museum of modern art. The encyclopedic museum considers the potential for the equality of all objects, and therefore the possibility for new definitions.

History is to be written using the wisdom of Michel de Certeau.[19] It is always written from the present, which allows him to shed a specific light on certain aspects of the past. This pertains as well to the current discussion on the encyclopedic museum: history is a dialogue with our contemporary, multicultural lives.

The Online World

In the first decade of this century, and increasingly into the second, Google has made itself the metaphor for the Internet, and therefore for a comprehensive encyclopedia of images and knowledge. This is an alternative answer to the encyclopedic museum—but now on a screen, and not three-dimensional, and not actually present in front of the viewer. Knowledge and things are placed on even footing, but things can be organized according to different structures. In that sense, the paradigm is inverted: Google is the library adopting the structures of the museum. This is why the California company has been quick to explore the possibilities of hybridizing its museumlike nature with the world of museums, putting together what might be closer to an objectless encyclopedic museum, in the sense of a museum that would encompass everything and organize it. Google Art Project, founded in 2011, now known as Google Arts & Culture,[20] currently encompasses more than six million pictures, from fourteen hundred institutions, including many of the world's leading museums.

At the same time as the world of communication changed, so did the world of art. The world of contemporary art has made itself into an ever-growing bubble—which every contemporary art has always been, since the seventeenth century[21]—that is based on the belief systems of modernity—of the spiritual value of an artistic work and its maker, whatever the work, whatever the maker—which has made thinkers and the general audience wary of the intrinsic features of the things, gestures, experiences, and protocols that are qualified as artworks. Contemporary art has engaged deeply with issues of museums, their history, and their dark or glimmering stories, and it has made the museum itself into an object for creation and thought.[22]

The encyclopedic museum, by definition, stands between the ethnographic museum, the picture gallery, and the "museum of art and culture," which has been, ominously, reused by Google to name its initiative. Being a hybrid of these different models, the encyclopedic museum offers a platform to reassess the nature of works of art and objects to determine whether they can stand on their own—with narrativity enriching the experience, not primarily defining it. Such an approach allows for a comparative take on art, displaced from its modern monologue to a dialogue with design, imagery, and knowledge, and therefore rethought in its specificity from a conversation with other media.

Museums and the Public

Another side to that shift in art lies in the reality of museums themselves. As actual institutions located in buildings, they have to deal with a considerable increase in their audience, their constituency, and, therefore, their public mission. When the Grand Louvre opened in 1993, it was designed for an estimated audience of five million visitors a year over the coming twenty years; in 2011, attendance rose to ten million, and it was over ten million in 2018. Attendance has also risen proportionately in all major museums, which are cosmopolitan institutions; people from all over the world travel to visit them and return to their native countries, enriched from experiencing the multiplicity and the unity of the world.

Museums are reflections of their time, as is history, following de Certeau's definition. Therefore, it may be possible to think they have been present in our cities forever—an illusion they often give to many of us. But they have not. The challenges and demands of culture in today's world are different than they were in earlier centuries. Museums have their constituencies, and the work they provide requires them to be in dialogue with the shifts in our world. The encyclopedic museum's status as a place of contemplation and learning, rooted in its location but connecting itself to all others, might be the form of the present and the future.

Some the questions raised by this book are: When does the encyclopedia start and when does it end? Can we consider that the encyclopedic museum as a complete entity is a dream that moves away from us, that it facilitates the opening up of narratives from one object to a story, and on to many stories? What if encyclopedicization were a method rather than an outcome? What if the encyclopedic museum belonged mostly to the future?

The Methodology for This Project

It is a remarkable fact that there is very little bibliography on encyclopedic museums: James Cuno's *Museums Matter: In Praise of the Encyclopedic Museum*; the Louvre conference of 2011, which was published in 2016; the International Council of Museums (ICOM) statements and replies; Neil MacGregor's *History of the World in 100 Objects* (London: British Museum, 2011); some parts in Jean-Loup Amselle's strongly critical essay *Le musée exposé*; a number of publications on the Louvre Abu Dhabi, such as *Le Louvre*

Abu Dhabi: Nouveau musée universel?; and the catalog of the exhibition held in 2014 to celebrate the burgeoning institution, *Louvre Abu Dhabi: Naissance d'un musée* (Paris: Skira Flammarion, 2013). There are, too, some scholarly articles—such as Carol Duncan and Allan Wallach's essay, which uses the uneasy phrase "universal survey museum," and actually says quite little about the major issues with which such museums engage. But there is no account of the very high stakes that are performed in encyclopedic museums today[23] and the many ways of empowering them and exploiting their status as a forum for art and culture.

It felt timely to provide such an account by bringing together the voices that make the universe of encyclopedic museums today and to represent them on a global basis. These include, of course, the voices of museum directors who lead the institutions that are traditionally described as encyclopedic, and who deal with these issues in thought and actions, from New York to Paris, Saint Petersburg, London, Dakar, Delhi, Los Angeles, and Mumbai. As such, we have aimed to include voices from multiple continents, in order to present accounts from both well-established and growing institutions.

Equally, we have aimed to consider the encyclopedic museum not only as an existing institutional reality, but also as a concept, a project, a way to think of the museum as a device for our cultures. We include the voices of thinkers who theoretically engage with the philosophical issues in terms of cultural policy, including Anthony Appiah, Bachir Souleymane Diagne, Homi K. Bhabha, and Partha Chatterjee; and of historians and museum scholars who can place those issues in historical perspective, such as Marc Fumaroli, Krzysztof Pomian, Bénédicte Savoy, and Kavita Singh. We also hear the voices of artists Camille Henrot and Grayson Perry, who in their projects *Grosse Fatigue* (2013) and *The Tomb of the Unknown Craftsman* (2011) directly tackled the structures of the encyclopedic museum and used them for making art; as well as the contemporary art curator Massimiliano Gioni, who titled the 2013 Venice Biennale he curated *The Encyclopedic Palace*, and who deals with the encyclopedia from a creative point of view, orienting it toward the past in order to deal with contemporary art in a new way. Others who lent their voices are Amit Sood, the director of the Google Cultural Institute, responsible for the company's "encyclopedia of art online;" *The Economist*'s culture editor Fiammetta Rocco; and political leaders and activists who are engaged with world museums, such as restitution activist George Abungu, UNESCO director general Irina Bokova, and Zaki Nusseibeh, the cultural advisor to the Ministry of Presidential Affairs of the United Arab

Emirates, who has played a crucial role in spearheading the project for the Louvre Abu Dhabi.

Each of these men and women answers questions that relate to their own facets of experience as well as to the major issues at stake in their institutions. Some of them are obvious contributors for such an inquiry—James Cuno, Philippe de Montebello—while others are unexpected.

In a way, the question of the encyclopedic museum is as much a philosophical one as it is historical and political one.

What is at stake is what we see as art and the way we value it. But it is also our politics, the relations between cultures, and the way we exist as human beings in relation to our past, our present, and our future. It is a model and methodology of museum that offers remarkable potential, in art as well as outside the arena of art. By gathering the words of such leading figures, some of them speaking personally, other on institutional terms, we have aimed to evaluate the field that the encyclopedic museum finds itself in today—as opposed to the one it found itself in ten years ago, when it was first consciously defined as an institutional model. It does not rest simply on one methodology—whether one of the contemplation of art or of the learning from an artifact—rather, it confronts different methodologies and blends them. It does not follow only one hierarchical canon and its model allows for the reshaping of our categories. It would be irrelevant to wonder on the status of cosmology or nature in an art museum. The divisions are quite set. In the encyclopedic museum, these fields of knowledge are to be set in motion, and we are to question how we see things and strip bare our preconceived ideas so we can reach the objects for the many stories they can tell us. The art museum was rooted in a time of relative rarefaction of the audience—a time of aesthetes who aimed to spread their passion. This time is not gone, but objects are now mutant entities existing in and facing a digital age. History is open again.

The nature of the encyclopedic museum model needs to be defined not exclusively from the old European and American models, but from the polyphony of world voices and approaches in order to ensure that the encyclopedic museum is a free field for debate as it pertains to our open and self-aware world. It is a model of extreme possibilities—discursive, visual, institutional, online, practical. The encyclopedic museum's presence and function extends far beyond the capital cities that were once its exclusive sites to include many world cities and virtual locations.

The encyclopedic museum today is a paradigm as much as—perhaps even more than—it is a reality. It offers a method of looking at objects in relation to each other and signals the permeability of things between them. It is a way of looking at the collections and at the mission of a museum, unearthing and establishing their history. Defining the encyclopedic museum can be done in many ways—historically, philosophically, museologically, or politically. Every inquiry can offer a different take on humanity, and every attempt is a layer added onto the conversation of who we are and how we can live together. This book, a miniature form of encyclopedism in thinking about the museum, aims to open questions and to celebrate the fact that encyclopedism is not an end; it is just a starting point.

1. Samuel Huntington, *The Clash of Civilizations and the Remaking of World Order* (New York: Simon & Schuster, 1996).
2. Such is the title of his much-debated essay, ending with a question mark: Francis Fukuyama, "The End of History?," *The National Interest* 16 (Summer 1989): 3-18; and of his 1992 book, *The End of History and the Last Man* (New York: Perennial, 1992). Fukuyama himself has changed his approach, most recently in his *Political Order and Political Decay: From the Industrial Revolution to the Globalization of Democracy* (New York: Farrar, Straus & Giroux, 2014).
3. Charlotte Chastel-Rousseau, Laurence des Cars, and Dominique de Font-Réaulx, eds., *Le Louvre Abu Dhabi: Nouveau musée universel?* (Paris: Presses Universitaires de France, 2015).
4. Jean-Loup Amselle, *Le musée exposé* (Fécamps: Lignes, 2016).
5. Jean Chatelain, *Dominique Vivant Denon et le Louvre de Napoléon* (Paris: Perrin, 1999).
6. Pierre Rosenberg, "Le musée universel entre nationalisme et universalisme," in Chastel-Rousseau, Cars, and Font-Réaulx, *Le Louvre Abu Dhabi*, 37–44.
7. See François Jullien, *On the Universal, the Uniform, the Common, and Dialogue between Cultures* (Cambridge: Polity, 2014).
8. Carol Duncan and Alan Wallach, "The Universal Survey Museum," *Art History* 3 (December 1980): 448–69.
9. David M. Wilson, *The British Museum: A History* (London: British Museum Press, 2002).
10. R. F. Ovenell, *The Ashmolean Museum 1683-1894* (Oxford: Oxford University Press, 1986).
11. Dominique de Font-Réaulx, "Le Louvre, modèle singulier pour le musée universel?," in Chastel-Rousseau, Cars, and Font-Réaulx, *Le Louvre Abu Dhabi*, 45-62; Jean-Loup Amselle, "Le musée du Louvre: Un "universel" à géométrie variable," in *Le musée exposé*, 45-65; and Félix Fénéon, "Iront-ils au Louvre: Enquête sur les arts lointains," *Bulletin de la vie artistique* 24 (15 November 1920): 662–69, 25 (1 December 1920): 693–703, and 26 (15 December 1920): 726–38.
12. See, among a large number of publications, John Henry Merryman, ed., *Imperialism, Art, and Restitution* (Cambridge: Cambridge University Press, 2010); Derek Gilman, *The Idea of Cultural Heritage* (Cambridge: Cambridge University Press, 2010); Jeanette Greenfield, *The Return of Cultural Treasures* (Cambridge: Cambridge University Press, 2013); and George Abungu, "Declaration

on the Importance and Value of Universal Museums, 2002, published in *ICOM News* 1 (2004): 5.

13. The museums were the Art Institute of Chicago; Munich, Alte Pinakothek and Neue Pinakothek; Berlin, Staatliche Museen; Cleveland Museum of Art; Los Angeles, J. Paul Getty Museum; New York, Solomon R. Guggenheim Museum; Los Angeles County Museum of Art; Paris, Musée du Louvre; New York, The Metropolitan Museum of Art; Museum of Fine Arts, Boston; New York, Museum of Modern Art; Florence, Opificio delle Pietre Dure; Philadelphia Museum of Art; Madrid, Museo Nacional del Prado; Amsterdam, Rijksmuseum; Saint Petersburg, State Hermitage Museum; Madrid, Thyssen-Bornemisza Museum; New York, Whitney Museum of American Art; and London, British Museum.
14. On the relation of the museum to the nation: Dominique Poulot, *Musée, nation, patrimoine, 1789-1815* (Paris: Gallimard, Bibliothèque des Histoires, 1997).
15. Zaki Anwar Nusseibeh, "Les musées universels d'Abu Dhabi: Perspective historique," in Chastel-Rousseau, Cars, and Font-Réaulx, *Le Louvre Abu Dhabi*, 15-36; Alexandre Kazerouni, *Le miroir des cheikhs: Musée et politique dans les principautés du Golfe Persique* (Paris: Presses Universitaires de France, 2017).
16. In Jean-Loup Amselle's words, on the back cover of the book.
17. Glenn D. Lowry, *The New Museum of Modern Art* (New York: MoMA, 2004).
18. On the global contemporary museum: Marsha Goss, "The Solomon R. Guggenheim Museum's Approach toward Contemporary Curatorial Practice," PhD diss., West Virginia University, 2014; Michael Kimmelmann, "The Globe-Straddler of the Art World: The Guggenheim's Thomas Krens," *Museum International* 51, no. 1 (January 1999): 51-55; David Dolan, "Cultural Franchising, Imperialism and Globalisation: What's New?," *International Journal of Heri-tage Studies* 5, no. 1 (January 1999): 58-64; and Joseba Zulaika, "Krens' Taj Mahal: The Guggenheim's Global Love Museum," *Discourse* 23, no. 1 (2001): 100-118.
19. Michel de Certeau, *The Writing of History*, trans. Tom Conley (New York: Columbia University Press, 1992).
20. Available at https://www.google.com/culturalinstitute/. And its statement of purpose: https://www.google.com/culturalinstitute/about/. On the Google Art Project: Elizabeth C. Mansfield, "Google Art Project and Digital Scholarship in the Visual Arts," *Visual Resources* 30, no. 1 (January 2014): 110-17.
21. Michael North, *Art and Commerce in the Dutch Golden Age* (New Haven: Yale University Press, 1997).
22. Among many exhibitions are *Grayson Perry: The Tomb of the Unknown Craftsman*, British Museum, 2011; and Walid Raad's three-year collaboration with the Louvre between 2013 and 2016.
23. Some attempts exist and remained in a limited approach and framework; among the most notable is Kavita Singh, "The Universal Museum: View from Below," in *Witnesses to History: A Compendium of Documents and Writings on the Return of Cultural Objects*, ed. Lyndel V. Prott (Paris: UNESCO, 2009).

Origins and Practice of Encyclopedic Museums

1

1

Marc Fumaroli

Professor emeritus, Collège de France

Donatien Grau: What's your position on the question of the encyclopedic museum?

Marc Fumaroli: I confess I don't very much like taking a "position" in public or even in private—particularly in this case, as the concept of the encyclopedic museum strikes me as neither sensible nor timely. The most ambitious museums, the Louvre and the Metropolitan Museum of Art, have a hard enough time managing their visitor flows and adding to their collections, which cover a vast area (though not exhaustive, either geographically or historically) to want to grow further. Moreover, how would they find room for all the intellectual disciplines—literature, the arts, the sciences, technology? Fortunately, a mammoth "encyclopedic" museum is neither conceivable nor, above all, desirable. Imagine the Louvre supplemented by the Musée des Arts et Métiers, the Musée du Jardin des Plantes, the Planétarium, and so on. Imagine the Met in New York joining forces in a Central Park cleared of its trees with the Smithsonian Institution, Washington's Library of Congress, and other jewels of American museography.

The gap between the imaginary encyclopedic museum and the major museums with which we are familiar, which are generalist in only a very relative sense, was once filled by the universal expositions, which were ephemeral (in other words, the opposite of the museum), and emphasized the rise of Atlantic civilization between 1850 and 1937, each one representing the last word in modern progress everywhere and of every kind. Charles Baudelaire was not above publishing a review of the Paris exhibition of

1855, and in 1893 Henry Adams devoted some anxious pages to the Chicago World's Fair. Monumental relics of these expos can be found in Paris (the Eiffel Tower, the Grand and Petit Palais, etc.), Chicago (the Museum of Science and Industry), and elsewhere. The institution survives to this day but lacks of its former radiance.

In 1970 the Met put on a vast exhibition called *New York Painting and Sculpture: 1940–1970*. Organized by Henry Geldzahler, it was accompanied by a hefty catalog in which Clement Greenberg claimed for New York the suzerainty over the arts that had previously been exercised by Rome and Paris, in turn. A copy of this catalog landed on Georges Pompidou's desk at the Élysée Palace and the president saw red. He ordered the director of the Musée des Arts Décoratifs to mount a rival exhibition, *Paris 1945–1970*, at the Grand Palais. This was a failure, not least because the opening was sabotaged by a detachment of artists who were furious at not having been invited. In his cabinet the president had a highly gifted alumnus of the École Normale Supérieure, Sébastien Loste, who was privately preparing a book on the world's fairs. Loste put to Pompidou the idea of attaching his name to a "permanent universal exposition" in Paris that would present the world with the very latest in (preferably French) arts and technology. This resulted in a competition whose jury selected the most "Brutalist" of all the submitted projects. The president was taken aback by the winning model but refused to overrule the jury. Valéry Giscard d'Estaing, who succeeded him in 1974, hated the project but didn't dare challenge it in view of how far the work had already progressed. In the upper echelons of the administration, people were vying with one another to argue with the greatest enthusiasm for a project that was all set to make New York jealous. The superb documentary commissioned from Roberto Rossellini, shot during the construction of the *pompidolium* and highlighting the aggressive character of its architecture, was prohibited from being shown, and remains so. The industrial design center withered away to the point of oblivion and the very cramped museum displays few of its accumulated riches, favoring instead exhibitions that beat the drum for "contemporary" Americano-global art.

Instead of building encyclopedic museums in the air, it would be better for us to focus our resources and efforts on the reality of our small- and medium-sized museums and on orienting the over-large public of our major museums—the development of individual taste, rather than all-out cultural tourism, being the ultimate aim of the museum as an institution. (2016)

2

Partha Chatterjee

Professor, Columbia University, New York;
former director, Center for Studies in Human Sciences,
University of Kolkata

Donatien Grau: Your work has consistently questioned the status of the narratives of history, and I would like to ask you how you feel toward the idea of the encyclopedic museum as this all-encompassing structure in which all human works would be gathered.

Partha Chatterjee: The idea of the encyclopedia stems from the project to include everything that there is to know. Does talking about an encyclopedic museum mean placing into one place the equivalent of the set of volumes in which all of human knowledge was gathered? Such was, indeed, the ambition of the encyclopedia.

The idea of museums as universal collections representing the entire world went away in the course of the nineteenth and twentieth centuries. It was felt that to place everything that is worth collecting under one single roof was an impossible task to achieve. It simply could not be done. Therefore, you now have specialized art museums, national museums, science museums, and so on. One can therefore wonder whether your questioning of bringing the encyclopedic museum into the present, or even into the future, is not trying to get back to an older idea. When confronting that idea today, we have to think of the reason that presided over the Enlightenment project of producing encyclopedias: the premise for inclusion in the encyclopedia was that it was something wondrous, because it was true.

The notion of truth has acquired a certain kind of sacredness: science and the newly discovered power of reason were considered able to provide true knowledge. This true knowledge needed to be put together in one place, and that place was to be the encyclopedia, which made completely irrelevant all of the older traditions of knowledge—the Scriptures, etc. Most of that was deemed useless and false.

The museum, too, in a sense had such a function as a pedagogical institution for people who can appreciate this wonder. But the idea of the wonder was performed in a different way: in the museum, the purpose was to draw people into a more serious encounter with what was true. Here, we have to take into consideration the separation between the museum and the library that happened during the nineteenth century.

This has to do with the way in which the world of science and the world of art were separated from each other. You had the much stricter, almost dramatic claims of science to say, "Yes, this is true, and this is what we know to be true." As such, the world of myth and religion, of representation, had no place here.

The kind of collections the British Museum might have had, which would have included things from the ancient worlds to the Islamic world and all sorts of other places, were considered worth studying as objects from the old world, but they were not science.

In the name of science, what had been the logical function of the museum was considered irrelevant: the museum of art was separated, as its function was not to speak about the truth. Even museums of history and cultures did not speak of the truth in the same manner that science would have done. The world of poetry, the world of history, albeit being separated, could have a place, but this place was not to be confused with science. That distinction began to be made.

This distinction is very problematic, as some old museums, such as the British Museum, continue to have objects that could be considered part of different types of collections. But new museums, created since the beginning of the nineteenth century, functioned according to this divide between science and art, and fed either one idea or the other—the truth of science on one side, and aesthetic contemplation on the other. Obviously, that has an impact on the idea of what the visitor is to expect from visiting these museums, and how he or she is taught by that experience.

Today this raises many questions. We might ask ourselves about how collections are presented and how necessary it is to implement a pedagogical focus to dispel myths, superstitions, and religious dogma. In fact, we need to get people to understand why something has been established as true in a scientific sense, even though there were other truths at other moments in history, which were not what we today consider to be scientific.

Encyclopedic museums have the power to return to their roots and question the very notion of the true, which no other museum can do in the same way. Today's museums have very different functions; the new encyclopedic museum could do something critical.

DG: The space of the encyclopedic museum would therefore be a sort of bridge between different forms of museums.

PC: That leads me to another question: Would it not be an interesting possibility for the encyclopedic museum today to bring back these two separate entities in the same place—science and humanist knowledge?

There could be two ways of looking at the truth of humankind. You could think of human beings as a natural biological species. There is a whole science of evolution, etc. Within a museum of natural history, you could easily see the human being as part of this natural world; the human being could be seen from a biological point of view, all the way to modern genetics. This gives one sort of understanding of what the human being is. Then, there is another sort of understanding—and here we return to the distinction made at the times of the Renaissance and of humanism. We can also see the human being as part of what has become known as the humanities: a species that creates intellectual and artistic works—philosophy, poetry, the arts, etc. The distinction is very strong. And one can ask: Could those two things be brought together?

Could the humanistic tradition, which would include human beings and their aspects of culture, art, imagination, etc. be brought back with the aspects of natural history, the biological aspects, within the same institutional space?

It is not simply a question of bringing the two collections together but also one of putting together a common pedagogical approach that would combine the scientific with the humanistic and make itself the purpose of the museum—the truly encyclopedic museum. This is the interesting question, it seems to me: Is there a way, at all, to bring those two divided fields together again, in the museum? The universities are still dividing these fields into faculties: you have a faculty of science, arts, humanities, social science. They don't necessarily go together, even in the academic world.

DG: One could argue, indeed, that the encyclopedic museum functions according to a very partial encyclopedia: it is the encyclopedia of what humans have made. The encyclopedic museum is a sort of temple humanity has erected to itself.

PC: Once the museum stopped being just a collection that very wealthy or very politically powerful people could access as a pastime—a sophisticated pastime but a pastime nevertheless—it became something that belongs to the public world. As a consequence, the pedagogical side of it is absolutely central. You cannot think of the museum without thinking of some educational project. My approach is inherently pedagogical: it would be an experience for visitors to think, and therefore from which to have a much wider approach to the world.

We now have to think of how we would bring together those objects, those pieces of knowledge that for the last two hundred years have been kept separated. Bringing them together would not mean simply becoming universalist—and not only in a humanistic way—but also negotiating that unity within a single institutional space. This is a major challenge.

One of the things that one might think of is this: rather than trying to do this all at once, it might be possible to think of specific things that are done in art museums and somehow find an interesting way of combining them with what would ordinarily be done in the science museum.

Could we think in terms of the use of technology, in terms of the use of many devices that combine the biological, the technological, the scientific, and what is considered to partake in the humanities—art, poetry? For instance, there is an interesting place where a questioning of art and architecture might be highly significant, as architecture is hugely technological and involves a number of elements that come straight out of the natural sciences. A museum of architecture from classical times to very contemporary times, which would combine this so-called aesthetic with the technological in interesting ways, could precisely open up this approach of trying to teach people about how the pursuit of purely functional requirements for living space or institutional space meets with creativity and imagination. This might be an encyclopedic museum in its methodology rather than its content.

We could include discussion of the building, the structure, the material foundation, budgets—how much money is spent on things is as much part of a building as the sketches one could fetishize. This is the crucial question: Can you combine this information with the whole aesthetic question of what is satisfying and beautiful?

One might think of other things, too, which would be seen as cultural products, technological products, and products of artistic imagination: cinema, music. It is a way to look into things. What we would need would be a more technical approach to the humanities, and perhaps a more aesthetic approach to the scientific.

DG: You develop an encyclopedic approach to the museum rather than an approach of encyclopedic museums as they are today.

PC: Possibly. But it is evident that in terms of the decisions of what to collect and how to collect, so-called encyclopedic museums are not encyclopedic in the terms of the Enlightenment they see as their origin. As a consequence, we need to think all over again of a museum that would be truly encyclopedic in the Enlightenment sense. What would be its characteristic? How would the principles of collection and display be different from the museum as we know it? Binding together the aesthetic and the scientific might well be the answer.

DG: If we compare your point of view and the point of view that was developed at the time of the encyclopedists, we can see that you are re-engaging with a certain notion of truth.

PC: Certainly. There is no way in which you can suddenly say, "Let's forget about scientific truth altogether. Let's go back to some idyllic premodern way of looking at the world." One simply couldn't do it. There's no way you can simply discard two or three hundred years of recent history.

This is how one has learned to understand the natural world as having its own laws, which are independent of human beings, which is the foundation of the whole idea of scientific truth: nature has its own laws. Even if human beings were to disappear, nature would still be there. That is not something that premodern people were used to. They would not have understood what this means. But we can't simply discard it and suddenly pretend that it never existed, as though we could go back.

It is much more a question of preserving the achievements of science, which is based precisely on the separation of the human world of will and imagination from the natural world in which imagination and will have little if any power. How does one preserve the achievements of modern science and yet bring it into some sort of meaningful unity with the world of the human imagination? That is the crucial problem the encyclopedic museum could address. My own approach would be that rather than trying to seek some kind of grand unity, which one could simply conjure up, it is probably a much better idea to try and pick specific areas—art, architecture, music, performance. These are fields where you can actually seriously engage with the question of developing specific technical principles of combining collection and display in order to achieve that more universal pedagogical function.

Let us take two examples: architecture and music. People build things. People make music. There were and are specific technologies involved in each of those activities. In a purely premodern world, the human and the infrastructural, or nonhuman, were not necessarily separated. They were all together. People may have believed buildings had magical properties. This is an important part of the premodern world. We couldn't simply go back and say, "Well, concrete has spiritual properties." That would be a meaningless statement in our world.

On the other hand, if one were to present a history of the way buildings were constructed in a traditional culture and the way it has evolved over time into the use of modern technologies with steel and concrete, and actually look at the way in which human beings in their practices make sense of what steel means, and what concrete means, one gets a much more interesting understanding of not only techniques but what it means to be human.

For instance, let's think of something like a motor vehicle: it is a very technological device. It is a machine. If you go to any non-Western part of the world and you look at the front of the windshield of a bus or a truck, it is plastered with dozens of amulets, charms, and pictures of gods and goddesses. The people who are driving don't think of the machine as simply a machine. It is part of a practice of life. That's where the categories of humanistic imagination and technological progress get completely mixed up.

Those are the interesting things people need to sense from objects, to become aware of them in a nonobvious way. The classic post-Enlightenment way of describing the behavior of the third-world truck driver is, "Oh, this is superstition. It has nothing to do with the functioning of the truck." Actually, that is not true: that is the way people use machines. There is a whole cultural apparatus in which machines get tied up with daily practices where you cannot separate the so-called cultural or humanistic from the purely natural or technological. Here we have to think encyclopedically, but against the way in which the encyclopedists of the Enlightenment thought about it.

DG: What you are suggesting can also be thought of in political terms: It means going beyond cultural borders.

PC: There is not a single unified political impact of this project. It all depends on how you would present it. It needs to be thought of as an educational project. Whoever puts up this museum space will need to have a certain idea of what sort of effect is intended upon the viewers, just as when you prepare a lecture demonstration in class you have a certain expectation of the effect you want to produce on your students.

The pedagogical purpose of a straightforward science museum is to get rid of unscientific superstitious ideas that people have about natural processes. You want to have that precise effect on your viewers who visit the museum—maybe school children and their parents. You want to show them that, in fact, natural processes are natural processes. They have nothing to do with gods and spirits, or our will, or anything of the kind. Nothing we do will have any effect on natural laws. Natural laws are final and unchanging. This is what science has established and that is the effect the science museum expects to produce. In a science museum, the power of humans is very much placed into perspective.

In the art museum, the culture museum, or the history museum, the power of humans is everywhere to be seen. We need to find a way for the positioning of humans to be respected and placed in a wider perspective. What do we want to project? How do we want to project ourselves as human beings? We need to encompass more than just an assortment of achievements in order to be truly encyclopedic. It is an educational project. The two approaches—science and the humanities—that were separated for two hundred years, right after the work of the first encyclopedists, have to be brought together. We have to be universalist again, and to re-engage with what universalism means. I am not saying that we can immediately set off and announce, "This is an encyclopedic museum for everything in the world." And it might be difficult to visualize this all-encompassing encyclopedic museum. It might be better to consider it methodologically, as a project, conceived in much more limited rather than grand spaces. (2016)

3

Krzysztof Pomian

Director of studies emeritus,
École des Hautes Études en Sciences Sociales, Paris

Donatien Grau: You've done a lot of work on the relationship between the nation and the museum. Why is the encyclopedic museum so popular today compared to other forms of museum?

Krzysztof Pomian: I don't altogether agree with the premise of your question, but perhaps it's a difference in terminology concerning the meaning attributed to the expression "encyclopedic museum." Because if we take it in its fullest sense, to denote a museum uniting the macrocosm and the microcosm, the *naturalia* and the *artificialia*, nature and culture, then none of the major museums is encyclopedic. They all start from the separation of the products of those two creative forces nature and mankind, a separation introduced at different eras in different countries: in the eighteenth century in the case of the Uffizi in Florence and in the second half of the nineteenth century in the case of the British Museum. Furthermore, there are museums that have been exclusively art museums from the very outset, for example the Vatican, the Louvre, the National Gallery in London, and the Hermitage. Contrary to appearances, the encyclopedic museum in the full sense of the term survives today only in the form of small establishments, some of which unite nature and culture under the same roof. However, this form of encyclopedism, if the term can still be used in this case, is of merely local reach: it applies only on the scale of a given locality or region.

The entire history of the museum since the eighteenth century has been one of abandoning encyclopedic ambitions in favor of differentiation and specialization. This is attested by the appearance of museums of history, of science and technology, of medicine, of the army, of the navy, of flight and space, of the postal service, of the railways, of the automobile, of memorable personalities, etc., etc. These museums constitute the majority of the world's museums and, taken together, are probably the most visited, although due to a shortage of data, it's not possible to be categorical on this point. The effects of differentiation and specialization can also be seen in the division of the major museums into a growing number of departments dedicated to different periods and cultural regions or specific types of object, these departments enjoying a considerable degree of autonomy (varying from case to case) within the relevant establishment. Indeed, visitors to the Louvre or various other major museums are actually visiting several museums without necessarily knowing it. From this point of view, there is no great difference between the Louvre and, taken as a whole, Berlin's Museum Island, except that the Germans are more federalist and decentralizing than the French. But does the juxtaposition under one roof of different departments that lead their own independent lives without (or very rarely) consulting one another, or the juxtaposition of several museums within the same part of town, permit us to talk of an encyclopedic museum? I think not. In my view, there are no longer any encyclopedic museums if one takes the original sense of the term. A further argument for this is that the viewing circuits of the major museums aim to present the visitor not with an encyclopedic vision of whatever the given subject is, but with the history of a specific civilization—ancient Egypt, Mesopotamia, China, India, Greece, the Aztecs—or of a well-circumscribed field of art: medieval art, painting, or objets d'art of this or that country from the fifteenth to the eighteenth century.

In short, a universal museum that claims to unite under one roof the art of every known civilization and of every period of the history of humankind is not an encyclopedic museum. That said, the question you ask is a valid one: What makes universal museums popular? What is it that attracts millions of visitors to them? To be clear, we ought to add that universal museums are not the only ones in this category. The same applies to certain museums that display the art of a particular country—the Rijksmuseum in Amsterdam, the State Russian Museum in Saint Petersburg, the Tretyakov Gallery in Moscow—or period, such as the Prado in Madrid, which offers the best display of European painting of the fifteenth to eighteenth century. My answer, not very original I fear, is to say that all these museums owe their appeal to their concentration of masterpieces of art, a large number of which can be seen during a single visit or several. What are these masterpieces? They are works that, as a result of their intrinsic qualities or history, are spoken about more—far more—on a global level than any others, that are reproduced more than others, that are imitated, pastiched, and parodied more than any others. A single masterpiece is enough to attract crowds of people; if you have dozens, these crowds of visitors become gigantic and can be counted in the millions.

Why do so many people feel the urge to go and look at masterpieces? I think it's because masterpieces are regarded as manifestations either of extraordinary beings or of the capacity of man or nature to surpass themselves, to produce something rare, unique, exceptional, extraordinary, something that testifies, through the characteristics that lend it these qualities, to a departure from the usual run of events. To see such objects is to be transported into a dimension quite distinct from the everyday, and thus to ourselves feel even momentarily removed from our normal walk of life, elevated, ennobled, hallowed.

Another factor that contributes significantly to the appeal of any museum (and especially to that of the major art museums) is the building that houses it, which can be distinguished either by its history—as with the Louvre, the Prado, the Hermitage, and the Vatican museums—or its architecture, which can itself can be a masterpiece under the definition of the term we have just provided. Such is the case with Frank Lloyd Wright's Guggenheim Museum in New York, Renzo Piano and Richard Rogers's Musée National d'Art Moderne in Paris, and Frank Gehry's Guggenheim Museum in Bilbao. Nowadays, in the case of certain museums, it even seems that the architecture is the main attraction. In general, attempts are made to amplify this effect by organizing temporary exhibitions whose purpose is to bring together masterpieces in order to supplement the relative poverty of the permanent collections.

The growing number of museum visitors invalidates the diagnosis made years ago by Kenneth Hudson, one of the observers who reflected most and best on the museum—within the limits of British empiricism. Hudson maintained, in public as well as in private conversation, that evolution had revealed the diplodocus to be a condemned animal. And, consequently, that diplodocus museums, such as the Louvre, would eventually disappear. Today there's nothing to justify this prediction. Or at any rate, if such museums are to disappear, we're perhaps still at the stage where the diplodocus is alive and well and giving no indication that it's condemned. For the time being, these museums continue to enjoy enormous public appeal. They've become unrivaled magnets for their cities and countries, attracting tourists and, with them, money.

An econometric study has been done into the economic effects of the new Rijksmuseum. This has shown that the museum indirectly brought people in who then spent considerable sums on transport, hotel stays, restaurants, entertainment, shopping, etc., and has already recouped the 300 million euros spent on the renovation. It therefore follows that the investment was profitable. Without being in a position to confirm the accuracy of the calculations, this seems to me perfectly convincing. I've long believed that museums, customarily regarded as money pits for public or private funds, over the last few decades have become institutions that provide a strong return on investment. Not all, obviously. But certainly the major establishments such as the Louvre, the British Museum, and the Metropolitan.

I therefore believe that in economic terms, these big museums are not condemned. And in our society, the only form of condemnation that really counts is economic. Because they're profitable—not directly, on the basis of their own revenues, but thanks to the benefits of the tourist flows they induce—the major museums have every chance of surviving. I believe not only that they will survive but that they will increase and appear where as yet there are none. There will be more than there presently are in China and India. There will be such a museum in an Arab country—not simply an imported product lacking any connection with the society in which it has been implanted, as in the case of the Louvre Abu Dhabi, but one that will have been genuinely made with what is available locally. There will be several in Latin America, and not only in Mexico, which already has some of exceptional quality. But once again, strictly speaking, these are not encyclopedic museums.

DG: You talk about the new museums that could emerge in an Arab country, in Latin America, in Asia. What would be the models, the development possibilities for these new universal museums? And what would distinguish them from the national museums?

KP: The models have existed for a long time in Europe and the United States. The real problem is their assimilation by societies that, unlike China and Japan, have only the treasures of princes or temples and not individual collections. And some of those societies reject the depiction of human beings and even of any animate or inanimate being, an attitude supposedly imposed by the religion they profess. Resistance to the art museum will certainly be stronger in certain strictly Muslim countries. But even there, it's likely that this will fade over time. Moreover, perhaps types of museum other than the art museum will be adopted in those places: the museum of natural history, for example, of technology, of local traditions.

As for the status of the national museum, this was attributed at the outset to certain universal museums or museums that have become universal. As its name indicates, the British Museum falls into this category. As does the Louvre, which for a while was called the Muséum Français. Museums that are rightfully national museums don't always flaunt the fact. In the United States, some of the museums of the Smithsonian Institution don't bear the epithet *national* as part of their names, despite being national museums in the same way that the National Gallery of Art in Washington is. On the other hand, museums that are not national in terms of their legal status are sometimes considered by public opinion to belong to the nation as a whole rather than simply the city in which they are located. A good example of this is the Metropolitan Museum of Art, a New York institution par excellence that is at the same time emblematic of the United States.

It's impossible to talk about museums without taking into consideration the individual history of each establishment, which varies greatly from case to case and is always directly determined by the history of the country in question. And in the case of the museums we're talking about here, it's a long history. Even the Metropolitan Museum is more than 140 years old. Even MoMA is approaching its centenary. Most of the other museums mentioned here go back more than two centuries; some Italian museums will soon be five hundred years old. When one takes over as the head of such an institution, one also inherits its entire history. And this is not something immaterial. It's a weighty history inscribed in the very fabric, in the content of the collections, in the display of the objects and the division into departments.

When you instigate a revolution in a museum, it lasts for a century and is often an initiative connected either closely or loosely with the vicissitudes of the country in which the museum is located. This is because the big old museums carry different connotations, including political connotations, which have become sedimented over the course of time. All the major institutions we are talking about are the palladia of their nations and are seen as such: this is why every event that affects them negatively, for example war, leaves its traces—wounds that never heal. There are no prescriptions for works of art pillaged during the Second World War. It's a political problem, a problem of public opinion. In this sense, all these museums are national museums because what affects them affects the collective identity that we call the nation. They show the nation not in its particularist but in its universalist guise, taking part in the community of nations, that which is, or was once, called "civilization."

Despite the fact that it no longer calls itself one, the Louvre belongs to the group of French national museums; indeed it is the very embodiment of the national museum. It was conceived from the very beginning as resulting from the opening up of the royal art collection (consisting mainly of paintings) to the nation, equated initially with the sum of the French king's subjects and subsequently with the sum of the country's citizens. And no one has ever contemplated housing it anywhere other than in the Louvre, the kings' palace, in the heart of the capital, despite these premises being completely unfit for such a purpose. In fact, it would be impossible to find any worse a building in terms of the organization of the museum. It was only with the creation of I. M. Pei's pyramid that it has become somewhat more practicable. Never—in all the debates held in the eighteenth century and later—was the idea ever voiced that it might have been sensible to build a new museum and abandon the Louvre to some other use. This goes to show just how important a place is occupied by art in the French national identity—and not only the identity of the French elite.

Until the mid-nineteenth century, the Louvre opened to visitors on Sundays alone. During the week, only foreigners (upon presentation of a passport) and copyists were admitted. In 1825 a Russian writer, the elder brother or possibly the uncle of Turgenev, noted in his journal after taking a walk in the Louvre, "It was Sunday; I went to the Louvre; there was a crowd there because the Louvre is open to everybody." He stresses this because it was clearly something out of the ordinary. At the time, the Hermitage was a very difficult museum to gain admission to. In Moscow there was virtually nothing. "I saw," he continues, "peasants and poor day laborers in rags before a painting by Correggio." I've always regarded this as being too good to be true, but the fact remains that the people came to the Louvre. And the people started visiting the National Gallery in London as soon as it opened because it was far more democratic than the Louvre in its early days. They were not always terribly well washed and didn't know how to behave, hence a series of comments and notes on the education of the people emanating from representatives of the "educated classes." This demonstrates that the nation's symbolic appropriation of the institution of the museum and its contents occurred not only on the level of the elite but also, to an increasing extent as time progressed, by the people.

DG: Today, the public has changed, and it is interesting to see how the museum has opened up. It was the point of contact between the nation and the outside world. This very broad public that visited the museum is now an international public.

KP: The museum public is the least-known thing of all. When you look at the so-called sociology of museums, you can find out how many men or women frequent the various museums, along with their age, occupation, level of education, etc., but to the best of my knowledge no one has ever carried out a proper longitudinal and in-depth study of the museum-going public, how it reacts to what it sees, and what it remembers long after a visit. In truth, we know very little about the museum public. What we know, as a result of strolling around many a museum observing the public and its behavior, is that every language under the sun can indeed be heard in such places, and from this we can infer that the public is a cosmopolitan, international one. Does this mean the natives have deserted their museums? I have my doubts about that. Do they go back to them? Which museums, and where, do they revisit? To what extent do the ticket prices and long queues put keen museumgoers off making a return visit? This is where a good in-depth study would be extremely interesting. The fact remains that the museums that present a nation in its universalist guise attract an international public. But they also attract just as many locals.

DG: Do you think the museum will evolve in the light of the changes in the definition of the nation, in the definition of humanity?

KP: The museum is heir to the triumph, in the eighteenth century, of the idea of Man as a fundamentally historical being. And I say "historical" rather than "subject to evolution." The admission of man's historicity provoked a radical change in the hanging and overall organization of museums—in the Louvre, for example, where the historical principle was introduced in the hanging of paintings in the wake of the Revolution of 1848. The Germans had arrived at that just a little earlier, possibly because historicization had been in the Berlin air with Humboldt and Hegel.

The idea that the objects on show should be grouped together not in order to please the eye but in order to situate each one in its proper place and time, and in so doing to make clear the relationships between them and the changes in these relationships—the idea, in other words, of making the museum an instrument of historical intelligibility—had been gaining acceptance ever since the end of the eighteenth century. It looks to me as if it's starting to be challenged today. This can be seen not so much in the museums themselves as in the temporary exhibitions that are increasingly being organized not necessarily along historico-chronological lines but according to other criteria. It's likely that sooner or later, changes will occur to the actual contents of the museums and the way in which they are ordered and presented. It would be unnatural if they did not. (2016)

4

Mikhail Piotrovsky

Director general, State Hermitage Museum, Saint Petersburg

Donatien Grau: How do you see the challenges ahead for the universal and encyclopedic museums, such as the State Hermitage Museum?

Mikhail Piotrovsky: The principle of the universal museum by itself is a challenge. We as universal museums challenge the idea of unifying globalization: the world is one world, but it is also very diverse.

Different cultures can connect together in the world of the museum. Each culture has its own place. The museum sows a seed. When you go abroad, it may be that you will not appreciate any culture in the same way as you do when comparing it to something similar, albeit very different, which is just nearby. You will not appreciate Indian culture from going to India in the same way as you will by seeing Indian artifacts in the museum.

In the Metropolitan Museum of Art or in the Hermitage, you can appreciate how beautiful these cultures are. We need to fight against the limitations of national museums, which speak of their own nation. This is why it is so important that national museums be separated from universal museums.

We need to protect this right to have different cultures in one place, and serve the universality of human beings. And yet, we should not forget that as universal museums we are children of empire: the Louvre, the Hermitage, the British Museum, even the Met. The Hermitage is the legacy of the Russian Empire and has been preserved as such under all regimes ever since. We should not shy away from the Russianness and the imperial past: they are our history, and perhaps they also gave us our raison d'être. There was something inclusive in the notion of empire that made it possible.

We need to accept the fact that the encyclopedic museum is a hybrid being: it constructs universality but it also builds on the legacy of one nation, which at the time was more than a nation. There is no reason to be ashamed of that—and it actually opens up many more possibilities: it makes us able to serve our national history in a way that is not limiting, and to serve human history overall.

DG: Is there a specific purpose to the encyclopedic museum today?

MP: Such museums translate one culture into another and explain it. That's why they are a good vehicle to overcome all the negative aspects of globalization. Museums fit into the globalization period. These universal museums are global in principle. Cultural globalism is only part of this general globalism, which is not exactly the best thing in the world. Most people hate it, and we see that its results are making the world more primitive. We have somehow to promote difference of cultures.

I tend to say to my American counterparts: "You give us McDonald's, and we give you Hermitage," because I've been opening Hermitage franchises in different parts of the world. This is the idea. In the world, we have to develop the idea of difference, of different cultures, and different attitudes to different cultures. Since we have Hermitage branches in different places outside of Saint Petersburg, we also bring our interpretation of our multicultural time in the history of the world.

We can live without empire. It's fine: you keep cultural relations, you keep this celebration of different cultures. The museums of empire, the imperial museums, kept this idea that different is beautiful. That's the most important thing that we have to preserve, especially now that the world is changing. People and cultures must be different. Different doesn't mean "enemy." Different just means "enjoy." You have to learn to live in different cultures. Then you become a normal person—a complicated person. Only complicated persons are good for the twenty-first century. Simple persons, primitive ones, will not keep our humanity surviving.

DG: There can be a conflict between national and universal history, notably in the case of restitutions. What is your position on that?

MP: I don't think that there is a conflict, but there certainly are misunderstandings. All these ideas of restitution, in general, of returning all the pieces to the sources from which they came, I think, are not relevant, and they do not serve the construction of history that an encyclopedic museum is supposed to provide in a unique way. These issues of restitutions only came up after encyclopedic museums showed that roots matter, and history is important: as far as the Greek sculptures are concerned, everybody was collecting them all over the world without even noticing where they came from. The Greeks were selling them without any origin. Museums established that origins matter, and now people ask for restitutions.

We at the Hermitage have made a choice: now everything must stay in the nations, and in the places, maybe, where they are discovered. And yet, for what happened in the past, we cannot disrupt a history that took place and has led us to where we are now.

After the Napoleonic wars, some leading members of the public wanted all the art taken by Napoléon to Paris to be returned. Alexander I [of Russia] said, "No, let us leave it there. First of all, let's not outrage France because we do not want trouble. Let's keep them in a good mood. And, more importantly, Paris is in the middle of Europe. Everybody can come and study culture there."

With the legacy of the world, we need to be aware of what happened before—and here, it seems that the czar teaches us a lesson that still matters today. Let's not dismiss this lesson. The encyclopedic museum is an ideology: certain institutions must show all cultures together. I don't think that we need to have more universal museums, but the ones we have now must stay and must be protected. This situation of the encyclopedic museum as a repository for objects from the world comes with strings attached: we have a duty to teach the public.

DG: How do you do that?

MP: A museum is the most democratic institution in culture, in the world—unlike theater, where you have seats, and for which you need a lot of knowledge. The museum is like a library: you have space for everybody. You have the museum in itself, you have great art, you have art you do not know about but would like to study. Now you even have restaurants and cafés. In European museums you have the architecture, you have the glory, you have history.

People from each level of education can get something: children go there. They can look at all these beautiful things or just at the furniture, it's enough for them. And if you are very sophisticated, if you have seen a lot, in the Hermitage, you can look at everything, up to the ceilings, which are wonderful.

Teaching the public in a museum means developing permanent education. You can't just finish university and be declared fully knowledgeable. You have to broaden your knowledge. The museum is exactly the place where you can do that without much effort: you come to lectures, you come to exhibitions, you study the catalogs. There is always something new, always some important addition to your knowledge.

I think it is crucial to develop teaching in museums, in the same way as it is crucial to develop museum scholarship: museum teaching and scholarship are very different from university teaching and scholarship. There is a sense of practicality, of materiality in museum teaching and scholarship that you would not necessarily have at a university. As encyclopedic museums, in order to fulfill our mission to the public, we need to keep it ongoing.

DG: This idea of teaching relates to the digital world, which can be used as a means of teaching.

MP: People spend a lot of time explaining to everybody that it's practical: that having good pictures on television, on the screens, and in books is not a problem for museums. I agree. But we as museums—and again there is the difference from universities—are places for objects. When people come to us, they want to see the real things. They're queuing to see the exhibitions. Even when they really can see everything on the screen, they still go and wait for hours and hours to get into good exhibitions. Therefore, we need to place an emphasis on that materiality. The virtual world, I would say, personally, is a thread of lies. There, we all live in a situation where somebody wants to make us think according to his own opinion.

Museums—that is, their specificity, their glory, their duty—deal with original objects. We want people to understand the importance of original objects. The specificity of the museum is to provide something that is different: I am thoroughly against any type of display that has things on a screen and some wonderful object in the middle. If you do that, you mix things, and you confuse the mind as to the real, actual importance of objects.

If we want to have those three-dimensional teaching facilities in a museum, we need to separate them from the actual works. There is nothing necessarily wrong with getting people to use them, but they must be separated. Some lines should not be crossed. With objects, whatever they are, you have the smell of history—that is what we, as museums, use in order to serve and teach the public. It is the same thing with being located in a historical building: I always say that the palace should not look too much as if it were a set for a television film. In the virtual world, everything is like television. And it's virtual, it's all a lie.

Only museums, I think, deal with original things, original objects. They are here to balance the pressure of the times we live in. We want people to understand the importance of original objects. In certain corners, some things must be a little wrong. You must see that it's a living entity. Real palace, real history, in front of the virtual one. I think this is one of the most important challenges we are facing.

DG: Do you think that other encyclopedic museums can be created?

MP: I don't know whether there will be many more encyclopedic museums. It is the empire and not the republic that loves to have different cultures inside of it. We have national states. National states oppress all other nations. It's just a nation as a nation, and not an empire, which is a very different political idea. Maybe globalism will help to make such museums. We'll see what will happen in Abu Dhabi. It's the only example of a universal museum that people are trying to build ex nihilo.

There is a potential, but we will see. It's very difficult, because you must have this love—as the Romans had, or the French had—for all the different cultures to be brought in together. We have the universal museums. Then, at the next stage, we have the national museums. Now we have the local museums, one in each place to keep all the monuments. We try not to move them from their places. (2014)

5

Philippe de Montebello

Director emeritus, Metropolitan Museum of Art, New York; professor, Institute of Fine Arts, New York University

Donatien Grau: The encyclopedic museum as it is defined today is based on the dream of bringing old cultures together under one roof. Do you think it makes sense at all?

Philippe de Montebello: This is not a "yes or no" answer. On one level, it makes no sense and never made any sense: not any more sense than the *Wunderkammern* and the *Kunstkammern* of the past that were completely arbitrary assemblages of treasures for quasi-scientific purposes according to the time—mostly the sixteenth and seventeenth centuries.

From that time we then move into the Age of Enlightenment and into the thought of turning collections of objects into much more accessible tools for education, using for that purpose works that are all, in a sense, wrenched out of their context, considered to be fragments of a civilization, and which can never represent the whole of a civilization. The object is only one single manifestation of a civilization or of a culture.

The museum in itself is like a mosaic of any number of fragments brought together with the idea that a critical mass of such fragments of our cultures will give us, in the aggregate, a fairly complete picture of civilizations, as the aspirations of man are expressed in visual terms. That is what differentiates art, obviously, from natural history, from literature, and everything else.

At this point, one can say that the encyclopedic museum still is the best thing that we have: there is no other mechanism by which to preserve and to display what we consider to be the best achievements of humankind.

The encyclopedic museum will increasingly be, in the future, a library of objects that are the tangible vestiges of every effort made in human time, including, now, the present time.

The most important aspect for me of the encyclopedic museum is not its use at any particular moment but its archival value, its value as the container and the preserver. At any particular time, any number of practices of politics, of the museum might be misguided. But its archival mission remains, whatever happens.

We are now, for example, at the moment when entertainment is privileged over seriousness—when the whole museum world is more concerned with numbers and attendance than it is with fundamentals. Those are passing fashions and it will change as long as the museum as an institution continues to preserve, to conserve; and there is no indication that it is not going to do so.

These works of art are the primary physical evidence that we have for the study and understanding of mankind. Then they remain enormously valuable. My view is one of the very long term: any particular use or activity a museum engages in at any particular moment and time is almost irrelevant—except once in a while, for the provision of scholarship for catalogs, either of the collections or of exhibitions.

DG: You mentioned the archival value of the museum: there seems to be more room in this archive for some cultures than for others. The encyclopedic museum would be more Western-oriented than it would be oriented to any other culture.

PdM: It is a common misconception, but it is certainly not correct. Look at the whole plan of the Met, and I wager that you will find far more space devoted to the art of China, of India, of Japan, of Indonesia, of Egypt, of the ancient Near East, than to European art.

Even in the architecture of museums it is wrong to say that encyclopedic museums are Western-oriented: at the Metropolitan Museum of Art, you begin with the ancient world, and the ancient world is not in the West. The ancient world in the first fifty or sixty years of the history of the museum is Egypt, Greece, and Rome. When you enter the Met, the whole ground floor is devoted to Egypt, the entire north side of the museum, and to Greece and Rome is on the south side. We now also have what used to be strictly called ethnography, again not European art: the arts of pre-Columbian America, of Africa, and of Oceania. If you go upstairs, you have, in the center, the European paintings, but you have American art to the north—perhaps derived from Europe, but still not European. The entire rest of the north of the building is Asia.

And then you move southward on the second floor and you go through all of ancient Near East—Mesopotamia, Iran, etc. You move farther south and you have the arts of Islam, from the caliphates of southern Spain all the way to Mughal, India. In fact, you will not see an overwhelming presence of Europe, and especially now that the modern wing is very international and includes works by African artists, such as El Anatsui, and works by Chinese artists.

DG: You mentioned the example of the Met. Can you generalize to other museums?

PdM: The situation is obviously different from museum to museum: the Met is very different from the Louvre. The Louvre, in fact, is not a legitimate encyclopedic museum: it is essentially a European museum starting with Egypt, Greece, northern Europe. But we need also to be aware of the history of the Louvre, whose Asian collections were separated to create the Musée Guimet. We have to remember that human intelligence does not necessarily dictate how these museums are. To a large extent, museums are dependent on the vagaries of place and time.

You are dependent on the availability of collections and the works of art. There may be a wish to be as comprehensive as possible, but it may be that you can build generation after generation without being able to acquire the works in any number of different civilizations and cultures.

The museum is a palimpsest of different intentions at different times: now, for example, in our particular generation, there is an increased emphasis on globalism. As a result, a number of museums, such as the Met, Denver Art Museum, Los Angeles County Museum of Art, and others, are beginning to collect what the Hispanic Society of America Museum and Library has done for a century: Colonial Latin American art from Mexico, from Peru, to the Cuzco School.

At any time you have different emphasis. The museum that I have described as a palimpsest, in the aggregate, with time, little by little, acquires greater universality as you add up all of the decisions made at different moments of its history. At the present time, at the Metropolitan Museum, for example, you have an encyclopedia that is missing very few letters.

DG: Do you think that the encyclopedic museum is a more important topic now than it was before?

PdM: Those of us who grew up in the encyclopedic museums and devoted our careers to them are seeing a world that is in fact moving away from the encyclopedic museum. It is already made. You already have Paris, Berlin, London, and so forth. With the exception of Abu Dhabi and one or two other places that are trying to build general encyclopedic museums, we have been experiencing a huge shift to specialized museums, and mostly in contemporary art. Almost every museum that is built is a museum of contemporary art, and you find them in most cities that also have encyclopedic museums. This is all a matter of shifting priorities, shifting tendencies. The pendulum always swings.

Even encyclopedic museums are fixated with contemporary art. The Met is doing more and more in contemporary art. The Louvre introduced contemporary artists into its galleries. The British Museum invited them to curate exhibitions. It is also the case with the Hermitage, where contemporary art is playing a bigger role.

DG: Do you think it is at all possible to conceive new encyclopedic museums?

PdM: No, I do not think so. Because of the national property, heritage laws, the interdictions of export from countries like Greece, Turkey, and Italy, from which it has become impossible to acquire ancient works, or Nigeria and many other countries. The combination of the restricted national and state laws and the increasing decline of the availability of works makes it very difficult. Obviously, the artworks kept in an encyclopedic museum are not being created anymore since they are historical works. With a lot of money, one can create very small institutions that can resemble somewhat an encyclopedic museum. But none of them can possibly have the critical mass in any area and make any sense at all as an institution comparable to those already existing.

DG: How do you see the status of objects in encyclopedic museums? Are they artworks or documents?

PdM: The very point of the encyclopedic museum is that objects there are at the same time artworks and documents—all of them. Let us remember that, in a way, the museum is in fact the inventor of art by very virtue of the transfer of objects to the museum, separated from their original use, whether in a cult, a Buddhist temple, a Catholic church, a monument, or a political setting. Most start their life as functional objects, albeit displaying a high degree of artistic sensibility. I should also add that in so many parts of the world, the original function of myriad objects has also long ceased to exist as civilizations come and go, so—

This phenomenon is accentuated with Marcel Duchamp, the shovel and the urinal. Every work in an art museum is a work of art because it would not be in the museum if it were not a work of art. It has been pointed out more than once that objects as different as a Louis XIV chair, an English silver tray, a Poussin landscape, and a Buddhist sculpture have their place in the museum because they have acquired the common denominator value of being "art."

They are documents in the sense that from these works of art one derives a form of knowledge, an understanding of the civilization and the individuals who made them. The encyclopedic museum allows a traversal through time and space in order to understand interconnections among cultures and among works of art.

DG: Encyclopedic museums tend to feature a certain notion of universality. Does it make sense today?

PdM: You could almost say that universality itself is a construct. I belong to people who are fundamentally museum skeptics. It is true that there is great notion of movement, of interrelationships, of influences back and forth the trade routes. Nonetheless, most works that you see in museums are created in relatively small, confined areas, spaces, villages, cities, studios. We see them side by side in a foreshortened history of time and space, in a geography that is arbitrary and largely artificial.

Let us think of representations of a Buddha created miles away by three different cultures, one in Gandhara, one in Japan, one in China. There may have been certain influences, as images do travel, but the craftsman sitting on his tatami mat on the floor somewhere in Japan, in a small area next to a temple in Kyoto, creating an object, is nowhere near his colleague in Suzhou in southern China also creating a Buddhist object. Nor are they anywhere near the sculpture in Gandhara that looks like a Hellenistic portrait of Alexander the Great. There is a forced shortening of those major elements of time and space. We have a juxtaposition, a coeval existence of works that were created in silos and operate far apart.

One wonders sometimes just how accurate a picture of the world is presented in the encyclopedic museum. One wonders how we would apprehend the world's civilizations if the museum did not exist.

DG: Encyclopedic museums come from empires and tend to be instruments of global power today. How do you see the relation of these museums to power?

PdM: Museums and, to a large extent, art, as we today have baptized it, are born often of power and fortune. Most of what we call art was created by rich patrons, whether it be the papacy, the church, the temples, the princes, or kings and emperors. So art itself, with notable exceptions, is born to a certain degree from being a luxury, of both wealth and power.

It is wealth and power along with the sense of nationalism that created the Louvre and the British Museum, whose name is not a chance—read British Empire. The concept of the museum is a Western construct, and even when we see it in Africa or Asia, it is borrowed and copied from the European model.

The growth of the encyclopedic museum in the nineteenth century is the result of the imperial practices of the major nations of Europe and later in the nineteenth century, of the United States. National museums, whether in Cairo, Athens, or Istanbul, were an outgrowth of the Western European model and largely followed the Western European interest in the cultures of the East, when they developed a keener interest in their own history. On that note, let me remind us of what the West has returned or repaid in knowledge (the understanding of ancient civilizations by deciphering their writing, whether cuneiform or hieroglyphic), especially as the local populations were largely indifferent to the artifacts that were transported to the West in the nineteenth century. While it is true that encyclopedic museums were fed by imperialism, it does not mean, as is so often written, that today's practices are still imperialist in nature. On the contrary, museums have gone the extra mile in presenting the art of the Other.

The museum plays a crucial role in bringing together cultures equally—the only institution chartered to protect, maintain, conserve the objects that are the physical primary evidence of the achievements of mankind. There is nowhere else, with the exception of all of the world's churches, temples or monuments, where you can turn in order to see the original, authentic objects, not simulacra, not digital images, but the authentic objects that you can study in all their physicality.

DG: How could localization impact the notion of the encyclopedic museum?

PdM: We are at a stage in history where in slightly more than two hundred years we have created worldwide a landscape of museums more or less as they will be for the next few millennia short of some external cataclysm—war, natural disasters, whatever it may be. The large bulk of the works that can be collected has been and is now in the museums where it is likely to remain. I don't see that there's going to be a great change or a great shift. In that sense, the actual landscape of museums is not going to change. And remember also that what has been preserved, whether in collections or in museums or in situ, is but a tiny fraction of what was once on this earth —so much has been lost.

In Athens they are in vicinity of other Greek works and it would be comparing Greek art to Greek art. So the Greekness of Greek art emerges more in the Louvre, in London, or the in the Met, where in galleries just a few yards away from the Greek works, are works from Mesopotamia. The Greekness of Greek art is clearer moving from the Assyrian galleries of the British Museum into the Greek galleries, into the Roman galleries, and into the Chinese galleries.

They are two different experiences, one of great concentration, penetration, and engagement with one culture—the national museum—and the other of a kaleidoscopic view of the world in the general museums. I don't see that it can change. (2015)

6

Grayson Perry

Artist, trustee of the British Museum, London

Donatien Grau: It seems to me that *The Tomb of the Unknown Craftsman,* the exhibition you conceived at the British Museum in 2011–12, was a statement on the encyclopedic museum. Would you agree with that idea? And what are the conclusions you drew on the nature of this type of museum?

Grayson Perry: The British Museum is the museum of museums. Let us think of a place where there is so much stuff that everybody could find themselves in it. Let us think of a place where, if you want to build your own story, your personal story, you can see aspects of yourself reflected in all the artifacts you may encounter. That is what a museum is—and an encyclopedic museum by definition.

That encyclopedic museums are designed for them is not something viewers or visitors are necessarily aware of and, by using myself as an example, I wanted to alert them to the extraordinary wealth of experiences in that type of museum. Therefore, I decided that instead of the normal method of an artist making an intervention into a museum, and responding to the collection, I assisted the collection to respond to me, as a viewer coming into the world of the museum.

I knew the British Museum was so universal that there were bound to be things that would fit and work. I set out with a menu of objects I wanted to find, and I found them. I also allowed things to happen on the way. The fact that the British Museum has up to eight million objects made me think: "There will be something that relates to this, this, this, and this." I set little themes, and I was right. I allowed serendipity to take its course. Whenever I saw anything on the way that inspired me, or I liked, I took that as well. I was very, very subjective. As an artist, I was a viewer, ready to experience the very human gift of the encyclopedic museum.

DG: Did your experience enable you to draw lessons in terms of how the encyclopedic museum should evolve?

GP: I think that the first evolution should be from the point of view of the public acceptance. There should be an acceptance that everyone who goes into the museum can speak for himself or for herself. The most enjoyable way is to look for the things that satisfy you. Don't try to like things you don't like. When you go into a museum, people should be told, "You don't have to like it all."

Museums and art collections often are so vast and so varied that you can use them as a cultural mirror in most of a way. If you are feeling in a certain mood or are wanting to think about a certain thing, usually there is an appropriate artifact or artwork to do that. You can use that as a universal resource for the individual.

If you go in there with a request, hopefully the museum will answer it. Those requests are not necessarily just about facts. They might be about a certain texture, a certain emotion, a short story, a subject matter, an image, a symbol. You will find it in the encyclopedic museum, because it is so vast. It is the purpose of that museum to enable you to have that broad range of experiences and possibilities: in there, everything is possible, for you and for others.

Of course, objects themselves have their own true, factual stories, but you can use them as things that weave together to reflect your own personal narrative. At the same time, you are part of that world, historical antecedents of your own experience. It's good for people to feel like they are allowed to see the museums through their own lens. They don't have to see it through the academic historian's lens, or the artist's lens.

When I did *The Tomb of the Unknown Craftsman,* I was trying to give permission to people so that they could experience the museum in an infinite number of ways, depending on how they approached it. I think that freedom comes from the people themselves, and it comes from the museum as an institution.

For me, what makes it work is that in the end, you have got to be very specific. You have to say, "I choose this object," and not take it away with any abstractions or ideas—look at the object, enjoy the object, and be in the moment with the object. Looking at the object, being in its presence: that is what the encyclopedic museum is about, and all those very specific things about the object are what makes it fascinating.

When you are in their presence, you understand that they are very specific things. While they remind you of what universality means, their specificity invites you to challenge the very idea of global culture. These objects are definitely from their time and their place, and from a specific person, whether that is the artist or craftsman that has made them.

That very specificity is the joy of them in many ways: they are not appealing to some abstract, vague, global, philosophical idea. They are of their time, and they are not embarrassed to be of their time. And yet, they are universal.

DG: It seems to me that there is a need to prepare the audience to engage at that level.

GP: Yes. Most people who come to museums want to tick something off on a tourist trail. They want to stand in front of a famous object in the museum, maybe take a picture on their iPhone and move on, whereas a lesser portion of people are looking for various different things when they go to museums, depending on who they are.

One of the missions of museums is to invite the visitors to go from that level of engagement with the artwork into another level, which is the one that is truly life-changing. It is a long process. It is about a deeper engagement with culture that takes a long time, over maybe even a lifetime. I have an investment in it because I am an artist. Therefore, I go to the museum to steal. That's why I go.

I look for things I can copy, look for categories of objects, or textures, or patterns, or images, symbols that I can borrow, appropriate, make another version of, re-update. That is what I'm constantly doing. I am aware that it is a very particular way of going into a museum. And yet, anyone could do it: not necessarily to make art, as I do, but to include those images, those patterns, those textures into their own lives. I am not saying that is appropriate for a mass way of seeing museums—and yet, it is a crucial possibility.

What you need is a trigger: once that trigger is placed, people start to have a bigger interest in culture, and therefore are willing to learn more about the cultures and objects they are interested in. They follow a passion, or a curiosity, down the trail.

The museum itself is a wonder. It is all big and huge, but it starts getting exciting when you follow it down the rabbit hole. You go, you get interested in a particular thing, and you start learning about it, the stories involved, whether it be a badge or an Egyptian amulet.

I get the feeling that, today, people want to go to museums because it is a thing that you do. It reflects a certain cultural status upon you. Museums need to try to get people down into the rabbit hole, from this social aspect; they need to make the social element an intimate one.

DG: What would you feel is the specific challenge for museums?

GP: It is an interesting time for museums. Particularly in the United Kingdom, they are mobbed. We have two of the top five museums in the world here, in terms of visitor numbers—the British Museum and the Tate Modern.

They have become like the Jim Morrison grave: people come to pay homage, sometimes not really knowing what or who they pay homage to. The function of the museum is for them to get interested, and from there to get them to try to know exactly what they pay homage to, to engage with society.

It is important to think of what the person is getting out of it—not just the actual aesthetic enjoyment but what is the museum doing for them socially? Demographically, who are the people coming to them? When I think of different museums I always feel like if they threw a party, what sort of person would they be? What is the headline of their place in society? Are they the grand old man? Are they the trendy young man? Are they the aging hipster? Are they the flashy nouveau-riche person who's got more money than taste?

There are plenty of those museums these days. The encyclopedic museum would probably be an incredibly grand but polite, well-informed person.

This person needs to think about his identity: he has got to stay the same and yet to appeal to young people, to move with the times. With tourists coming from all over the world, more and more museums are going to become the theme parks of Europe, with their nice old buildings and their fantastic collections. This possibility is a threat and it is an opportunity. How are they going to cope with it?

And the answer, there, I think, is, once again, the individual. The grand, polite, well-informed person needs to be generous and ready to speak to anyone, while the crowd is coming at him. That is the great challenge for the encyclopedic museum of the future. (2015)

7

Thomas Campbell

Interviewed when director, Metropolitan Museum of Art, New York

Donatien Grau: The Metropolitan Museum of Art is located in New York. How important do you think the location of an encyclopedic museum actually is?

Thomas Campbell: It is critical. Theoretically you could have an encyclopedic collection somewhere obscure and inaccessible, but it would not have much impact. At its best, an encyclopedic museum is defined by the breadth of its collection, the range of expertise of its staff, and the international nature of its audience.

The Metropolitan is blessed by its location in New York—one of the most dynamic and international cities in the world. Internationalism has played a critical part in the evolution of the museum's thinking over the years. The expansion of our collections and programs continues today to challenge, and they inspire growth and awareness in new areas.

Being in a vibrant, multicultural city is not essential, but it's a very significant factor in the success of a vibrant encyclopedic museum.

DG: The difference between a museum and an encyclopedia lies in the fact that the one is a book—two dimensional—and the other features artwork, which is three dimentional. How much do you think this difference matters?

TC: It is absolutely critical. A museum is about objects—ideas, of course, behind the objects, but first and foremost. That is the contrast also with a university, where you are dealing with the realm of ideas. We bring people face to face with objects, and that is the starting point of our scholarship, research, and programs.

In an age of digital information, where we are overwhelmed by information, it is essential to always bring people back, whenever we have the opportunity, to the physicality of the object. Being in the presence of an object is very different from looking at pictures of it or looking at slides of it. It will be larger. It will be smaller. It will be dirtier. It will be shinier. It will be harder.

It is somehow arresting to be in the physical presence of a work of art or a significant cultural artifact. It is a portal. It commands attention if you get your audience in the right frame of mind, in a way that the reproduction of an object can rarely do.

DG: The encyclopedic museum stands between the art museum and the ethnographic museum. What relation do you see between the object as document and the object as artwork?

TC: It is a very interesting question, and perhaps I have a slightly different take on this to my predecessor: for him, the criterion of access to this museum for objects was that they should first and foremost be art objects.

In fact, I feel that the objects that are housed here are of a very broad spectrum of different kinds of objects: from objects that were made intentionally as art objects, to all sorts of objects where artistry was a component in their making. They had a functional intention that, very often in the past, was the motivation for that creation.

I think we need to be constantly aware of that duality—the artistry involved in the production of an object, but also the context in which it was made. Why it was made. What it signified. The investigation of those two interlinked elements is one of the dynamics that means our work is never done.

Not only are we learning more about these cultures of the past, but taste is always changing. What we consider to be aesthetically pleasing is constantly evolving. What might be a great art object for one generation may be a historical curiosity to another. It is our mission and our responsibility to be constantly accessing that calibration.

DG: As director of the Metropolitan Museum of Art, you have done a lot of work on the online experience of the visitor. What can be the online version of an encyclopedic museum?

TC: The digital realm is opening up whole new possibilities to us that we are still only beginning to understand. For me, the most intense part of what we offer will always be bringing visitors into the presence of works of arts or significant cultural objects. Digital provides us with a way of preparing them for that visit, providing them with different kinds of information during that visit, or indeed allows them to follow up and learn more after that visit, whatever age they are, whatever level of interest they have and whatever level of education. That's one huge step that we are exploring.

Beyond that, the digital realm allows us to reach out to audiences who may never come to the museum. Our mission is in part an educational mission and in part a proselytizing one. Digital images are a wonderful tool for us to reach out to people, touch them, engage with them, and stimulate them with curiosity about art and about history. Even if they have no opportunity to visit a museum, we can help encourage them to be interested in local cultural objects, museums, and artists in their own locality.

We are pushing forward toward an online museum, both in terms of getting our collections online and exploring different kinds of cross-collection publications that will engage audiences from the scholar to the school child.

The third realm we are just beginning to explore is engagement: we are well established as the authorities' voice. How do we engage and encourage further discussion with our audiences? We are exploring social media, how we can use Facebook, Instagram, Twitter, all of these new forums to engage audiences and develop discussion. All that is part of our mission as an encyclopedic museum.

DG: Then, what relationship should the encyclopedic museum have with its audience?

TC: We have many audiences and there will be different kinds of engagement with all of them. If there is one defining element, I suppose it is that we should be constantly stimulating curiosity, whether it is a great scholar, a first-time visitor, a school child, a retiree. We want to create a physical or a virtual realm where our audiences can relax and not feel self-conscious, and where they feel empowered to be curious and to explore without fear of judgment.

It is a trusting relationship. We are, of course, a voice of authority, but we do not want to be a patronizing voice. We want to be informative not prescriptive.

DG: How do you see the role of research in an encyclopedic museum as opposed to the university?

TC: Research is absolutely essential at a vibrant, successful museum of any kind. If you've got great objects, you can open the doors, and the public will come. To make the collections relevant, to engage an audience with the collections, the objects need to be presented thoughtfully and beautifully. The sort of information you put in around them needs to be informative and engaging to stimulate curiosity.

I think that scholarship and research allows us to constantly refresh that relevance. The information that may seem relevant to one generation can seem anodyne and trite to the next. As the world evolves around us, by returning to historical artifacts, I think we can constantly discover new things.

The predominant tastes and assumptions of one generation are so frequently overturned by the next. Ongoing scholarship allows us to continually be refining and holding on to the core elements of knowledge, the canon, but allows us also to expand it.

One of the great assets of institutions like the Metropolitan, the Louvre, the British Museum, the Hermitage, the Berlin museums is that they house a faculty of art historians, conservators, scientists, and educators who are tackling a broad range of subjects and who are applying a wide range of methodologies.

If you are open minded, you cannot help but be stimulated by that dialogue. It will challenge individuals within their own discipline to look at the parallels, whether they are geographic or temporal, and to constantly bring fresh perspectives to sometimes very familiar, very famous subjects.

DG: What is the role of the canon in the context of an encyclopedic museum? Is it the place where the canon can be challenged?

TC: One would hope that in a great museum you have an exhibition program, a scholarly program of lectures, and classes that explore the existing canon but are also open to voices that can challenge it. Take my own work as a curator—which is just one example among many here: I became an expert in European tapestries. When I began studying the subject in England, at the Courtauld, I think there was only one person in a museum position in Britain who was expert in European tapestries. Around the world, the number of experts can be counted as only between twenty and thirty.

In coming to the Met, I was privileged to organize a series of very significant exhibitions and to publish major catalogs in association with them. That really drew the attention of a broader audience to the significance of the subject.

Along with the work of my peers, that has helped open the eyes of the next generation of art historians to the way that tapestry, a very significant form of figurative art, coexisted with painting, fresco, and other forms of figurative art. That is informing the canon. That is just one example of many which can happen in our museum.

DG: The principle of an encyclopedic museum is that it decontextualizes things and recontextualizes them—as you do with tapestries. How does one deal with such responsibility?

TC: Whether it is religious art from the churches, cathedrals, and chapels, whether it is funerary monuments intended for Etruscan tombs, whether it is furnishings and wall panels made for the great homes of the rich from around the world, you are indeed dependent on removing many objects from their original context.

You have a responsibility to inform your audience about the context in which these objects were likely created and used. Then, of course, you have, as far as that is a challenge, to communicate the atmosphere of a cathedral, around an altarpiece. At the same time, you have the remarkable serendipity that, by having so many objects from such diverse origins and cultures in close proximity, you encourage dialogue and a comparison process that operates at both a conscious and a subconscious level. It can be deeply enriching at a scholarly level and to a general visitor.

DG: The encyclopedic museum is an art-historical paradigm, but also a cultural paradigm in a political paradigm. How do you see the connection between all those different models that are brought into this institution?

TC: Our goal is to collect works of art and to promote understanding of them. Inevitably, at a cultural level, we reflect the tastes and the opportunities of our predecessors. The Met, for example, in its early decades was heavily inflected by an interest in the ancient world and the European world. It was only much later that we made a concerted effort to expand our collecting into Asia, for example. The Met collected modern and contemporary art during its first forty years of existence, then famously pulled back from it in the early twentieth century. We are now playing catchup and engaging, to a much greater degree, with the modern and contemporary. In an active and healthy institution, one would be constantly exploring what it means to be encyclopedic, and expanding in areas that might have been neglected in the past.

We are very actively building now, for example, post-conquest Latin America, and Native America, two areas that have been neglected in the past. We need to be aware of the cultural blinkers that have operated.

Politically, the Met is very fortunate in that, being independent, we do not depend to a significant degree on government funding, so we are able to act independently of government direction. Our program is entirely unrelated to any political agenda. One can't help but be aware of the degree to which some of our European counterparts have received funding and encouragement to support a political agenda, whether it is in relationships with the Middle East or as an expansion of trade and political discussions with nations around the world. That has helped them, of course. It helped them expand their agendas in some respects, but it also defined them. We need to be self-conscious about the degree to which we live in a political world, and preserve the integrity of our educational mission.

DG: What is the role of narratives in an encyclopedic museum?

TC: It is sometimes challenging. We have so many narratives here. Some are discrete, and can be told within a sequence of localized series of galleries, such as the story we tell about the evolution of arms and armor. Others are harder to tell, because collections are dispersed across the entire institution.

Just to give one example: our collections of Indian art are dispersed between our Islamic collection and our Asian collection. We also have numerous objects made in India, for export, in our European and American departments. It can be challenging to make connections across these silos. One solution is exhibitions, where we can take objects from around the museum and create tight narratives in temporary exhibitions.

Another is through cataloging, which traditionally has been in books, but of course now is increasingly online. Another is through guides—audio tours that take our visitors through different parts of the collection. I think that with the advent of digital media, we have to be open to the fact that people are proactive, they're going to be creating their own narratives. We have a group called Hack the Met that regularly brings tours to the Met. They are not licensed by us, but they bring people around and tell their own stories. We have numerous tour groups that do, more or less, the same.

There is no single narrative. We can tell some of the overarching narratives that we think are important. We can tell some of the specific narratives that our curators feel are pushing forward the boundaries of scholarship. But we should not be closed-minded: we need to try to make our collections and information about them as broadly accessible as possible so that our information and our objects can become part of larger narratives that have been constructed by other people.

The museum, ultimately, is a combination of its collection and of what it makes of them. Having a vibrant curatorial body, a faculty, is absolutely critical to having a meaningful voice. You can be a tourist destination with great works of art, but the danger is that you just end up being part of a tour bus stop, with millions of people tripping through the galleries to look at one or two objects. I think it is healthier if one is a destination where people come and have multiple experiences, not just ticking off the famous objects.

DG: How does the paradigm of the encyclopedic museum relate to the contemporary museum, with which it shares a lot?

TC: Leonard Lauder made a resonant comment in respect to the Met and our ambitions to engage more fully with modern and contemporary art: "How can you be an encyclopedic museum if you stop collecting in 1900?"

I am sure that the leadership of the Met, back in the early twentieth century, when they decided not to collect the modern art of Europe, felt that they were building up an encyclopedic mission. Stopping in the present day, that was absolutely fine, but with the hindsight of an additional hundred years, we see an extraordinary sweep of creative activity that could have been just left behind, if the Met had not started collecting twentieth-century art again after the Second World War.

Assuming that institutions like the Met will be around for, hopefully, many decades and centuries to come, if we are to be true to our mission to be encyclopedic, we need to continue to extend our collections with modern and contemporary art. It has to be in proportion to our responsibilities across the broader collections. The art of our time is informed by the art of our past. Just as the understanding of the past brings insight to the present, it also works the other way.

The creativity of the present, for many audiences, helps to open their eyes to the realization that the art of the past was once contemporary. I think that it is a dynamic relationship that we would ignore at our own peril.

DG: The model of the encyclopedic museum is based on the perception of an interconnected world. Does that make it particularly relevant now, finding an interconnected world?

TC: Yes, I think it is a very important factor. For much of the nineteenth and the first half of the twentieth century, the growth of museums around the world, but primarily in the Western world, was characterized by a flow of objects from elsewhere to Europe and America.

Since the Second World War, we have seen the industrialization and modernization of much of the rest of the world; in the last thirty years, there was the rapid growth of middle-class populations in Latin America, Africa, Eastern Europe, and across Asia. With that development has come growing local audiences and curiosity for the art and culture of these different regions, with a result that we are seeing an explosion in the creation of new museums around the world.

One result of this growth is a new focus on the trade and the illegal movement of objects from these different areas, and this has fundamentally changed the collecting activities of museums in the Western world. Our role is evolving. Institutions like the Met, the Louvre, and the British Museum have the good fortune, through historical circumstances, to have accumulated these extraordinary international collections.

Looking to the future, the growth rate will be greatly reduced. Equally important will be our relationships with museums, not just in the Western world, but also elsewhere. The Bizot Group [a group of predominantly European and US art museum directors] is thinking about how it can become a more international group.

We and our peers are all involved in different initiatives, whether it is programs of loans, and exhibitions going to Asia or elsewhere in the world. Our own initiative, the GMLC, Global Museum Leaders Colloquium, brings directors from around the world to the Met for a two-week colloquium, building up a network of museum leadership, a new kind of network.

Looking at international engagement is a very important part of our health in the future.

DG: People relate the word *encyclopedic* to the eighteenth-century Enlightenment, knowing that as a concept, the encyclopedic museum appeared much later. Do you think that museum model emanates from the Enlightenment, and do you think that dissemination is still relevant now?

TC: In part, it emanates from the Enlightenment's curiosity about all aspects of human knowledge. In America it was the founding spirit of the Met, museums in Philadelphia, Chicago, and many of our other peers that were created between 1870 and the 1920s/30s. These institutions were looking back at European models, but with the vision of stimulating education in the United States, or being international, embracing the breadth of human cultures.

Today, that mission is ever more important. We are highly connected, through digital media, news streams, current politics, and ease of travel, with events around the world, in a way that would have been inconceivable to our ancestors. At the same time, we have never been more exposed to the prejudices, the extreme points of view, the radicalization of viewpoint.

We have a responsibility to play a critical part in education, in countering that ignorance and that misunderstanding. We have a potential to educate people about cultures, not only about their own culture, but about other cultures with which they are not familiar but which are having such impact on their lives. Just one example of that: back in 2011, we reopened our Islamic galleries after a very extensive renovation and rethinking of the presentations of those collections. It was about ten years after 9/11, obviously a period in which the notion of Islam has become a dominant, highly polarized issue in the world.

Many Americans had little knowledge of the Islamic world of Muslim religion before 9/11. After 9/11, their perception was inflected by a very polarized situation. What we were seeking to do in our Islamic galleries was to show a much more nuanced understanding of the differences of culture across the Islamic world, and the great aesthetic and cultural achievements.

It is very interesting that, since we opened those galleries in 2011, attendance in those galleries has been as strong, and continues to be, as if it was a temporary exhibition, reflecting the huge curiosity of our audience, who wants to learn and to be informed about this part of the world that is so impactful on their lives. (2016)

8

Kaywin Feldman

Director, National Gallery of Art, Washington, DC

Donatien Grau: Do you think that the history of encyclopedic collections is a burden or a fortune?

Kaywin Feldman: The history of encyclopedic museums is neither a burden nor a fortune, it is simply the past that has shaped who we are today. When the Minneapolis Institute of Art (Mia) was founded in 1883, city leaders strove to create a cultural organization such as might be found in Europe. The period from 1900 to 1925 saw a huge museum boom all across America, as communities recognized that a great city needs an art museum, orchestra, library, and zoo. With the classical temple-like building designed by McKim, Mead & White, Mia opened its doors in 1915.

American museums like Mia were created very much in the image of European precedents. We filled our galleries with European works of art, as though we were holding up a mirror to show what our civilized aspirations should look like. A review of the first 2,000 objects Mia acquired in its first twenty years reveals that 65 percent of what they collected was European. American art made up 26 percent of the collection, and less than 9 percent came from the entire rest of the world. The museum's interest in non-Western art grew until 1950, when much of the "ethnographic" art was deaccessioned, which happened in many other American encyclopedic museums at this time. Mia's non-Western collection did not expand significantly until the arrival of Evan Maurer as director in 1988 and the museum's collection focus shifted significantly away from Europe. Due in large part to the early collecting focus in China and Japan by the Museum of Fine Arts,

Boston, which set an example for encyclopedic museums across America, these cultures were collected more readily and early on by encyclopedic museums and they escaped the wave of deaccessions in the 1950s.

Many museums assume that our past must be our destiny. Cultural institutions tend to be conservative by nature, but the complicated governance structures in America, involving boards of directors, elected officials, volunteers, community stakeholders, donors, and staff, make it even harder to navigate change and innovation in museums. There are so many mixed agendas and expectations that influence an American museum's leadership in charting the institution's future direction. The American funding model means that donors are very often given a heavier collection and program influence than is often healthy for the museum. And that influence tends to be conservative and focused on maintaining the status quo.

This tension between patrons and the museum's future direction is more striking today than at any other time in the encyclopedic museum's history because the pace of external societal change is faster than ever before. I frequently argue that the status quo is actually the riskiest place to be. Consumers, many of them cultural omnivores, born in a digital and globalized world, have different needs from and expectations of cultural institutions than their parents and grandparents had. Somehow, our museums must understand the broad range of societal needs and attempt to serve all audiences.

The challenge for contemporary leadership is to work with and program for our loyal traditionalists who fund the museum and the younger audiences who expect innovation, relevance, transparency, and agility. When I ask our patrons and trustees if they would like to see younger and more diverse audiences at the museum, they respond with sincere enthusiasm. The difficulty is that they expect these younger audiences to behave exactly as they do and to have the same expectations for the institutions.

I am encouraged by the new leaders in America's encyclopedic museums and their commitment to navigating change. The hard part will be for these leaders to manage relationships and the number of stakeholders with vastly different opinions about the role and identity of the encyclopedic museum. A sustainable future for our museums requires both a committed donor base, often composed of our loyal traditionalists, and an engaged younger, diverse audience. The necessary balance between these two audiences is why I frequently say that this moment of museum leadership is no time for cowards.

DG: It is difficult, one could say impossible, for a museum to be fully encyclopedic. How encyclopedic is an encyclopedic museum?

KF: The term *encyclopedic* is problematic, and we would do a service to our field if we came up with a better word. *Encyclopedic* is certainly much better than the other adjective that is often used: *universal*. I admire the aspiration of the encyclopedic museum to be comprehensive in the representation of information. Calling ourselves universal, on the other hand, proposes that we serve and represent all people and all things in the world. This representation would be impossible for any museum, and it is arrogant and imperious to claim that we do.

It is easy to admire the benevolent desires of our founders and predecessors in their goal to represent diverse world cultures. I do believe that many of our founders had an altruistic belief that they would serve the community by exposing citizens to new cultures and new worlds. But we rarely acknowledge the singular perspective from which they came: the white European and American male point of view. These men defined *culture* and *museum quality* for generations to come. They not only decided what would be included in their museums, but also what and who would be excluded. One hundred years later, we are still reluctant to acknowledge—let alone change—that bias.

American museums' early collecting biases still impact our institutions today, and the majority of the collection objects in our supposedly encyclopedic museums were made by white men. It has been widely acknowledged since the arrival of the Guerrilla Girls in the 1980s that our museum collections contain a paucity of work by women artists. The field is actively trying to address this, but we are still inconsistent. For example, I find that while we often hold curators of European and American art accountable for acquiring work by women artists and artists from traditionally minority cultures, we rarely apply the same requirements to curators of non-Western art, and most especially Asian art.

Several museums have not only stepped up to add artwork by women and artists of color to their collections, they have deaccessioned and sold work by white male artists in the collection in order to do so—including the Baltimore Museum of Art and the San Francisco Museum of Modern Art. I admire the courage and commitment of the leadership at these museums; nothing signals change like applying resources to the problem and making sacrifices. When I speak about the need to acquire more work by people of color, I sometimes hear museum stakeholders express the fear that this would mean we are "lowering our standards."

It is predicted by demographers that America will become majority people of color by around 2043. This is exciting news for our museums, as we have the opportunity to grow our audiences and broaden our impact. We cannot assume, however, that increasingly diverse Americans will find the same appeal and relevance in the museums that were established several generations ago, to serve a very different America. We must change, grow, adapt, and pivot in order to meet the needs of our audiences today and in the future. We must also ensure that our staff and board members fully reflect the diversity of our communities so that we can actually represent and attract diverse audiences.

Part of this change must surely be an acknowledgment of our history, our biases, and our points of view. As a group of thoughtful museum staffers has recently campaigned, "museums are not neutral." We do a disservice to our museums and our audiences when we pretend that art, culture, and history are not difficult and replete with both beauty and horror—and everything in between.

Last year, a trustee in Minneapolis asked me why society expects museums to resolve the trauma of identity politics in America at this contentious moment in time; he thought it was an unfair responsibility to delegate to museums. Museums are indeed at the center of this societal and demographic change, and art museums are a primary locus of meaning and identity. A stroll through any one of our galleries offers a glimpse of both individual and collective identity, including joy, fears, dreams, love, desire, violence, hate, and hope. The good news is, we matter. The bad news is, we matter.

DG: There have been consistent discussions, in the last decade or so, to find new ways of displaying encyclopedic collections. Do you think they are relevant? How could they be shaped and implemented?

KF: In large part, the encyclopedic museum as structured today reflects an outdated world view. We often organize our collections by both medium and culture, and this classification suits an earlier understanding of the world, before recent migration and political and societal changes. And contemporary artists often disregard boundaries of both medium and geography. Maybe people have never actually fit in the convenient categories that museums have assigned them for organizing our collections and it is simply more apparent today how irrelevant—and sometimes dangerous—those categories are.

For example, in a recent lecture about contemporary art from the Middle East, Glenn Lowry acknowledged how difficult it is to define this global art as a region anymore. There are many artists originally hailing from the Middle East working in other parts of the world, such as Europe, Africa, and America, whose work comes out of a Middle Eastern tradition or heritage. Many artists from this region are not Muslim, so they cannot be referred to as Islamic artists. And of course, there are many artists who are Islamic and who live in the Middle East but work in an entirely different tradition and whose work is not considered representative of the region. We don't actually have words anymore to reflect the great movement of people, religions, and ideas around the globalized world.

I do believe that people want museums to make sense of their collections and organize the objects and the chronologies and geographies that they represent in a meaningful fashion. Our visitors want us to do that work for them and to help them to have a window into the works of art that we are presenting. There probably isn't a correct or rigid approach to this meaning-making anymore.

In Minneapolis we addressed this challenge by inviting experimentation and variety into our organization of the collection. Mia's primary galleries are still broadly organized by geography (Europe, America, China, Japan, and Africa) and installed chronologically. The museum, however, regularly introduces new organizing concepts and experimentation within galleries and in discreet nearby galleries. For example, in a Medieval Europe gallery, there is a case with examples of carved ivory from a variety of cultures, including fourteenth-century France, nineteenth-century Nigeria, seventeenth-century Mughal India; and twentieth-century Denmark. The accompanying label discusses the historic economic value of ivory—considered "white gold"—across global cultures and also highlights the current threat to the elephant population in Africa due to today's booming black market for ivory. The installation, therefore, is intended to remind visitors of commonality across time and culture, while also highlighting an important contemporary issue.

In another part of the building, curators at Mia worked across departments with single-gallery installations focused on a broad theme. The museum explored expansive topics, including nature and the environment, representations of the sacred, and globalization. Mia encouraged curators to propose gallery installations within the selected theme and to work together collaboratively with other departments. For example, in *The Art of the Sacred*, the curator of old-master drawings worked with the curator of

African art to produce a gallery about pilgrimage, including works of art from medieval Europe and seventeenth-century Ethiopia. And in *The Nature of Nature,* the curator of Japanese art worked with a European print curator on an installation titled *Eat, Prey, Love,* about birds of prey and their targets. For visitors who were frustrated by this thematic approach, they could wander our traditional galleries, organized by geography and chronology. Mia understands that there is not a single correct response to the opportunities provided by encyclopedic collections today and that visitors arrive with different needs and expectations, so variety and experimentation are key.

DG: A significant aspect of the discussion on objects today is provenance and the history of each object presented. How do you think this should be addressed?

KF: Over the last twenty years museums have become more transparent and ethical in collecting behavior. When I started in the field over twenty-five years ago, the curatorial ethos was to do whatever it took to secure a great object. I am proud to acknowledge that American museum collecting practices have changed profoundly and that colleagues across the country follow strict ethical guidelines in their collecting procedures today, whether they are contemplating an antiquity, a potential national treasure, a sacred object, or a work that might have a gap in provenance during the period of the World War II looting by the Nazis during the Holocaust.

Of course, current and future ethical collecting does not address possibly problematic objects already held in museum collections. I remain optimistic that museums are reacting ethically and responsibly when alerted to potential provenance issues in their collections. We are also starting to see museums investigating provenance and occasionally preemptively offering to return objects to source countries even before claims have been made.

We are potentially on the cusp of even greater change in how we view museum collections, nationalism, and patrimony. American museums have watched very closely the recent decision by France's President Emmanuel Macron to return to Nigeria twenty-six Benin objects that were plundered in 1892 from the Kingdom of Benin that have been held in the Musée du Quai Branly-Jacques Chirac. President Macron acted immediately after receiving the 2018 report by Senegalese economist Felwine Sarr and French art historian Bénédicte Savoy, *Rapport sur la restitution du patrimoine culturel afri-cain.* The report supports the shocking statement made by many experts that over 90 percent of the material culture of sub-Saharan Africa remains preserved and housed in collections outside of Africa. Critics have noted that the report only addressed the boundaries of Europe and Africa, ignoring consideration of the cultures of Oceania and Latin America, among other parts of the globe.

In the aftermath of the report's release, governments and officials from Ethiopia, Senegal, Cameroon, Ivory Coast, Greece, and Easter Island, among others, expressed their expectation that objects would be returned to source countries from museums and private collectors. Several European museum directors responded thoughtfully about the complexity of the issue, but without any consensus. Hartmut Dorgerloh, general director of the Humboldt Forum in Berlin, wrote in the *Art Newspaper* that the discussion of colonial heritage is "as challenging as it is overdue." Amen.

I had hoped that the report might spur some timely, difficult, and meaningful conversations about cultural property, provoking new and honest discussions about objects, museums, interpretation, and partnership. Increasingly, younger audiences want museums to be transparent about how they have come to own the objects in their collections and why they were acquired. Traditionally, museums have been silent on these issues. The lively discussions following the release of the restitution report seem to have subsided, with surprisingly minimal impact on museums. Books have been and will be written on the topic of plunder and restitution, from the ancient world until today. Human history is a complicated and violent story, and museums will face this contentious matter for years to come. Transparency, frank discussions, and open minds are the only successful path encyclopedic museums can take on this journey.

DG: You have worked as the director of an encyclopedic museum, in Minneapolis, and now of a national museum, the National Gallery of Art in Washington, DC. What role do you think the national effect has played, plays, will play in encyclopedic collections?

KF: I am proud to lead the National Gallery of Art, which has long been on the vanguard in provenance research. Nancy Yeide, former head of the department of curatorial records, dedicated much of her career to impactful research into the looting of cultural property from Jewish owners by the Nazis during World War II. Her presentations and publications about provenance research have helped countless museums in Europe and America proactively address provenance issues in their collections.

The National Gallery of Art does not claim to be encyclopedic and only collects painting and sculpture from Europe and America. This narrow collecting focus does exempt the Gallery from some of the thornier issues facing museums with antiquities, indigenous sacred objects, and global collections. Having worked in encyclopedic museums in the past, however, this moment offers me an opportunity for "balcony view" reflection.

I always had difficulty with true/false and multiple-choice tests when I was in school, as I could always argue the gray area in between the black-and-white correct answers. And I believe the gray area is where the most interesting substance of questions resides. As the repositories of the human lived experience across time and across continents, museums exist in highly ambiguous and often contested space. It is imperative that we recognize the challenges and opportunities presented by our collections and the work that we do. The cultural history that we nurture and present is simply too important and too precious to ignore its inherent complexity and nuance.

DG: You dismiss the expression *universal museum,* and are critical of the contemporary relevance of the term *encyclopedic*. What would be the right new word? Or what should it convey?

KF: I have to say, I haven't yet arrived at a word that I think is accurate while also being both interesting and comprehensible to the lay person. I sometimes refer to "general" art museums, but this is a particularly uninspiring term. Perhaps *global* is a better adjective to describe the model of the encyclopedic museums; it suggests an expanse beyond the United States but does not necessarily commit to a complete representation of all world cultures across all time. A few years ago I spoke at a conference in Szechuan, China. I was the only participant who wasn't from China, but because I was there, it was billed as a "global" museum conference!

DG: It seems that, from your experience at Mia, the response to the criticism of the encyclopedic museum is to be local, within the institution itself. What do you think?

KF: I do believe that the character and mission of a museum should be rooted in the history, identity, and values of its local community. In general, over 80 percent of American museum collections are formed through gifts, and the majority of these gifts tend to be from collectors residing in the region. Our collections are shaped by our communities, but so are the programs and strategic directions of the museum. When directors fail at the job, it is often because they have not paid enough attention to the concerns and values of their local communities.

In my move to the National Gallery of Art, several reporters asked if I would repeat everything that we did in Minneapolis after I arrived in Washington. I always explain that my job is to learn the museum, which has a history, a culture, values, and committed stakeholders. I want to understand the Gallery and apply my skills and experience to help our team achieve their highest aspiration for the museum and our audience.

DG: You talk about the importance of nuance in museums. How can it be manifested in an encyclopedic museum?

KF: Nuance is increasingly hard to find in our world today. The way that we see and explain the world has become so polarized and absolute that it is often assumed that if you are supportive of one direction, it means you are against another direction. Our contemporary paradigm seems to enforce that one must be either for or against. I prefer the "yes, and..." thinking that has come out of improvisational comedy and which demonstrates that there are multiple simultaneous possibilities. When I tell patrons that I am committed to diversifying the collection, they often assume this automatically means a complete rejection of the museum's collection of European old masters. I do not understand why one cannot value the art of Europe while also celebrating artwork made in America by people of color. Stating the importance of one does not in any way exclude the importance of the other.

Nuance is also found in context. It has long been pointed out by intellectuals and art historians that museums display objects torn from their original context, which gives them new meaning. For example, seeing religious art in a modern, secular museum context, whether an altarpiece removed from a Catholic church or a Bamana *boli* figure, whose sacrificial encrustations give the object a spiritual quality, is a different experience than the one intended by the artist when the work was created. Museums rarely acknowledge the distance between the artist's intention and historical culture and the current circumstance of display.

Art museums sometimes fetishize the masterpiece to such a degree that we ignore the original context and maker of the work. While some works can be admired for purely formal qualities alone, museums can offer so much more. I am a fan of the quote by Sir Francis Bacon that "some books are to be tasted, others to be swallowed, and some few to be chewed and digested." I believe the same to be true of works of art, and it is the job of the museum to help our visitors to taste, chew, and digest as they please. (2019)

9

Mari Carmen Ramírez

Wortham Curator of Latin American Art and
director, International Center for the Arts of the Americas,
The Museum of Fine Arts, Houston

Donatien Grau: The encyclopedic museum is known to embrace all cultures, and aim for a sense of completion. What do you think of this ambition?

Mari Carmen Ramírez: If postmodernism taught us anything in the last three decades, it was to question all sorts of metanarratives and to doubt the legitimacy of accounts that lay claim to any form of universality. With regards to this question, what is at stake implies distinguishing between the desire to promote the artistic values and achievements of human civilization and the ability of museological institutions to effectively represent them in their collections and programs. The idea of a museum that embraces all cultures for such purposes is undoubtedly a noble ideal, hard to encompass over the long term, and impossible to implement in the short term within the restricted limits of the gallery space. Such an institution presents itself as a place where viewers can connect with cultures across time and space in a stimulating dialogue. James Cuno—the most passionate advocate of this type of museum today—argues that encyclopedic museums are places for people to identify with others and build a shared sense of humanity as well as a common history through art.

Yet, in light of the troubled history of these so-called encyclopedic museums, we must be careful not to oversentimentalize such an ideal at the risk of appearing naïve. Indeed, at the plain level of practice, the notion of an encyclopedic museum presents us with an extremely tall order that very few, if any, institutions have lived or can aspire to live up to, particularly in the twenty-first century. Regardless of the widespread use of the term in the United States, it is hard to think of any museum in this country that is truly encyclopedic. Not even the Metropolitan Museum of Art—generally perceived as the gold standard for this type of institution—can fully claim this characterization. Far from embracing and displaying objects from *all* cultures, the presumed universality of these kinds of institutions represents in fact a particular ideological construct or abridged canon that originated in the Enlightenment. While so-called encyclopedic museums may indeed do justice to the core values of this construct, they cannot pretend to reflect the totality of artistic or cultural expressions that have contributed to human civilization or to the myriad ethnicities and nationalities that make up global society today. I thus agree with George Abungu when he says that museums who claim this type of universality are really fighting to preserve their own legacy, not the world's.

It is not a coincidence that encyclopedic museums only exist in the United States and Europe—the traditional enclaves of Western culture—and that the very concept is alien to entire regions of the world whose cultural legacies do not always constitute the core of these institutions' comprehensive collections. These faraway domains include Asia, Southeast Asia, Africa, the Middle East, and Latin America. While it has become a commonplace to point out the nexus of these museums to colonialism, such a relationship cannot be overlooked in any discussion of these institutions. We must not forget that encyclopedic museums were originally established to showcase the spoils of wars and political strife that resulted from conquests, invasions, and plundering by countries like England, France, and Spain. The abducted treasures from these horrific conflicts adorn the galleries of many encyclopedic museums. References to imperialism and colonialism are thus deeply embedded in the very origins and history of the term. Again, in this context, the idea of a museum that embraces all cultures can only be a naïve, fallacious construct.

Nevertheless, I would argue that this dark historical background is no longer the biggest challenge confronting these institutions. For reasons that are both practical and ideological, it is no longer possible for museums today—whether in Europe or the United States—to embark on this type of universalizing ambition. Stringent patrimony laws, a significant increase in repatriation suits, substantial cuts in funding, a decrease in connoisseurship and expertise in art-historical periods before 1900, and hyperinflated art markets have seriously limited the range of objects from distant past or present cultures that museums of any kind can acquire. Long gone are the days when these institutions could accession comprehensive collections to fill in for entire periods or cultures. Moreover, there is the increased surge of nationalism across the planet that is threatening to turn back the purposeful goals of globalization, placing in jeopardy both the nation-state and the very notion of a global culture. In societies increasingly veering toward tribalism (Russia, Spain, and the UK, among others), even the notion of a global museum is in serious jeopardy.

DG: We all know that this model is geographically localized. And yet it has spread all across the United States, and many museums feature encyclopedic tendencies without describing themselves that way. How do you feel about the actual presence of this model?

MCR: There is no doubt that the Enlightenment model persists with all the limitations I have described so far. However, I am more interested in bringing attention to other societal factors that are significantly limiting the viability and relevance of this model for twenty-first-century multicultural societies such as the United States.

We must remember that in this country, the emergence and proliferation of these museums went hand in hand with the push by white liberal elites to educate large swaths of the population in a geographically vast, culturally heterogeneous country shaped by consecutive waves of immigrants from all over the world. As important as this prime civilizing goal was for the early history of this country, I believe it may be time for a close scrutiny of its function today. A series of factors, even paradoxes, must be taken into account when assessing the relevance of these rarefied institutions to US society today. Those that come immediately to mind include demographic transformations and an increasingly steep educational gap. However, we must also consider the ascendance of a new paradigm based on "the contemporary," and the impact of the digital age on the way visitors experience the museum and its collections in real time.

A paradox comes to light if the mission of so-called encyclopedic museums is considered vis-à-vis the transition from a white majority society to a "non-racial majority" society, a term coined by demographer William Frey. According to a 2016 report from the Pew Research Center, since the 1980s more than 59 million immigrants arrived in the United States mostly from Asia and Latin America. Today, more than 14 percent of the US population is foreign born, compared to 5 percent half a century ago, in 1965. Racial and ethnic diversity in the United States is a feature of many suburban and rural areas, not just city centers. In addition to this, and to compound things further, a 2015 Census Bureau Report showed that by 2044 whites will no longer comprise a racial majority whatsoever in the United States. By then, the nation will be made up of a racial kaleidoscope. Today the hint of this unstoppable tendency can be perceived already in demographic groups such as children younger than five and the under-thirty population. Since 2010, a significant decline in numbers has led white populations to become minorities in key voting states such as California, Texas, Florida, New York, Georgia, and New Jersey. Not surprisingly, another report issued in 2010 by the American Association of Museums' Center for the Future of Museums underscored that the group historically constituted as the core audience for museums (non-Hispanic whites) is—if not on the verge of extinction—fading as a public audience.

Most encyclopedic museums in the United States are located in multicultural and multiracial cities with populations representative of cultures or regions that were either left out or were the victims of the Enlightenment's imperial thrust. African American, Latinx, Asian, Hindu, or Muslim communities have no particular investment in this Western set of values. Their artistic interests correspond to quite different historical or cultural matrixes encompassed by the term *Otherness*. Like many other types of museums, encyclopedic museums are thus caught in a dilemma: Should they continue to uphold the abstract Enlightenment values that have shaped their mission and collections for decades, or directly address the present-day needs of their richly diverse audiences? The implications of this process are bound to transform encyclopedic museums as we know them today. It is undeniable that these institutions embody a particular world view that, despite presuming to be accessible to all social classes and groups, ultimately responds to the needs and aspirations of privileged sectors of US society. So, in the absence of any majority group, who will determine next the mission, programs, and scope of the encyclopedic museum? Are these essentially white institutions capable of assimilating the world views and traditions of different groups already embedded in this society, albeit still alien to its traditional fabric for being historically marginalized? Of course, further contributing to this complex scenario is the intrinsic heterogeneity of these immigrant groups. For instance, the Latinx communities encompass a plethora of races and nationalities held together only by Spanish language, Catholic religion, and a shared history of colonialism. On the contrary, for Asians, language and religion do not provide a common foundation whatsoever. In other words, what I am trying to say is that the intrinsic heterogeneity of these groups, as well as their competing ideological and social agendas, make adjustments to the mission of encyclopedic museums a rather urgent, complex, and difficult endeavor at any level.

A second factor contributing to the crisis of these institutions is the significant gap in shared cultural values that characterizes US contemporary culture as a result of changes in educational curricula that have steered middle and higher education away from the humanities. I remember *New York Times* art critic Holland Cotter brilliantly arguing this point in a recent article where he observes how, even a generation or two ago, the myths and religious subjects that form the basis of, say, Italian Renaissance painting would have been familiar to a general public, thanks to surviving public-school variations on a classical education. But with changes in schooling in a country that has grown increasingly secular, viewers of art predating Impressionism typically don't know what they're looking at. Such a process has been compounded and augmented by the advent of the digital age and the need it has created for instant, experiential gratification on the part of the viewer (paying audiences) upon whom museums today depend for survival, thereby creating a different set of conditions for these institutions to engage with their public. Audiences have for the most part left behind the curiosity for glorious objects from a remote past in favor of the type of accessible interactivity with enticing objects and installations associated with contemporary art.

This brings me to a third, even more critical factor: that which concerns the ascendance of the phenomenon of "the contemporary," understood as the consolidation of a new paradigm that resulted from the ascent of globalization as the hegemonic world order after 1980. Such a phenomenon has further complicated the scope and range of action of encyclopedic museums, bringing about what may be tantamount to an existential crisis. The roots of such a crisis are grounded in the juxtaposition between a narrow-minded notion of culture based on a closed, easily packaged notion of the past and one that is in full-blown progress, unfolding in the actual present. In line with the presumed dissolution of nationalisms brought about by international processes, what is contemporary appears to stand for a neutral, acritical art seemingly devoid of a historical past or an overriding style. Unlike the fixed stylistic and elite-based hierarchies favored by universal art or modernism, what is contemporary implies also an art promoting stylistic plurality as well as ethnic and cultural diversity.

As a result of all these factors, encyclopedic museums are currently struggling to find a new course that will allow them to reinvent themselves for the twenty-first century. Where these venerable institutions once considered contemporary art to be fairly insignificant in the millennial course of history, they are now seeking to shake off the dust and ride the fast-forward trend by building annexes, opening curatorial departments, and incorporating curators of contemporary art into their staffs.

DG: The encyclopedic museum is not just an institution. It is also a model. How do you see the relation between the institutions themselves, as they exist, and the model as an idea?

MCR: Emergent constituencies like Latin American and Latino—as well as African, African American, Asian, and Islamic—not only embody the art needs of the increasingly multicultural communities in which these institutions operate, but they also have the power to shape the museum's malleable identity, as we understand it today. In this context, rather than engage with the ongoing problematic notion of an encyclopedic museum, it makes more sense to turn our attention to the concept of an ecumenical museum—that is, a museum where the diverse constituencies that make up the city or nation are actively represented not as objects of display but as shareholders of the museum's identity. Such an all-embracing model confronts the past not as a closed legacy to be neatly packaged in a museum visit but as an intrinsic part of an actively unfolding present that is all-inclusive.

Conceiving of such institutions will require significant changes to the current ambitious and worn-out model through which these museums operate. At the level of governance this involves diversifying boards of trustees and administration rosters; at the level of displays it entails reconstructing the past from the perspective of the present; at the programmatic level it requires outreach programs extending into every single community any museum serves.

Some fundamental issues must be emphasized. What is at stake is not institutional branding or audience development but rather the articulation and implementation of a different axiology, one forcing the museum to directly engage at the intellectual and practical levels with different sets of cultural values embodied by the new audiences. Indeed, the critical issues boil down to these questions: In a no-majority society, where not one single group dominates both the grand narrative and the social discourse, how can art museums provide a flexible environment for true intercultural exchange among diverse racial, ethnic, and gender groups to take place? How can they make their treasured collections of universal artifacts relevant for underrepresented audiences? How can the art museum compensate for the type of exclusion that results from economic or ethnic bias? The answers to this bundle of questions must be sought not in the assimilation or conversion of underrepresented groups to the mainstream values embodied by the so-called encyclopedic museum, but rather by the establishment of equal avenues of dialogue and exchange. It is my belief that the museum must learn about the values and symbols informing these communities as much as the communities must learn from an everlasting, undeniable Eurocentric legacy. In the process, the encyclopedic museum will inevitably come to reality by reinventing itself. (2019)

2

Encyclopedic Museums around the Globe

10

Irina Bokova

Interviewed when director general, UNESCO, Paris

Donatien Grau: The encyclopedic museum, such as it exists today, is based on the idea of gathering together all the world's civilizations under one roof. Does it make sense to do this?

Irina Bokova: The role of museums as research institutions and institutions for the dissemination of knowledge remains essential in the current world context, in which the development of empathy, understanding, and tolerance toward other cultures is more necessary than ever. This has become the minimum that is required of every citizen of our globalized world. In this sense, the museums that collect, study, and put into perspective collections of great diversity, accompanied by the related knowledge, with the aim of serving the public interest, are fulfilling a key role, whether we call them "encyclopedic," "thematic," or "universal." Every culture needs access to its patrimony, to its history; at the same time, not being able to look beyond this patrimony and discover different horizons would be a form of imprisonment and a considerable impoverishment. Furthermore, this capacity to put oneself in perspective with relation to other cultures and peoples corresponds precisely to anthropologist Claude Lévi-Strauss's definition of humanism. This position is shared by UNESCO's member states and partners, and in May 2015 it was called to mind during the discussions held at the intergovernmental meeting of world museum experts for the elaboration of UNESCO's new international Recommendation Concerning the Protection and Promotion of Museums and Collections.

DG: The encyclopedic museum model has been a focus of debate over the last ten or so years. To what do you attribute this debate? How would you position yourself with regard to it?

IB: This fascination with the subject of the encyclopedic museum is connected to a profound change in the way the museum's mission is perceived, and to the scale of the socioeconomic and political changes that have been affecting the role and diversity of museums for decades. It reflects the changing ways in which publics and nations view both their own histories and the Other. The internationalization and regionalization of museums and their collections are complex processes that drive the debate. The growth in world tourism, in particular the development of heritage and cultural tourism, is also feeding these reflections. Furthermore, the emergence of new powers is encouraging certain states to lay claim more forcefully to their culture and heritage, to combat the trafficking of works, and to demand the restitution of objects—not least from encyclopedic museums. This is why the debate about museums can never be separated from the sometimes violent or tumultuous manner in which these collections have been formed over the course of history. It also explains why this is such a complex field. It's clear that no private or public encyclopedic collection should be authorized if it relies on the plundering and trafficking of other peoples' cultures. The challenge is therefore how to guarantee that cultural objects are able to circulate in a fair and legal way that allows the diversity of the world's cultures to be discovered without cutting peoples off from their heritage.

DG: Encyclopedic museums bring together objects from all over the world. Are they legitimate ways of representing the world in its entirety?

IB: The encyclopedic museums attempt to represent humanity's natural and cultural diversity, and play a key role in the protection, preservation, and transmission of patrimony. In this sense, the desire to represent collections in such a way as to embody a certain universality is legitimate. However, no establishment, museum or otherwise, can claim to represent the world in its entirety. What counts is discourse and the way in which collections are presented. Faced with the diversity of the world, such approaches are an invitation to understand and see. This can also be done without using objects: new technologies and the use of documents, archives, and videos have opened up a new field of expression for museums. It can also be done by means of a very small number of hybrid objects that shed light on the interactions and influences among cultures. European chests decorated with precious stones or ivory from other continents; Buddhist statues whose facial features or hairstyles reveal Greek influences, etc. The Greeks, incidentally, had different terms to denote entireness: *pantos* (all) and *holos* (whole), that is to say, entire in extent and entire in terms of comprehensiveness. The encyclopedic museum is not so much a museum that exhausts itself embracing the entire world as one that is capable of explaining the fundamental relationships and structures that govern our world in order to help citizens find their place in it.

DG: Can the idea of universality on which these museums are based still be justified?

IB: Whether the universality of the collections is a valid notion or not is a question that varies from one museum to the next. No museum can be universal in absolute terms, as it's impossible to cover every period and every region evenly. What justifies the notion of universality is more about how the collections are presented within the applicable limits. At a time when, in many parts of the world, we're witnessing a desire to turn in on oneself—all too often accompanied by rejection and fear of the Other, by racism and anti-Semitism—it's important to cultivate this desire for the universal, which impels us to search for what we have in common. This idea is more topical than ever.

DG: The provenance of objects can be problematic, precisely because they come from all over the world. What, in your opinion, should be the policy of the encyclopedic museums toward this question of provenance?

IB: UNESCO is fully committed to the fight against the trafficking of cultural goods, and museums are a key partner in this fight. In compliance with the letter and spirit of the convention on the prevention of illicit importing and exporting of cultural property, adopted in 1970, and by way of a supplement to the UNIDROIT convention, adopted in 1995, UNESCO's position is to raise awareness among museum professionals and other, private actors about the provenance and traceability of the acquired objects and to eliminate any ambiguity over the origin of these objects.

DG: Do you see the encyclopedic museums as museums of art or of civilization? What consequences does this identification have on the status and impact of these museums?

IB: I'm not sure that this categorization is of any great importance. What strikes me as important is the way the collections are interpreted, presented, and placed at the disposal of the public. Nonetheless, I think the relationship between the visitor and a work in an art museum is more about a notion of aesthetic value that, in this precise case, transcends the identity value (whether of a cultural, historical, or even religious kind), which is, it seems to me, perhaps more sought after by and perceptible to the visitor to a museum that focuses on civilization.

DG: At present, the encyclopedic museums are all located in Western countries. Is it possible to conceive of an encyclopedic museum anywhere other than in the West? On what principles might such a museum be founded?

IB: There are other museums in the world with a claim to the label "universal museum": the Bardo National Museum in Tunis and the Hermitage Museum in Saint Petersburg. We are also seeing the development of museums of universal character such as the Louvre Abu Dhabi, whose development policy is based on the principle of sharing and partnership. It's also important for the encyclopedic character of a museum to be able to assume an educational role, fostering an openness toward the world and a better understanding of the history of humanity. It's therefore important for the collections and the way they're presented to be guided by the principle of presenting cultural heritage as not only part of a desire to amass the biggest collection of objects but, most importantly, from the perspective of a dialogue between cultures. By this I mean the development of more global narratives that focus on the connected history of the different peoples and cultures throughout time in a way that stimulates reflection on the world as a dynamic organism composed of different cultural, scientific, and historical contributions, and in constant evolution. By adopting this approach (in the spirit of Fernand Braudel's phrase "Every part of the world reflects the history of the world as a whole, is affected by it and comes to terms with it"), a museum can position itself beyond national differences.

DG: Does the critical situation in which cultural heritage finds itself in some parts of the world reinforce the importance of the encyclopedic museum as a repository of the world's past?

IB: André Malraux wrote, "The museum is one of the places that conveys the highest idea of mankind." It is precisely for this reason that today the museum is a target of choice in times of conflict: because of the ideal it represents; because of its mission of passing on the most important aspects of history. After all, the works transcend the differences between individuals and the places where they live many times over and attest to the diversity of human history.

Those museums in possession of collections from the affected regions have a key role to play in safeguarding this shared patrimony and in making citizens aware of its value—in particular, by making available to their younger audiences the different aspects of those civilizations and cultures whose diversity is under such grave threat today. Instead of the term *repository,* which conjures up the image of a safe filled with humanity's treasures, I prefer the notion of a platform for exchange and dialogue. When we see the destroyed heritage, the plundered and stolen objects, knowing that elsewhere in the world there is an example in a glass cabinet offers scant consolation. The most important thing is to ensure the circulation and sharing of knowledge about these objects so that everyone can understand the significance of Palmyra, of its funeral stele and their role in the dialogue between East and West, and of what they tell us about our contemporary societies. This educational role is performed by the museum but it needs to reach far beyond, into schools, into the media, into the public space.

DG: The encyclopedic museums are located in a particular nation. How should we picture the relationship between these museums, in their universality, and the state?

IB: The museums on the encyclopedic model are, above all, the products of nations that express their position on and perception of cultures from elsewhere—not only where the historical aspects are concerned but also with regard to contemporary actors connected with these pasts represented by the collections. They are also important contemporary instruments of diplomacy in that they create and maintain relationships among the nations through the collections and all the exchanges around them.

DG: Given the way our world is changing, does it need more encyclopedic museums? If so, why?

IB: Given the way it's changing, our world needs more places where, with the aim of fostering a global consciousness, knowledge is circulated and the diversity of cultures is put into perspective. I'm convinced that museums have a vital role to play in the pursuit of the common objective of erecting bulwarks of peace in the minds of the men and women of the world. In this sense, it's not only the number of encyclopedic museums that's important, it's the promotion of an education to the citizens of the world and the recognition of the museum's role in social inclusion, sustainable development, the promotion of creative industries, and the sharing of knowledge. This calls for financial and human resources as well as the incorporation of museum policy into global development policy. (2016)

11

Fiammetta Rocco

Culture editor, *The Economist*

Donatien Grau: You are the culture editor of a leading political and economic publication. How do you stand on the idea that all cultures could coexist in an encyclopedic museum?

Fiammetta Rocco: I would have to take a step back first and sketch out why we are having this conversation at all. One of the reasons we are having it is because, although these museums have roots that go back to Mesopotamia, in the sense of objects being collected together, they evolved out of the Middle Ages through very specialized cabinets of curiosities, cabinets of art—things that were secret and were for very few people to look at, to peer into great temples of culture of the nineteenth century. Now, 150 years later, we have more museums than we have ever had. We have more people going to museums than have ever gone to them before. So why is that?

It can be seen from two very different perspectives. In the West, or in the Old World, Europe, and America, museums have something that stands above technology, above modern invention, above fashion, above all modern ways that we might have of manipulating culture and ideas. They are collections of objects that were made in their time and have not been fiddled with. They still come to us with a certain integrity from the past.

In the developing world, in the world where museums are a newer invention, they are safe places for objects—many countries here have seen incredible turmoil and destruction. Museums represent a certain pinnacle of education. Therefore, they are seen as centers of sophistication—things to aspire to. They also serve in either newly created countries or very fractured societies as visible, physical manifestations of a sense of pride Human pride does not necessarily have to be nationalistic pride.

They also serve as a way of creating a unified story. There are problems with this, I realize: When you start saying "a national story, national narrative," how much do you have to hide? How much do you have to compromise?

None of this is perfect. This is going to be a thread through everything that I say. It is not a perfect construction, but in its imperfections, it stands for something. It has an appeal that we see every single day. The encyclopedic museum is the universal museum. The encyclopedic museum, the dream of bringing cultures together under one roof: Does it make sense? Yes, of course it makes sense. Can you do it? It is very difficult. Is it perfect? No. Is its imperfect manifestation better than if it did not exist at all? Of course.

Even though I see all their troubles and problems, they are very human to me. They are imperfect, but they keep on trying.

DG: To what do you ascribe the current emphasis on encyclopedic museums?

FR: It's interesting that they came to the fore in the nineteenth century at the same time as newspapers and novels. Art, in a way, helps us understand the Other, foreigners, things that are different, people who have varied backgrounds, who come out of a unique wellspring.

The greatest encyclopedic museums were formed in the nineteenth century, and they brought us news of the Other. Today, with the great emphasis that there has been over the last half century on trying—and undoing—the brickwork of empire, and colonialism, and empire building—all that had been used politically and culturally to create a particular world view—they are more relevant than ever.

We have spent half a century trying to understand other people—people whose sexuality or religion or culture or language is different, whose race and ethnicity is not like ours—and trying to place our own cultures not on top of others, but within a world in which other cultures exist as well. That is the appeal of the encyclopedic museum today.

DG: You mentioned imperial history: encyclopedic museums are also imperial museums. How does the imperial root relate to the fact that they are supposed to present a universal view of the world? Does it compromise their moral integrity?

FR: It's certainly true they arose in Britain, France, Germany, and Russia. And to a certain extent, not altogether differently, in America. There was a time of empire building and the clash of empires. I would say two things about that, which again have to do with imperfection: We cannot and should not destroy them. That would not work.

Empires come and empires go. Ever since the end of the Second World War, an enormous amount of human endeavor has been exercised in trying to understand the rise and fall of empires. The greatest universal museums are ones that have a constant sense of selfinquiry. That is the only way to deal with the imperial beginning.

Empires. Do they make it problematic? They are problematic in the same way that our entire history is problematic. Do we like the fact that we are descendants of imperialists? We have to deal with that the best way we can.

Do Americans have tremendous trouble with their racial past, their slavery past? Of course. We see it every single day. That can't be eradicated any more than the nineteenth-century encyclopedic museum in our great cities can be eradicated. What should they do?

If you go to museums—you would see this most strongly in anthropological museums about other cultures—and if you do not engage in any kind of endeavor of self-inquiry, they project a static, unevolving, unchanging view. To me, those kinds of museums are dead.

DG: We use the phrase *encyclopedic museum* as if we were talking about a whole. Is there a unifying pattern that would bring all of them together?

FR: I think we should start with the museums themselves, their situation past and present. They certainly have different identities, different personalities. The Louvre is a museum that is filled with art that was effectively looted from a neighboring European country. The fact that France chooses not to make an issue of this makes it possible to behave as if treasures carried away in invasion and war are somehow part of the deal; it has allowed the Louvre to continue on in the twentieth century and into the present. Face it: it is an extraordinary art museum full of treasures, but the elephant in the room is how a lot of these were acquired.

The British Museum, like many things British, grew out of them accidentally. It was not planned that way or dreamed up that way. The British Museum has always been a museum of cultures with some art—not great pictures, but sculpture—from the statuary of the Parthenon right down to armchairs made in Mozambique out of AK-47s by artists who may also be deemed to be craftsmen or reusers of war material.

The Met grew out of a new society, a moneyed society, an industrialized society that was also trying to show that it was sophisticated. Having great European art was one of the trappings of that sophistication. All Europeans were very happy to sell to rich Americans.

This is the origin. But now, you have an enormous board of trustees, whose first job is to stump up a lot of money. The new money is in new businesses, new industry, new areas of finance. People who are not necessarily interested in old European art or interested in contemporary art: so the Met, in order to chase the money, is going into contemporary art. Why? Because it wants to seize the moment and build up an endowment.

We need to think about these specific situations in order to describe their politics—which are not simply grand world politics. They are also very direct, straightforward ways of governing an institution. I see what we would call "universal museums" as having acquired art along the way, some of them more diligently than others.

DG: Since you mentioned that it is important that they come from empires, and should acknowledge it, how are they to deal with their history?

FR: There are various aspects to this. Empires, emperors and imperial courts are concentrations of power—economic power, as well as political power. There has always been a system of patronage, in terms of artists, craftsmen, makers of cultural objects. Therefore, a lot of what has ended up being acquired by encyclopedic museums like the British Museum, the Met, and the Berlin museums have been the great works from other empires around the world.

Inevitably, there is a concentration of attention on what could loosely be called the "chaps and maps" view of history, and not on more fragile components, voiceless people, underdogs of all kinds. That is one side of it. Are our encyclopedic museums in a way perpetuating the idea that only this physical cultural legacy matters, or do they have another aspect?

The Louvre, the Met, the British Museum, and the Berlin museums are enormous centers of scholarship, which is a more discreet, and yet perhaps more powerful, contribution.

DG: These museums feature a certain definition of universality. How should they relate to that ideal of universality today?

FR: A simple ideal must be that the things that unite us are greater than the things that divide us, however that is expressed. There is a huge role, for example, for universal museums, encyclopedic museums in the West, with not just their scholarship but their practical capacity of training people.

There is a very practical contribution they can make to other parts of the world, ensuring they provide real help to other countries, particularly countries at war—countries facing economic and political strife—to look after their own cultural legacies.

DG: How do you think they can relate to the fact that now, more and more of the discourse and more and more of their approach relates to universality, whereas the history and their holdings are incredibly different and mark a very clear emphasis on some civilizations over others?

FR: Unless you have that constant effort, self-inquiry, it is very easy to perpetuate that old construct. Part of the self-inquiry might manifest itself in two ways. One is that the acquisitions and holdings are ongoing, and they evolve over time. Having holdings of African and Polynesian art does not mean that you cannot focus on their value and their deepening.

The essence of scholarship is to be involved in, to push, to encourage, and to nurture conversations between cultures that were considered to be less important and to recognize that some of those conversations nowadays do not necessarily take place from the outside back to the metropolis, rather they are taking place along various parts of what we have looked at differently, what we used to call "the outside."

There is, for example, not one modernism, but many modernisms. Why should one not study Gutai at the same time as one studies modernism in America, modernism in Europe? There are now many conversations going on across the Indian Ocean, across South Africa, India, and the western part of Australia about what the Indian Ocean world is, which has nothing to do with what the European metropolis represented. That is very much a discussion for the encyclopedic museums. First of all, one needs humility and the willingness to be a listener in those conversations. You do not always have to speak.

DG: Encyclopedic museums, as they are now, are considered to be instruments of global power, what is known as cultural diplomacy. How do you see the tendency of these museums to be instruments of cultural diplomacy and power?

FR: There would be various different stories to this. Museums are never going to be a central part of the great diplomatic movements between nations. At the very best, they can be helpful. Usually afterward, we see or hear about certain things to be done, or shaped, or influenced, or moved. It is very difficult for these museums to continue maintaining that their right to exist is solely because of their holdings, and for no other reason at all. Their reasons for existence need to evolve, just as any other do.

One rather practical, simple way of doing this is for them to give back a huge amount in knowledge, training, and assistance to museums—many of which are just starting out. The real cultural diplomacy lies in this support; it is not in the trading back and forth of objects. It is in helping India, or Abu Dhabi, or China build a trained generation of their own of people who not only care but are knowledgeable and will then go on and train their own youngsters.

DG: Many civilizations are not represented, or not properly represented, in the collections of these museums. Do you think this absence should be acknowledged?

FR: Maybe it is that I am very fortunate in the work that I do and in the fact that I now live in London. I grew up in Kenya. There was no museum other than the national museum, so I did not see a great museum until I was in my late teens. Probably when I came to university in the United Kingdom.

My grandparents were both artists and, having grown up in that culture where museums were very important, we were able to pass it down. In a sense, I have always seen the encyclopedic museum as being a family of different relatives who have different attributes. You go to each of them for different things.

Sometimes we ask: "Should there be only one encyclopedic museum that shows everything?" That is never going to happen. Each museum has a different strength. Do you go to the Met for their African holdings? No. you do not. Do you go to the British Museum for great French painting? Absolutely not. Their diversity is part of their attraction. This issue of completion is a non-problem. We need to talk about the museums that exist and what can be done in them.

One of the extraordinary things that I remember from going to the British Museum, the Met, and the Louvre when I was in my teens was that incredible sense of wonder, not just at seeing things but at almost mainlining knowledge, and information, visual information, but also intellectual information.

Now, I have a daughter who is twenty. If she wants to take a great injection of the information, she is going to go to Google. She is not going to museums. What should encyclopedic museums do? It's the question for all museums, but it's particularly relevant for encyclopedic museums, because of the broadness of their arena. What should they do to engage this generation? That is the biggest question that they have to answer. They are not wholly addressing this question, or perhaps not addressing it as energetically as they should. That chiefly may be because they are still run by a generation of people who are pre-Internet.

DG: Do you think that new encyclopedic museums can be founded?

FR: Should every country have one? Clearly, it is a very difficult thing to do. It does not make sense. How different are they in individual countries from their national museums?

There is a huge section of the world where national museums are of vital political and educational importance, the only place where we are able to see some art and visual culture. But the question is, how do a national and an encyclopedic museum interact? Do they coincide?

In fact, the whole question we are talking about here is about Abu Dhabi. Is what Abu Dhabi is doing a good idea? They are building a national museum. They are building an art museum and what they call a universal museum—the first universal museum in the Arab world. The national museum is going to be the story of the nation as seen through the life of its founder. That speaks to a society for whom the patronage and protection of a founding father figure is very important and unifying.

They are still writing the script of what the universal museum is going to be. It opened to the public on 11 November 2017, but much work remains to be done. Across twelve galleries, the museum presents a chronological and thematic narrative of world history. The shift from hunter-gathering to sedentary life produced the first villages, symbolized here by a monumental 8,500-year-old plasterwork statue with two heads, lent by Jordan. That led to the first great powers in the fertile valleys of the Tigris, Euphrates, Nile, Indus, and Yellow Rivers around 3,000 BC, which, in turn, led to the first empires, the universal religions, and the continental trade routes. Pioneering voyages offered new perspectives on the world and, in time, new ways of living and governing. For the Louvre Abu Dhabi, globalization is a very old idea and a cause for optimism. The Gilbert Stuart portrait of George Washington, which the museum bought from the Armand Hammer Foundation in Los Angeles, is a rare version with a rainbow in the background. The early galleries, with similar objects from similar periods, although coming from very different places, are very effective.

The Louvre Abu Dhabi is the first universal museum to be built in the twenty-first century and the first in the Arab world. Manuel Rabaté, the French director, describes it as an "adaptation or renewal" of the Enlightenment idea that led to the original universal institutions—the British Museum, the Hermitage, and the Louvre in Paris. Some may feel it is a bit rich for a country that has limited free speech and a history of using imported indentured labor on its construction sites to ask people to "see humanity in a new light" or "recognize ourselves in each other," as exhorted by the posters advertising the Louvre Abu Dhabi on the main highway to Saadiyat Island. But its fans are passionate.

They see the Louvre Abu Dhabi as a pillar in the effort to turn the UAE away from its dependence on oil and toward becoming a modern, knowledge-based economy. It will be an important local employer, especially of women, and not just in menial jobs. Hissa al-Dhaheri, the deputy director, is an Emirati woman, as is the finance director. The 60-strong staff is expected to grow to 150 by next year; many more will be employed indirectly. And it will be a draw for foreign tourists; 4.4 million visited Abu Dhabi in 2016. The city is already a busy transport hub. The emphasis on culture distinguishes it from the shopping malls and glitzy commercial tourism of Dubai, an hour down the road. Most of all, the LAD is seen locally, and by neighbors like Saudi Arabia, as a bastion against what it regards as the forces of evil: Islamic extremism and Iran. That Abu Dhabi feels itself under threat cannot be underestimated, and the iconography of fear runs through the museum—from Abel Grimmer's 1595 painting of the Tower of Babel to the final exhibit, Ai Weiwei's Babel-shaped *Fountain of Light*.

It is not simply a cleverly branded product that the Louvre exported to the Middle East. They want it to be the first universal museum in the Arab world. It is a tremendous ambition, and it will be impossible to judge for at least a generation.

DG: If the new museums, like Abu Dhabi, are to be founded, what should their approach be? They have to start from scratch, or near scratch.

FR: If they are prepared to be as ambitious as they could be, they stand at an extraordinary moment in history. The old notion of encyclopedic museums is growing out of being a Western construct.

It does not have to be. For the very first time you have the possibility for an encyclopedic museum not to be an imperial construction. Therefore, in its way, it could be a great experiment. That is the first time that we see dialogue between cultures that speak many languages. Latin, English, or French is no longer at the top. It is much more of a dialogue, not of equals, but of histories and historical experiences that, at least, deserve mutual respect and recognition.

DG: Does the world as it evolves need more encyclopedic museums? Why?

FR: Do we need more buildings full of objects that have been collected together, many of which can't be displayed because there is no room or there is no money? I am not entirely sure. Do we need more cultural dialogue, more exchange of specialties, training, and education?

Of course we do. What can we do in the West, in the great city museums of Europe and America, while we watch the Jihadists, the Islamic state, tearing down statues? We can sit and wring our hands.

We can train Iraqi and Syrian archaeologists, curators, people who have the knowledge to deal with emergency protection. We can prepare them for a time when these things will be returned to safer hands. If we train four this year, they will train twenty. Those others will train another hundred. That's the best thing we can do. And that is something the encyclopedic museums, as places for the scholarship of objects, can take on now. (2015–17)

12

Zaki Nusseibeh

State minister, United Arab Emirates

Donatien Grau: The encyclopedic museum, as it is defined today, is based on the dream of bringing all cultures together under one roof. Do you think it makes sense at all?

Zaki Nusseibeh: Yes, it does. It makes sense because the world is becoming smaller all the time, and because it is important for different cultures and different countries to know more about each other. No one will ever be able to recreate encyclopedic museums the way they were done in the eighteenth and nineteenth centuries. What you can do is create a museum that attempts to bring different dimensions from the various cultures around you, and do it in a way to give an insight into all those cultures, and relates them to your own culture, in order to make your own public, your own people, understand better what is happening around them, and in order to make people who come from overseas understand what is happening in your own country. It is a space for that sort of dialogue, more than any other form of museum.

DG: Often, the encyclopedic museum is seen in opposition to the national museum. Do you think the two models are antagonistic to each other?

ZN: I would not see them as antagonistic. They are two sides of the same question. The national museum, obviously, can tell more of the history of a nation, but it would not make sense to do it in exclusion of everything that has happened abroad. The history has political, cultural, economic developments, and all these cannot be considered in exclusion of other nations. In

Abu Dhabi, we are doing a national museum, the national museum of Sheikh Zayed. But we are doing it at the same time as we are building a Louvre in Abu Dhabi, which is going to be an encyclopedic museum.

An encyclopedic museum is designed to really look across the cultures of the world and to try to say that there are many points of convergence that we need to look at, and there are many points of difference to consider in order to understand them better. This is something that is as relevant today as it was two years ago.

The encyclopedic museum, for instance, will bring arts, culture, and artifacts from different eras, different periods, and different parts of the world, whereas the national museum will focus on what is happening within one's own country and region, and how that relates to the events happening in the world.

Obviously there are points where things will be parallel. If you look at the concept of religion, for instance: one way of looking at it would be within the nation, within the story of the national development. The other would be in the story of human evolution or human development. There will be points where they touch, and there will be points where they diverge. And this approach can be adapted to many other topics.

DG: The localization of the museum seems to be a very important component of its meaning.

ZN: If we look specifically at our region of the world: in order to go visit museums, we have to travel abroad. There are very few museums as such in the region itself and in the Gulf, and no encyclopedic museum. Therefore, having one that is homegrown will give the opportunity to young people to discover art, to think about it, to understand the world better.

There are two sides to that issue. We are talking, on the one hand, about education, formation, and, on the other, about a long-time investment in culture.

It is important to have this museum localized in your own country because it plays a very clear civic function, and I am thrilled that we are building it at this time of our history. One of the things that excites me when I come to Europe and I go to the British Museum or to the Louvre in Paris is that they are no longer seen as hostile, anemic, cult places. They are places where children come, play, run around, and look at the same time at these different cultures of the world. It is the marvelous story of mankind. How did it evolve? How did it develop? It is important to have it located in our region so that our young people can be exposed to it, and can benefit from a museum that is also designed for them.

DG: Are there things that should be done specifically for a certain location in an encyclopedic museum? Are there different versions of encyclopedic museum that might be more inspiring than others?

ZN: Yes, some museums, for instance, focus on a historical narrative or a geographical narrative. It will be interesting to poll each museum, to compare their underlying narratives, to decipher what they want to showcase.

In the case of Abu Dhabi, it is not going to separate the different geographic regions of the world, but rather going to look at them together and to feature, within one period, what was happening in these different parts of the world. What was happening in China? In Africa? In the Gulf region? What was happening in North America in that particular time period?

This is an interesting way of trying to bring once again these different strands of culture together, to look at them and to find out where the common points of convergence and where the points of divergence are.

DG: The one thing that is very specific about the encyclopedic museum—which is also known as the *musée universel* in French—is this idea of universality. Do you think such an idea makes sense, and that it could be perceived in the museum?

ZN: Personally, I believe that the story of humankind is universal. We sometimes tend to look at it as a construct and disregard it. It is an illusion of intelligence: we forget that most of us originated somewhere in Africa. Sometimes, when you look at the DNA script of different individuals, you can see that it is very similar; it would be interesting to take DNA scripts of many individuals living in different parts of the Middle East, whether in Israel, Palestine, or Syria, and then try to find out where they originated from and how they came together.

We forget that, in the very end, the story of humanity is one. For many decades, there was a Eurocentric vision of the world that tended to look down on the cultures and on the national evolutions of the different parts of the world that were not Europe. Today, we have a new narrative and it is evolving. It is crucial to bring it through.

I believe it is particularly important to convey a universal message, and to state clearly that we are all part of the same family of mankind. This, incidentally, is something that was central to the ideals of Sheikh Zayed, the founder of the United Arab Emirates. And here you see how the national narrative and the encyclopedic narrative can interact.

We belong to this same family of mankind regardless of the different religions, creeds, colors, races, or backgrounds, and therefore there is a story, there is something to look at here and to say something about.

DG: You say "a new narrative." How would you describe it?

ZN: It is fascinating to know, for instance, what was happening in the Gulf region 12,000 years ago. Sometimes, one looks at a place like Abu Dhabi and tends to put it within a narrative that only considers what happened with oil, forgetting the thousands of years of evolution of this community. It would be interesting to look at what was happening in Dibba AlHisn or in Dilmun, then look at what was happening around us in Egypt and Babylon, and try and see the points of contact. What were the points of convergence between these different things?

It is interesting to look, for instance, at an old Talmudic script and an old Quranic script: to look at the embellishments that were imbedded into the writing of these manuscripts, religious or sacred, and to find out where the points of convergence in those were. There are many stories to be told. We can only tell them once we look at human culture, human evolution, as a universal one.

DG: One thing that is interesting is that alongside the trend for the encyclopedic museum, there is a trend for the contemporary museum. How do you see the relation between the encyclopedic museum and the contemporary museum?

ZN: There are parallel narratives in both kinds of museums, and both models dialogue, if they are taken from the right point of view. There has been a great interest for the contemporary museum in the Gulf region. In Abu Dhabi, for many decades, art and human creativity were looked at from a Eurocentric perspective. What mattered was only what was happening in Paris, London, or New York: that was accepted as art. There was a neglect for what was happening everywhere else in the world.

We have found out in the last thirty or forty years, I think, that a new interest has developed internationally, in part thanks to people who have these visionary ideas of coming out to the region and looking at what is happening. At that point, you can see that institutions, such as the Guggenheim, Tate Modern, and many others, adopt new narratives.

For the first time you have perspectives from a Lebanese artist, a Sudanese artist, or a Syrian one. Again, in those contemporary museums, the message that comes across tells you that the creative energy of humankind is a universal story.

At a time when we have so many conflicts that are sectarian and turn religion into an ideology, it is crucial to go back to the foundation, to the base—which the human story, the human culture and journey, are really the same.

Contemporary art, from that perspective, is contemporary with what is happening in Iran, India, Pakistan, and Sudan, and in countries that people did not traditionally associate with contemporary art. Therefore, you can see that the message you find in a contemporary museum and in an encyclopedic museum is the same, and it is particularly relevant to feature it now.

DG: The encyclopedic museum is perhaps, of all museums, the most political. How can one deal with the political element of this model?

ZN: The traditional encyclopedic or universal museums tended to look at it from the perspective of their Western superiority, to say that they collect artifacts from cultures of primitive or underdeveloped regions of the world, in order to bring them together and to look at them. This approach led to a separation of the different cultures, the one from the other.

I think there is a political narrative that goes in the other direction, which is to say that many of those cultures have borrowed from each other. They are the many contributors to the one main stream of human civilization: ancient Egypt, ancient Mesopotamia, ancient China, and ancient Africa are all as important.

The political narrative is to say that, although we are living today in an era in which these sectarian differences have become brutal and bloody, we have to go back and look at this universal history of mankind, and accept the idea that we are one family, that we are on a very vulnerable earth and that we need to work together in order to survive. In that sense, there clearly is a lesson that the encyclopedic museum is teaching us.

DG: You consider the encyclopedic museum with a great deal of hope. How do you think it can have an impact on the world, since it hosts only a limited number of visitors?

ZN: To begin with, it will have an impact on our own people, and that is important: it opens the world to them and it brings the world to them. Also, it will affect anyone who comes to that part of the world. Already we have seen very rich exchanges between everyone who came in and became part of this project.

Initially, many of the professionals in Europe and the United States, whether it was in France, New York, or England, were hostile to the idea of coming out to a desert and trying to take what they saw as culture to an area that they considered almost did not deserve it. There was real racism in some of the initial reactions to these projects.

Now there is an engagement by different people, professionals from varied backgrounds, and an understanding that these rich exchanges are beneficial in both directions. If you consider that in Europe alone, Islam is the second largest religion, it is important for the institutions that are located there to tackle it. It has become fundamental to have a better understanding between Europe and the wider Mediterranean region.

Islam is not only a Middle Eastern religion, it is also a European one. In fact, Arabs are a minority within the larger Muslim population of the world. There are many narratives that come together, many strands that need to come together. It will have to happen.

The Emirates receives 15 million visitors a year, and 100 million persons pass through the airports. I can therefore be optimistic that it will make an impact universally.

DG: Encyclopedic museums are places in which objects are seen as both documents and artworks. In a sense, they challenge the idea that art as a concept is a Western construct. Do you think its impact is specific in that regard?

ZK: I do not think that art is a Western concept at all. There is rock art in Abu Dhabi itself. If you go out to Al Ain, to the hilly excavations that date back from four thousand years ago, you see some beautiful rock art showing some wonderful gazelles and people dancing. You go anywhere in Saudi Arabia and you can find this rock art that has been there for thousands of years.

In fact, the encyclopedic museum is designed to fight the very idea that art is a Western construct. What is true is that, within the Arab world, for instance, there is more emphasis on words than on representation itself. But does that mean there is no art? Art is a universal energy. Universal museums are trying to bring all those facts into one forum so that we can look at them historically, narratively, and can see how it has evolved. Yes, artworks are also documents, but does that mean they stop being artworks?

DG: It is a space for learning as well.

ZN: For learning, of course, for exchanging ideas, for making new discoveries, for entering a world of things that are new to you and have been there for centuries. This is what is exciting about museums and why it is so important that we go on investing in those forums. Not because they are iconic, prestigious projects—that is not why they are important. They are important because they are an essential part of the investment in education, locally, nationally, and also universally.

Museums today are not just forums where people come, they meet, they exchange ideas. Virtual technology makes it possible for museums to link each other, to link to electronic libraries that are available to them. The technological possibilities are fascinating—it's remarkable what they can make available for any part of the world to plug into this general managed society that we live in.

DG: An important element of the encyclopedic museum is the issue of power: when they were first built, they were displays of power. Do you think it is the same today?

ZN: I do not believe so because it has become unacceptable now for any country to show hegemonic urges toward other parts of the world.

Colonialization was accepted in the nineteenth century as a natural development of society: it is not today. You cannot go to a country, rob their art, and place it in your museums. That makes a major difference. I don't look at universal museums today as expressions of power, because the sources of acquisition are not the same. In these acquisitions, you could see the inequality between cultures and countries: some artworks were bought at high price, others were simply taken. That is obviously not the case today. There is a high price for all objects and not just for some, an investment in knowledge, and an investment in opening up the world for your own people, and giving them access to the rest of the world.

DG: An essential argument that has been made against traditional encyclopedic museums is that they are not encyclopedic at all. The different cultures are not represented in the same way or with the same relevance. Is that something that can be or should be corrected in the new version of the encyclopedic museum?

ZN: It is easier to correct in the sense that, obviously, there is no museum today that can aspire to become truly encyclopedic. There is no means for any new museum to be able to get access to all the artifacts, to all the cultures of the world. You cannot find all those hundreds of thousands of artifacts that are now in the Louvre or the British Museum. Therefore, you need to find other ways to elaborate the encyclopedia.

At the same time, the technological innovations that have developed also make it possible for any encyclopedic museum to truly enrich the content through a judicious mixture of what is on show physically and what is available digitally.

I know that some tourists and even scholars are against it and believe that what you see physically before you is the real content of any truly great museum. But such an approach does not contract the immense electronic possibilities. We are going to see more and more of this in the future: why not have three-dimensional projections of objects?

The electronic library of the world offers extraordinary possibilities: those millions of books that are being digitized should be used to complement the encyclopedic museum.

DG: The project in Abu Dhabi proved from its very existence that the encyclopedic museum is not simply a Western imperial construct, because it is the first real encyclopedic museum, at that scale, founded outside of the West. Do you think that new encyclopedic museums can be founded?

ZN: Why not? It is an important forum for learning, and therefore it is very useful. It is important to say that every part of the world has its contribution to a universal narrative, and that it is possible to have a universal museum created today. That it is still possible to be able to do it, but not in the same spirit that the initial encyclopedic museums were created in.

They were signs of great empires that went out and collected artifacts from different parts of the world as an expression of power, but also as a forum for learning. Even going back to the library of Alexandria, there was always the idea of needing a forum for learning available in one region, where people can come and exchange ideas. This is the idea we have to foster. It is something that we need on the continent. We need it today more than at any other time before.

DG: The issue of scale is crucial. Do you think there is a required scale for an encyclopedic museum?

ZN: Obviously, it needs to have an important collection. It needs to have a significant collection that tells the story it intends to tell, and therefore there is a minimum. The collection justifies the naming of any such institution—the grand name of being a museum, and, even more, an encyclopedic one.

However, you do not need to have as big an institution as the British Museum or the Louvre in Paris in order to have a significant institution. I think 70 to 80 percent of the world's museums have been built in the last forty or fifty years. Sometimes we tend to think that the museum is only a nineteenth-century concept, but many modern towns in Germany, Europe, in France and in England continue to open museums. Museums are an important part of community life, anywhere in the world.

DG: What should be the components of an encyclopedic museum built today? What would be their structure?

ZN: There is a collection that tells a narrative. I don't think that you can just bring different artifacts from elsewhere: in Abu Dhabi, there is a strategic partnership with the Agence France-Muséums, a collective of thirty institutions that work together on a scientific program, in order to be able to tell a narrative that is significant. You cannot just open an encyclopedic museum in the way you did it before, and try and bring to it everything that you can have access to. It is a collection, and it is a narrative. And, then, from that collection, there is everything else that goes with it. There is the library, the open forum, the ability to have people come in, to make it part of your community life, part of your educational system, the access to children, the narrative you can provide those children with. It is a collection, it is a forum, library. It is a virtual world as well, and it is part of community life, with services like cafés and restaurants. It should be a place where it is fun to go to.

DG: For a long time, encyclopedic museums collected mostly cultures from the past. Now more and more they are collecting the present, and the the Louvre in Abu Dhabi also has major works of contemporary art. How should it relate to the past, the present, and the future?

ZN: The real narrative is to say that the development of human-kind is a universal story: that we are related to each other, that there are certain paths that we have taken, some of them lead to great disasters, some others lead to a flowering of knowledge and understanding. We need to have the museum as an expression of optimism in the future. Humankind can work together as it did in the past and can achieve progress and advancement.

This museum shows that people can be together rather than being against each other. The hegemonic museum is no longer in fashion today. You are not showing that you are a great power that has collected trophies from the rest of the world, but you are saying that your story is common, your story is universal. We need to understand it as such in order to survive.

If you look around in the Middle East, with all the tensions that are going through there, and you think of the Sunni and Shiite divide that is so bloody today, what is it all about? Certain minor differences in some interpretations that happened fifteen hundred years ago.

Can it not be looked at rationally? The true spirit of religion, without its ideological misapplication, cannot lead to these tensions between people who share the same ideas, the same message, and the same history. There are many stories to be looked at in this light and, as a consequence, the present is part of those stories as well. It is a story moving forward in time, that we look at to be optimistic about the future. If you look around us today in the Middle East, you may think that the whole world is going to disintegrate around us. The encyclopedic museum is the place for us to hope. Time will tell its impact. (2015–17)

13

Michael Govan

CEO and director, Los Angeles County Museum of Art

Donatien Grau: You are a forceful speaker for the idea of situating the encyclopedic museum historically, and for reconsidering it.

Michael Govan: We have to think that every institution is a model of thought built at some particular time. I am always struck by the fact that art is more than 35,000 years old and museums as we know them are only a couple hundred years old.

I often say things to disrupt people's sense of certainty about the longevity of museums: when they look at museums, they sometimes think that museum equals art. Most encyclopedic museums carry the image of ancient architecture, and therefore they present themselves as having somehow existed forever. Honestly, the history of museums is short. They are evolving and will continue to evolve. They are simply frames for considering art.

Of course there is art made within and for museums, but most art was not made for museums. Museums are containers to collect and present art, and they were a construct of a particular time and place—in this case, the Enlightenment in the eighteenth century, having since been refined and revised only a little bit. We have not fundamentally changed the concept, which dates from before the invention of the airplane, the telephone, the Internet, and easy photography. It seems to me it should be agreed that there is no fixed model for museums. We are looking at a cultural construction of a particular place and time, which is subject to change.

Yes, I've been very forceful about possible change: not "the" change, as if museums were one thing and are to become something else, but more pluralistically, many possible changes. Encyclopedic museums tend to look the same. Every locality wanted a library of the exotic—things from outside their locality. But now photography, travel, television, and the Internet have changed the way we perceive the world. We need a more locally devised model. We should think less about the encyclopedic museum than about how a general museum of art of all time and place might exist, in my case, in a city like Los Angeles, right now. Critical thinking about our history leads to more contextually based definitions.

Some people say, "Oh, you are attacking the encyclopedic museum." Far from it: it's an amazing invention that is especially relevant to the future in a way that twenty years ago I wasn't so sure it was. When I went to school I learned that most institutions were the result of biased power structures that should be mistrusted. What I find now (maybe because I'm older) is that the institution we know as the museum can be an incredibly relevant construction for the present, if properly framed and properly accessed—which means: reframed.

DG: You have a plan now to rebuild most of your museum to make it more adapted to the present conditions. How do you rethink an encyclopedic museum like the Los Angeles County Museum of Art?

MG: We are right now conceiving a new building for LACMA that has, of course, to do with the need for a safe place for art, because our older buildings are no longer serviceable. But really our current plan is not about the beauty of a new building; it's about the beauty of the program.

What is one element of the program? The proposed building has an organic shape. Not just because it looks sleek and cool, and not just because it might echo aspects of the organic form of a lake (the La Brea Tar Pits next door, in particular), but because the organic form does not tend to have a particular front or back. Therefore, no culture is in the front, no culture is in the back. It is an architectural form that embodies a reframing of an encyclopedic collection that in older museums might be situated on a formal symmetrical podium—in a temple.

The grand staircases of New York's Metropolitan Museum of Art and many other large museums represent a world view that is not necessarily that of present-day Los Angeles. Therefore, a different form must be found today to present and arrange diverse art objects, because values and meaning are embedded not just in the pieces themselves but also in their order and arrangement, and the atmosphere within which they are shown.

At present-day LACMA we turned the display upside down and decided to start with modern and contemporary art on the ground floor, and then go up to ancient times. There is an arbitrary distinction about which way is north and which way is south, why we have a hierarchy of up and down, and why some cultures are considered lesser. If the world were turned upside down, would it be different? At LACMA, we attempt to flatten these geographical hierarchies, as well as to flatten the hierarchies among the different media of art.

It is a philosophically strategic decision to have encouraged the Academy Museum of Motion Pictures to be built next to LACMA: when visitors enter the museum campus, they will perceive that film merits the same attention as art. It does. But that isn't reflected in a traditional encyclopedic museum anywhere else. It's not that we're trying to add popular culture to high culture. Rather, I would question whether or not there is any distinction at all. Some commercial cinema can be considered high art as easily as a painting made in the name of high art can come to be considered, in the end, a product of popular culture. Really, what's in a museum is what lasts and inspires many generations.

One of my favorite examples of understanding the flexible nature of hierarchy and value in art comes from one of my trustees, the head of our acquisitions committee, Lynda Resnick, whose name is on the Resnick Pavilion, and who asked pointedly in an acquisitions committee meeting: "When was it that painting got to be more expensive than furniture?" Indeed, it used to be furniture was more expensive. Tapestries, for example, at one time were far more expensive than paintings, and then all of a sudden everything flipped. It's like a giant sign that says, "Remember, values are constantly changing."

Hierarchies are constantly shifting in time. One idea of the museum is to set the hierarchies at the moment. The other is to try to be less hierarchical. What I work on is the idea of flattening: flattening hierarchies of culture, of media, and of time. Models of time, for me, are perhaps the strongest, most powerful example of bias. Architect Rem Koolhaas's proposal for LACMA in 2001 was based on a totalizing horizontal time-space grid. It was a revolution in thinking to put all the artworks on one floor, but its European-Cartesian time-space grid contemplated that time was unidirectional. When you study Asian art or pre-Columbian ancient American art you begin to understand that time in those cultures is more like a circle. The

Aztec calendar or the Mayan calendar is a circle, whereas the encyclopedic museum tends to strongly show the arrow of time in one direction, from past to present. If I look at the world, I see one model of time in one set of cultures, another model of time in another set of cultures.

If I decide to organize the museum backward in European time or Cartesian time—contemporary first and old last—that's perfectly valid. I would argue it's even more true. To start at the beginning of our history and walk to the present is a strange thing. Every day I wake up and get out of bed in the present. It's a lot of work to construct the past and to be able to see the past properly. I would say that it's a more truthful organization of the museum to have contemporary art first.

These things are much more malleable—not arbitrary, but malleable—than most people think, or than the definition of museums implies in everyday practice. Art existed for a long time before encyclopedic museums did. Art will potentially exist for a long time after encyclopedic museums. Even artworks that we consider relevant today are seen as such not because they are absolute in their exposition of an idea but because they are open. They are less determined, less specific, and so people in other times can invest these objects with new meaning, whereas an object that is very specific to its time and place sometimes is less lasting.

I was recently asked about what might inspire my thinking about museums of the future. As we were sitting in a room with windows overlooking Fifth Avenue in New York, I thought about that place. On Fifth Avenue I see the beautiful Metropolitan Museum, the New York Public Library—all clad in closed-stone facades commonly used for museums, libraries, and banks in the late nineteenth and early twentieth centuries to convey their everlasting quality, that they were always around and always would be. In the case of a bank, you need to feel comfortable depositing your money there, suggested by an architecture that is ancient and permanent. I noticed the museum and the library have not changed, but every bank has abandoned its stone temple facade in favor of glass—transparency, the value of the present. Today the bank that's not transparent is considered to be suspicious, not safe and lasting.

When I look at that change in our value system, I think, yes, the museum should be glass. Its walls should be transparent, inviting people to take a look—like a store on Fifth Avenue before you walk in. So many people in Los Angeles don't know what's in a museum, not because they're unintelligent but because they never grew up going to museums. Why would you know what's in a museum if you haven't already been to one?

DG: But isn't there a risk that the public will be confused with turning things upside down?

MG: When we make an exhibition, as opposed to presenting permanent collections, we tend to be very good now at creating a narrative that one can follow. It's not always chronological, and it's not always by culture.

We find many narratives to go through art. Chronology can sometimes play a role, but usually other narratives are stronger, and then there are many exhibitions that don't follow those; but they always have a narrative. No one is saying you don't have to have a frame or a narrative.

The question is the bias of the frame of the narrative—how often it changes. You do not need to fix the collection in one narrative: you can present it in different ways over time. I don't mean changing the collection every week, but maybe every few years we could commit ourselves to the complete reinstallation of the whole collection, each time with coherent presentations so that the public is not confused and realizes there are many ways to read art and art history.

Recently we put all of our Latin American art together, ancient to modern, with a very strong geographic frame, thereby taking Latin American modernism outside of its juxtaposition with midcentury modern American or North American art. One may present it one way for a few years, and then another way for another few years. Maybe putting the permanent collection in motion is one way to be true to a diversity of approaches without being confusing.

DG: You worked in the ultimate global institution, the Guggenheim under Tom Krens, and now you lead an encyclopedic museum, which is a Western construct. How do you stand toward it?

MG: The encyclopedic museum is a totally European/Western construct, and in that sense most of the United States is part of Europe. It's absolutely an arbitrary construction of a culture that wants to have a coherent totality of knowledge, and an ordering system that accounts for everything. That's not necessarily a value in all cultures. It's interesting that in Latin America and in Asia there are almost no encyclopedic museums.

Some cultures maintain a place for mystery. There's a general understanding we now have in science that most of matter is not accounted for or seen. There are many ancient and other cultures that take for granted that we do not have access to everything. The European system of the Enlightenment is based on the idea that you can account for everything. It's one of the most subtle, beautiful, amazing systems of knowledge that's ever been invented. It's just not primary. It's not the only one.

You can ask whether or not that gives me great doubt in coming to work every day in an encyclopedic museum. The answer is, I used to doubt such museums. Thirty years ago I didn't have the experience to think about it, and again, context is everything. In a place like Los Angeles, which speaks hundreds of languages, living languages, and has the largest populations of other cultures and other nations outside the locations of those nations—whether it's Korean, Chinese, or Native American—there's great relevance to the breadth of what is offered versus the strategy that I took, for example, in making a museum like Dia Beacon, which was as narrow in content as any museum—twenty-one artists of the same era, each with almost a museum to themselves. Both models are equally compelling, properly considered in context.

I do not believe that the encyclopedic museum is the ultimate good. Why would it be absolutely better than its opposite—the intimacy of seeing the work of just a few artists in depth? Being able to immerse oneself bodily, physically in a narrow frame of time and ideas is a very thrilling experience. When you see the work of Robert Ryman in an encyclopedic museum, he is the guy who made the totally white painting, whereas if you see three rooms of Robert Ryman, you get to sense that every work is different, that they are like sculptures. You realize there is no such thing as white because you see the variation by subtle contrast.

DG: How do you announce the difference of your approach to the encyclopedic museum?

MG: Practically every big museum in every city has the same classical temple facade. You could confuse them if you were not an expert. One has a pediment, and one does not. One has double columns, and one might focus on Corinthian versus Ionic columns.

Architecture is one way to disrupt the certainty, and, even more greatly, to celebrate the uniqueness of a time and place, to make it more specific. It's a very specific gesture to place Chris Burden's *Urban Light* as the entrance to LACMA. You can read it in relation to the general definition of the museum as well as our specific museum. The 202 cast-iron streetlamps that comprise that sculpture come from 1920s and 1930s Los Angeles, and were specifically and diversely designed by the many cities of Los Angeles. As Burden says, "They were public art before they became public art." There are many different designs among the lamps because each city took unique pride in being differentiated. You could read each of them as a column. You could read them as the collection of the diversity of the cities, and as a multiple, pluralistic temple.

The artist placed all the tall lamps in the center. It does look like a temple, but it's transparent. It has no body, and yet it's monumental and lights up like a beacon. You can see it from an airplane landing in LAX. It gives up nothing in terms of spectacle. Yet it's made of the elements of the everyday urban landscape, not the elements of a high-minded temple. To present a work of art, not architecture, as the entrance to the museum, is another reversal.

That *Urban Light* is both a temple and not, high and low, art and architecture, is not confusing. It's both a thing and a critique of itself. Critiques keep things alive. It's not meant to destroy the encyclopedic museum; it's meant to critique the unconscious definition of the museum. That questioning is what keeps things alive.

DG: It seems that the encyclopedic museum is a very hierarchical museum and that you aim at turning that upside down as well: encyclopedic museums do not have to be hierarchical institutions.

MG: This is absolutely imperative now. Some people question why I, with architect Renzo Piano, put the bar and the restaurant outdoors right behind the ticket desk at the entrance of the museum. I'm quite proud of it. The outdoor gives a sense of community. We organize concerts, people stay there late at night. It is a proper plaza. What an encyclopedic museum should be is more than a place for art—it should be a place for public life.

There is very little that we have done here that has not been experimented with elsewhere. What we do is put it out front. With *Urban Light,* I said, "Put the security barrier behind the sculpture, so that the first gallery in the museum is open 24/7." You can shoot a music video there at midnight, which people do. Visitors create their own sense of community within an image of community: 202 streetlamps from all over Los Angeles.

How do you equate the otherwise foreboding entrance of the museum to community? For a start, you can simply reframe it with public sculpture. People's perceptions are shaped very much at the point of entry. It's so important. Artists know this. Robert Irwin taught me this. When you walk into a room, when you arrive at a place, you focus on the designs and symbols you see in the first moment, which provides a framework for seeing everything else. What I knew is that changing the frame would automatically change the reading of the same content.

DG: What is the specific function of the encyclopedic museum, then?

MG: The museum must be a social good. There are many people who can describe the museum and access to art as a form of social justice. Even if you do not share those aspirations, it's imperative that the encyclopedic museum should be constructed to be inviting to all, and inclusive of many diverse people as it presents many diverse objects of art. Community is not separate from the museum. It is the museum.

I know art can also be a private activity; there can be art in caves, where only special people are going to be part of that ritual. Is there a hierarchy between the private and public experience of art? Some experienced museumgoers will say they so much prefer museums that are small and empty—more like private spaces. I don't see why a museum can't be boisterous, busy, and casual, especially on the outside, and also be full of meaning and contain the quietest places of meditation. It seems to me that a good museum has that range of expression, carefully thought out, without conflict between busy and quiet, big and small, accessible and intimate. The encyclopedic museum is many things. It is a public square. It's a multicultural center for multicultural cities. It is the definition of community. It evokes many metaphors and makes them material. It can also be a place where one person can see a particular work of art and have an individual experience that's not shared.

It is true that big encyclopedic museums are fundamentally educational. But I don't like the distinctions suggested by the proliferation of education departments in museums—as if the museum wasn't educational. Perhaps we should get rid of the education departments, so that the museum in its entirety becomes considered as education. Let's take it back to what curatorial practice is, rather than seeing it as something you layer on top of curatorial practice.

DG: Encyclopedic museums are places emerging from the past. And it seems important for you to revitalize them with artists from the present.

MG: It is an obvious way to create a living energy for objects that might otherwise be a little distant. I hate the distinction of contemporary art from any form of other art. As if it were a breed, an animal or species of some kind. An encyclopedic museum is for all art, the present included.

Is it when you die you are not contemporary anymore? How old do you need to be to not be contemporary? It's a meaningless distinction. Why not just say that there is art, and artists. One cannot be separated from the other, whether or not the artist is living.

I promised not just to bring contemporary art into the box of the museum. Everyone brings contemporary artworks into such a position now. I've been interested in engaging artists into the workings of the museum, even into the design of the logo, or the installation of galleries. But that idea comes with a lot of work and a lot of questions: How much license do you take? Is it foreground or background? Is it in balance? What are you saying by that? I think it is a fantastic challenge, between creative life and the museum and the visitor experience.

I like to think of museums as places to inspire new ideas as well as consider old ideas. If I had a museum that artists were inspired by, and inspired them to make other work, I would call that very successful. Artists come to the museum all the time for inspiration—and to look at the competition. And encyclopedic museums, having such a wide range of art, are particularly relevant in that regard.

Artists have so much to offer in every way to help us think, look, reframe, reconsider, create perspective, inspire. We should restructure the museums to be quite accommodating of artists. Artists create awareness, which is part of what museums are supposed to. That's what good learning is, building awareness of the making of the humanity.

Franz West is an artist who plays with the idea that objects can be leftover from performance. He looks at an object and he thinks that it makes no sense as a sculpture unless you relate it to the body, as it's used in a performance. Then, he presents that mysterious abstract form on a table in a certain way that looks provocative. We invited him to install our collection of Oceanic tribal objects—which indeed are residue of performance and use, and can often look static and dead in a museum because they've been ripped out of their context. West created an artwork with his installation while at the same time presenting the tribal objects more clearly. It works. The objects are alive and do not suffer from it.

There is a flow of life and change of meaning constantly. Museums for a long time have tried to emphasize the fixity of the order of things. My essential emphasis is the continuous flow and malleability of those orders. (2014–15)

14

Max Hollein

Interviewed when director, Fine Arts Museums of San Francisco

Donatien Grau: You are a very prominent contemporary curator, and you started your career at the Guggenheim, under director Thomas Krens, who is considered to be one of the inventors of the contemporary museum. I first would like to ask you about the interaction between the encyclopedic museum and the contemporary museum.

Max Hollein: There are two ways to look into this question. First, the idea that a contemporary art museum can really encompass all the contemporary art production of the world, which is something that seemingly several contemporary art museums are trying to achieve these days, is an insurmountable task.

With the art being made in Africa, South Asia, Latin America, as well as in Europe and North America, it will not be possible to accomplish an overarching collection that really reflects contemporary art in this global moment. I know that the word *global* conveys a very different meaning from *encyclopedic*, but I think there's a certain correlation there. You have a challenge in the contemporary art museum per se.

The second aspect is that contemporary art museums have become, so to speak, a little bit foreseeable in regard to both their programming and what they put forward. The encyclopedic voice is even more contemporary than in a contemporary institution, because it is more charged and more reflective. It has a more interesting editorial voice that could be connected with the contemporary art production of today.

Some people think that there is a conflict between encyclopedic and global. I think the opposite. The encyclopedic museum dissects any kind of notion that there is one global culture into the reality that it consists of various different cultures that almost then, to a certain extent, create their own combinations into different groups.

DG: What is the editorial voice of the encyclopedic museum?

MH: The application of the concept of an encyclopedic museum is certainly not possible: the British Museum, the Metropolitan Museum of Art, at the end of the day, are not encyclopedic museums. These are very deep and rich collections, but they will not be able to show you the world and its history in all its complexities, and feature the whole cultural history of the world.

The interesting encyclopedic museums in the future will be very reliant, of course, on deep holdings, but actually will be more reliant on having a distinct editorial voice. Encyclopedic museums in the future will differ very much the one from the other, similar to how *New York Magazine* differs from *The Economist*. Both of these publications are trying to provide a certain understanding of everything that's happening in the world through a particular lens.

In a certain aspect, an encyclopedic institution of the future needs first and foremost to define its particular editorial voice that it wants to apply toward the culture of the past and the present. That kind of editorial voice, a mission, certainly differs from one institution to the other, based on its location, its history, particularities of its collection, etc.

If you look at the British Museum, it certainly develops a certain kind of wise and distinct narrative, an editorial attitude through its history of both colonialism and being one of the first public institutions at the same time.

This is the question: how you look, how works get into the collection, how they speak to each other. That has a very distinct editorial voice, if you really think it through and then apply it to each and every thing that an institution does in regard to its display of the objects, its programming, the arguments that are being put forward, as well as its educational mission.

The encyclopedic museum of the future will be much more subjective and much more editorial. The whole dream of having all of culture in one place is certainly a fantasy. Subjective means that it is already understandable or decipherable for the audience, for the visitor, whoever is the user. The museum has one opinionated voice, one kind of particular lens that I would say is a subjective perspective.

DG: It seems to me, from what you are saying, that the encyclopedic museum is not as much an institution as it is a lens, a way to look at things.

MH: We have come full circle in a sense that the whole idea of the museum and of the museum being an outcome of the Age of the Enlightenment. The idea of categories, of "schools," that would structure the museum is probably not the future. The future lies in a more narrative, more porous structure, which is not iterated from one place to the other.

Different institutions have different responses to that based on their particular setup. If you are the Metropolitan Museum, you have an opportunity for a different path than if you are a new museum in Shanghai trying to address that issue.

It is first and foremost a matter of where you are coming from and what the basis is. However, you can have a certain kind of encyclopedic voice or presentation that is not totally geared toward having the overall representation of the culture of humankind in objects. This overall representation is obviously an ideal, and the institutions that have brought the possibility of doing that—meaning the Metropolitan, or the Louvre and others—obviously are more party to that. To a certain extent, if you look at the Museum of Fine Arts at de Young, I would say that we don't have an encyclopedic collection. We have a fairly eclectic collection.

To really be able to speak in a more global way and a more encyclopedic way about our vision, we have to find a particular narrative—a particular editorial voice that's being applied to what we have. In that context, it's interesting for me that de Young's view, which, of course, is "our" encyclopedic museum in its original basis, is actually some kind of world's fair pavilion. De Young came out of the Panama-Pacific International Exposition of the turn of the last century. It looked at culture in all its different kind of manifestations. We look at art at the Legion of Honor, where it's really a representation of the visual arts in all that glory and aesthetic outcome.

DG: You are addressing a crucial topic, which is how the museum engages with the "religion of art," and how the encyclopedic museum, being more porous, offers a more interesting and compelling viewpoint.

MH: If you look at it through the contemporary art lens, you have the complexity of some artworks being very conceptual and speaking about things that are completely beyond the object and its manifestation. Others are much more about the art itself. If you look at Piero Manzoni's work as an artist, that's a different kind of object, and a different kind of context. It's a very different kind of artistic setting.

The encyclopedic museum, in a sense, is obviously not a visual arts museum per se. In the encyclopedic museum, the object itself can almost mutate into different levels of existence vis-à-vis the visitor looking at it.

On the one hand this is, of course, a piece of artistic excellence and an outcome of an artistic practice. On the other hand, it is a cultural artifact. It also is a visual memento, or a visual note, for a bigger and more complex story. It is much more about the context and the relationship, the readability of objects on multiple layers and on a more complex narrative.

As Neil MacGregor put out in *A History of the World in 100 Objects*, while the credit card is certainly not the highest aesthetic achievement—it's certainly not an artwork—it is a cultural artifact of major importance. It can speak about culture and different aspects that an encyclopedic museum and all of the visual arts should definitely address. You have these different thresholds here that are extremely interesting, which will make the encyclopedic museums much more interesting and also more challenging than museums that are geared toward a certain time. That's the interesting thing right now.

We all know that the idea of the museum is about two hundred years old, so it doesn't have a very long history. On the other hand, there has never been a time when so many museums were created for such a short time frame as the one covered by the contemporary art museum. There's obviously an issue ingrained in that. That means there will certainly be a fatigue, and there will be a longing to complicate the narrative. You can see that, even in the market.

I was fascinated the first time Frieze London opened the Frieze Masters fair next to it, and all the contemporary collectors were so excited to suddenly see contemporary works in a very different, and sometimes historical, context. That was kind of an eye-opener for a lot of these younger collectors, who have not even seen such connections. There is a deep longing for the more complicated, more complex narrative. That will mean a rise of the encyclopedic museum, at least in its mission.

It certainly doesn't mean that we will have thousands of encyclopedic museums of the same quality and depth as they will have at the Metropolitan, or the Louvre, or the British Museum. But there will be a longing to go down that path rather than have yet another forty contemporary art museums.

DG: I think that echoes a broader question: Why is this issue of the encyclopedic museum so important now?

MH: Why now? This is very simple observation, but I think that right now we have a change in understanding of the incapabilities of the encyclopedic museum. Fifty years ago there was still this fantasy that there is such a thing as an encyclopedic museum, there is such a thing as one narrative about the cultures of the world, that you could really display it in a valid form.

As an effect of globalization, and as an effect, of course, of the digital platforms—not only the accessibility of knowledge but also the ability to hear very different kinds of voices—it becomes more and more obvious that it's utterly impossible to be an encyclopedic museum of the world and for the world.

In that sense, though, the encyclopedic museum becomes more interesting and probably more relevant. What it does is it gives the responsibility to each singular institution to define its own particular attitude, narrative, perspective on the culture of the world, or however you want to define it.

There is certainly an understanding that if you look at museums of modern and contemporary art, which still try to resemble each other one way or the other, I think an encyclopedic museum these days will be much more about the world, but actually be more locally rooted in regard to how it presents its own argument, opinion, etc., about many other things.

I mean, without doubt an encyclopedic museum in Beijing would be very different—probably not so much in the kind of objects that would be on display but in what kind of narrative it would put forward—from an encyclopedic museum in New York, and an encyclopedic museum in Berlin, and London. I think that's something that, right now, is a unique and very interesting opportunity. It gives each institution a singular platform of unique narrative. That, I think, is fascinating.

DG: Do you think that an encyclopedic museum in Beijing is a possibility?

MH: It's, of course, an impossibility in itself. If you see an encyclopedic museum as having the requirement of being able to portray the most important cultures of the world, then it's an impossibility for any museum, and certainly for a museum in Beijing. I would define an encyclopedic museum as an institution based, obviously, on artistic objects or objects that stem out of cultural tradition, but which looks at the development of culture and the world from a particular vantage point. I think that it's not just possible in Beijing, I think it's even important that it happens over there. Will that mean that they will have also one of the really most important Western European old-master collections there? No. For me, that's not the issue.

If you go, now, to the British Museum and you see how much twentieth-century Chinese art is presented there, how much does it speak about the Cultural Revolution under Mao? I would say it's fairly minimal, but you get something else from the British Museum, you get something from the Age of the Enlightenment.

For me, one of the most fascinating attempts at an encyclopedic museum is the Museu Frederic Marès in Barcelona. He had a great sculpture collection, but he also collected everything else—cigar bands, walking sticks, fans—from his travels. He tried to assemble collections of everything. Orhan Pamuk was fascinated by some of this. This could be seen as an attempt at an encyclopedic museum.

Collections are important. Of course, the richer they are, the more opportunity you have, but I would say that for the encyclopedic museum, today, it's more important what kind of narrative you put forward.

If you compare it to the classical visual arts museum, in the latter it's not really the narrative that people expect from you, it's a selection. In regard to the encyclopedic museum, I don't think it's really the selection that people expect from you. Of course, you want to have the best objects, but the cultural narrative really is the key. That narrative can be certainly more succinct, more relevant, and more persuasive the better your collection is.

DG: When you are talking about the different narratives, what sort of narrative do you have in mind?

MH: It's a mixture of many things. It's an intellectual perspective that is ingrained within the institution and it reflects a certain sense of the values and histories that are part of the institution and location themselves.

If you are an encyclopedic museum in New York, you probably have a more capitalist narrative about the world than if you are an encyclopedic museum in a very different kind of cultural background. I wouldn't now prescribe anything, saying, "OK, well this is the one way you could compare it."

As curators and museum people, we all reflect on the art and culture of our time, and of previous times, through certain lenses of artistic merit but also social, cultural, and historical reference. I think it's the responsibility of each institution to ideally—that's probably why I used this analogy—form one editorial voice. To a certain extent, this could be also seen as if you're the editor of a really important magazine and you apply a certain editorial perspective to very different areas or very different subjects in economy, culture, and other places.

In a museum, you obviously look at culture, but you have to have a certain way of editing. The way that I see it, let's say for our institution—and that might not be the right thing for the British Museum, which has, of course, much better and richer collections—is that our collection will certainly always have a perspective of socioeconomic impact, wherever we can find it; also, there is a certain element of culture and counterculture, the misunderstandings of culture, given the location of San Francisco, looking at it from a very Western perspective and then from a perspective coming across the Pacific Ocean.

Our mission is more important than ever, due in part to the much bigger public presence of the encyclopedic museum. These days museums are probably the single platform where you can have a very deep cultural debate without polemics. They provide the platform where people with very different opinions who are usually very agitated about things assume it has this possibility of giving this opportunity to have that debate.

The museological approach is, of course, educational and it is about seeing any object as an opportunity, not only to reflect a bigger concept but also to question that very concept. I think that's a very twenty-first century attitude. Look at, for example, how Silicon Valley people think, with, on the one hand, their obsession about disruption but, on the other hand, also their way of looking at certain things as, "OK, what is the most likely outcome?" and asking, "What is the most unlikely outcome?" They also look at the most unlikely outcome because it gives them a lot of understanding of the whole issue. The mode of thinking is no longer linear, but has become dialectical. (2017)

15

Sabyasachi Mukherjee

Director general, Chhatrapati Shivaji Maharaj Vastu Sangrahalaya, Mumbai

Donatien Grau: You have devoted considerable efforts to opening up the CSMVS to encyclopedic practices. What led you to do that?

Sabyasachi Mukherjee: I think that in order to understand what we try to do it is essential to look at the context and the local situation. The first Indian museum, in Calcutta, was established in 1814. It was a good beginning, but the colonial government was not very serious about the uplift of Indian cultural heritage. The impact of Europe on Indian social and cultural life is very much evident. The concept of museums during this period remained more or less at discovery, exploration, and excavation level. Some provincial museums, somehow, survived with low maintenance but could not do anything productive to their contemporary society. The British government then constituted a two-member committee headed by S.F. Markham and H. Hargreaves in 1936 to review the conditions of Indian museums and to recommend possible remedial measures. After the independence, priority was given to agriculture, health, education, the social sector, and infrastructure development. Unfortunately, culture was never ever given any priority.

The resulting apathy by British rulers toward Indian museums was for two reasons—firstly, all the best pieces of the Indian art forms were taken to different museums in London, and secondly, because of the Indian ignorance about Indian art.

Though many new museums and university training institutes were established in different geographical locations in India and the subcontinent, the general approach of the government and museums remained unchanged even after sixty-eight years of Indian independence. We have to keep in mind the situation in which they were created, and the audience of that time period. The situation, in terms of politics, society, and culture at the beginning of the nineteenth to twentieth century was completely different from the situation of 2015. Most of the government national- and state-level museums could not change themselves according to the needs of the society or the changing landscape of the world.

Now, with globalization, the world is slowly becoming small because of different modes of technology and communication tools. We live in an Internet age; within no time one can reach any part of the world. Things are happening at a fast pace. The generation of this Internet age is unable to accept those early nineteenth- and twentieth-century models. The curation or narration made at that time was completely different. Today, museums need to be creative and innovative to remain relevant in a changing contemporary society.

When we see the visitors come to those museums, they feel neglected and rejected because the present contemporary society cannot connect with the old traditional presentations. Realizing the need to modernize the museum—its display, maintenance, visitor facilities, education and security—the museum began its modernization program eight years ago with the idea to transform the museum from a national-level repository of antiquities to an institute of international standards. The museum was established on 11 November 1905; the foundation stone was laid by the Prince of Wales—later King George V. The construction of the building began in 1909 and was completed in 1914. Due to the outbreak of World War I, the building was converted into a military hospital, but it was built for the museum.

It was initiated by the aspirations of the local people, in 1904. The fortune from the American Civil War helped Bombay immensely. Bombay became the main textile center, and made a fortune. The people of Bombay thought it was important to have a cultural space in the city, and they approached the British government: the British government agreed and made a statement in 1892. Then there was a meeting, and that initiative led to the foundation in 1905.

Collection is always considered as king, and it is understood by everyone that without the collection one cannot have the museum. Finally, the museum (then the Prince of Wales Museum of Western India) opened on 10 January 1922. The major collection came from the Tata family, a big business family, in 1922 and 1933. The founder of the Tata family, Jamsetji Tata, had two sons, Sir Dorabji and Sir Ratan Tata. Sir Ratan Tata, the youngest, had a deep interest in art and culture and had traveled all over the world. He purchased most of the antiquities and artifacts from different places, in consultation with experts; a major part of his collection was purchased from Christie's and Sotheby's. His elder brother, Dorabji Tata, donated his European collection to the trustees of the museum in 1933.

Thanks to the Tata brothers, today we get the opportunity to see an encyclopedic collection in Mumbai—a bit of everything: European, Chinese, Japanese, Himalayan art, a small Egyptian collection, collections from Central Asia and the Middle East. That helped us immensely. The focus was not only on the Indian collection but also on other world cultures. Since the museum is an autonomous body, it was difficult to undertake major projects and shoulder the entire financial responsibility without any state or central government support.

I was trained at the Victoria and Albert Museum, and of course that gave me a huge insight to respect different cultures and also to develop a universal approach. When I joined CSMVS as director of the museum, I started following the principles of the universal museum. The CSMVS has achieved several of its goals with a combination of indigenous skills and foreign expertise and not merely as a showcase of antiquities.

DG: You said you were trained at the Victoria and Albert Museum, but implementing such a view in India must have been rather different.

SM: It is true that the situations in London and India are completely different; even after the industrialization, the agricultural revolution, and the economic boom, we still have problems. What we wanted to do is to connect with different communities in understanding our role as a secular institution: we involved NGOs, different communities in our activities, program, and development. It has been observed that most of our traditional cultural museums and institutions were created in different times for different audiences than the ones they now have to serve. In the past, exploration, mapping, and the collecting and preserving of cultural goods were of major importance, while today museums are required to connect with society and represent the people they serve.

It was the first step in 2007-8 involving local communities: we all felt it was important for us to connect with the world. Our aspiration was not to become a national-level museum—I will not even say a world-class museum or a universal museum—but a museum appreciated by everyone. That was the whole intention, and then we started growing. We had to work hard to create infrastructure. When you plan international programs and exhibitions, you need to create environment infrastructure.

In 2008 we did the first international exhibition, *Indian Life and Landscape by Western Artists*. We collaborated with the Victoria and Albert Museum for the first time, and it was their first major exhibition in India. After that, organizing international exhibitions became a part of our culture. Every year we do one or two major international exhibitions on different subjects. In 2015 we organized an exhibition on Howard Hodgkin's connection with India, in collaboration with Tate—it was Tate's first exhibition in India—and there was another very interesting exhibition from a private collection in Zürich. Before that, we brought a Peter Paul Rubens from Belgium and the *Cyrus Cylinder* from the British Museum. The Egyptian exhibition *Mummy: The Inside Story* was a huge success.

Interestingly, these different exhibitions on world cultures started attracting Indian audiences as well as international visitors. The number of visitors in 2015 has almost doubled from the number of visitors in 2005.

We do charge admission fees. Once a week, we don't charge students. As part of our social justice policy, people from below the poverty line visiting the museum are always provided a complimentary ticket. By Indian standards the fee is perhaps standard, but yes, when you convert into foreign currency it is nothing. Today we charge less than a dollar, whereas in Europe and America they charge quite a lot.

The museum program has made us popular within and outside the city. Activities and events helped us immensely to connect with the world. This is one aspect of making the museum a place where things happen.

Another aspect we experimented with is how museums become, in time, a community space. The population of Mumbai today is between twenty-one and twenty-two million. Our museum is the largest in the city and one of the largest in the country. There is one city museum, and there are a few small institution-level museums. Unfortunately, the city could not create more cultural space. So we have a responsibility. We thought we should connect with people. In 2007–8, we started engaging visitors, connecting local communities through activities and programs.

But somehow we felt that the museum was not doing enough for other sections whom we consider special visitors, such as HIV patients, cancer patients, commercial sex workers and their children, construction laborers, municipal corporation workers, etc. How do we bring all these people in? They are an integral part of society. If society suffers, we all suffer. Then the challenge is: How do you involve these people? We do not have access to them, but there are NGOs. There are hundreds of NGOs working with them, and they are all specialized. Today there are forty-four NGOs working with us. We design education and cultural programs for these special visitors in consultation with the NGOs. Our job is to bring them to the museum. It has to be sustainable: it can't be just a one-day trip. We continue with a particular group for a year, and that brings little changes to their life, their lifestyle, and their thinking. They don't get such opportunities. And my experience has been fantastic. I used to observe them very closely when they attended programs. At times I felt they were more interested than the so-called educated and cultured people, because local educated and cultured people have everything, but they don't have much cultural hunger.

DG: How do you relate the fact that you are very deeply rooted in Mumbai and all the different communities of Mumbai, and the fact that you connect to the world through a very local and encyclopedic or universal museum at the same time?

SM: You connect people through your programs and activities, and education. Education is a very powerful tool to reach out to people. Through education you involve communities.

In my experience, money is not the issue. What is important are ideas and proper implementation. When we started doing all these activities and programs, we had a little anxiety over money. But we knew it all depends on how much interest you take in the project. You have to involve a few partners, so we tried to involve communities, press, and media, and we also encouraged and motivated them to participate in the museum's education program.

When people got to know our different modules and the success story, they started supporting us by sending checks, transferring money, without any complaints. Usually money comes with strings attached, but in this case, I really don't recall anyone having asked for anything. All our education programs are supported by people, individual donors. Now, after so many years, for the first time Citibank and Bank of America have come in to help us. Our two projects are very close to my heart. We are creating a new dedicated space for children—the Children's Museum, where we are creating a space within the space. The Children's Museum building will be designed by Rahul Mehrotra, the head of the design department at Harvard University. For the first time, we will be in a position to offer something to children specifically. Our collection is multipurpose, but a separate section will be devoted to children where they will be able to enjoy, study, and learn, and when they leave they carry some learning experience with them.

I personally believe in informal education. I am against established education. It's not correct for anyone to impose anything on anyone. I prefer allowing visitors to see and interpret. The curator's interpretation at a certain point disappears. You just give clarifications. Our approach is more informal and visitor friendly.

I was trying to understand the purpose of the museum. It is important for the institution to know its character. Looking at ICOM's definition, I accepted that it's a not-for-profit permanent institution in the service of the people and their development.

But what is the purpose? The purpose remains the same, whether it comes to an educational institution, a museum, or a cultural institution. Study, education, and enjoyment: that is the purpose. If you place too much emphasis on study and education, you will not truly enjoy your visit to the museum. What we are trying to do is to maintain a balance. The learning element is important, but it should not be so overbearing that at one point you feel like leaving the museum. How do you make it interesting and an enjoyable trip, where visitors come and spend more time? It's a challenge that one has to accept.

DG: The fact is that you were interested in connecting the collection to the world, and establishing a Mumbai version of an encyclopedic museum.

SM: The encyclopedic museum is a very colonial concept. We are trying to create a converging scene between East and West through our collection, through our activities and programs.

Looking at our collection, it may appear to you as encyclopedic, but to us it's a conversation between cultures and the people. The purpose of the conversation is to know and respect each other. Today we are losing such a balance in our world: nationalism is very common. How do we tell our people to respect different religions, different cultures, and different languages? That is only possible when you design programs, and it appears more like another intercultural dialogue. Intercultural dialogue is ultimately a conversation between individuals engaging in a relationship with each other. This dialogue's starting point is the present, from which it explores the past and imagines the future, guided by the needs and expectations of actual and potential visitors. It values not only objects or collections, but first and foremost, the individuals and the regions they embody—stories, ideas, emotions, values, desires, fears, and hopes.

It is okay to have to maintain your own identity. I respect that, but there is no harm in allowing different communities to interact.

DG: When I used the word *encyclopedia,* you said it was a very colonial point of view and that you had a different point of view, which is conversation. Are these points of view for the same realities? Or are these different realities?

SM: The first question is: Are you making a statement based on the purpose, and therefore on the activities and programs, or based on the collection?

When we look at our collection, we are indeed missing some important cultures. We have quite a strong European department, a strong Central Asian department, a strong Asian department. No Latin American works.

When you use the term *encyclopedic*, you need all the cultures reflected in your collection. What we are doing through our number of international exhibitions and activities is bringing in world cultures, to fill the gap, and then to provoke a dialogue. We are inviting people from different countries to come and share their experience, their views, so that people get an opportunity to know more about them and their culture.

It is not necessary to learn about a particular culture from art; it can also be through people, activities, programs, seminars, workshops, social and cultural interactions. Sometimes we come to know through food how different cultures see themselves and interact. Today some people say that at CSMVS the whole approach is more encyclopedic, and that is because of our activities.

DG: Do you think that, basically, the museum can be an encyclopedic museum without the collection? Or is there another paradigm that would not be the encyclopedic colonial museum, that would be a museum of conversations? Is it a supplemented encyclopedic museum, in which things are brought in to expand and make it an encyclopedic collection, or is it another model?

SM: I agree. The collection is the king. You just can't have a museum without a collection. But, with time, things are changing, and they are changing very rapidly.

My approach is to maintain a balance between the three-dimensional and two-dimensional objects and the conversation or the interaction. I cannot completely ignore the collection and create a museum of dialogues; what people need is a civic space where they get an opportunity to interact. Ultimately, you have to maintain a balance between collections and dialogues.

And yet, it is not necessary to have a representative collection from different nations. If your collection even covers 40 or 50 percent of the world cultures, you can fill the remaining 50 or 60 percent of the vacuum with temporary exhibitions, interaction, seminars, workshops, and activities. It is possible, especially today with technology and social media. But a completely separated museum without a collection, whether we call it a museum or a center for social or cultural interaction, is something you have to think about.

DG: I think that through these different cultures you are engaging with two ways of being inclusive: locally, globally. The two are connected, don't you think?

SM: I tend to say that "think global act local," is a slogan. It is a fact that no institute can sustain without the support of local communities. We connect with the world through the support of these communities.

If local communities don't understand your ideology, your philosophy, your approach, at one point you'll be isolated, and that will create huge political problems for the institutions later on. You may, with your personal agenda, move ahead by ignoring local people, local communities. It happened. And it created huge problems. My approach involves local communities, local people. You take them with you, you enlighten them, and create an environment where they can interact with the world. That should be the approach.

In Europe and America I requested that some of the directors conduct a survey on the participation of local communities in the development of the museum. How many local people visit the British Museum, the Metropolitan Museum of Art, and how many tourists visit the Victoria and Albert Museum?

The museum is not a tourist spot, it is a cultural space and allows local people and international communities to see, understand, and respect each other. If we turn it into a tourist spot, then automatically the commercial interest comes in. And then you start ignoring essential issues related to contemporary society.

This is one of the issues the world is considering seriously: how do we preserve the indigenous cultures? In a global context, the world is changing. We have lost many things, for example, letter writing and postcards. The postcard culture is gone. Very few people today handwrite letters. Every day we are losing some essential components of cultures, and now we are concerned about the preservation of continuing tradition. There are parts of the world, such as Asia, Southeast East Asia, Central Asia—known for their continuing and living traditions. Unfortunately, in Europe and America, they have lost their traditional arts and crafts due to the tremendous dependency on technology. Here in India, we have handloomed textiles: there are still weavers with the skills of hands to create a beautiful eight-yard sari. The production may be a little expensive, since it takes months to create one, but still weavers continue weaving traditions. The cultural heritage is under threat from technology, globalization, and power politics. We don't know how long the traditions will continue. That is the question.

Specialized museums, libraries, cultural organizations, educational institutes, and, more particularly, universities have a role to play because of their grassroots link with the life of the common people. They will have a special responsibility to honor the basic principles of different communities and a commitment to the cultural pluralism that can hold the world together. (2015–18)

16

Henri Loyrette

Director emeritus, Musée du Louvre, Paris

Donatien Grau: I would like to start by asking about terminology. One could take the view that there are two names for the same reality, the French expression being *universal museum* and the English being *encyclopedic museum*. What do you think? Are they, for you, one and the same?

Henri Loyrette: I don't think that's the case. The term *encyclopedic museum* indicates a classification; *universal museum,* an ambition. A museum can be encyclopedic without being universal and universal without being encyclopedic.

The ambition of the Louvre Abu Dhabi, for example, is to be a universal museum that covers all civilizations and all fields, from the dawn of time to the present day. It's not necessarily an encyclopedic museum; in other words, it doesn't follow an encyclopedia in the classification and arrangement of its works. The Louvre is an encyclopedic museum without being a universal museum, despite initially having the ambition to be a universal museum; this ambition was limited geographically by the creation of the Musée Guimet and the Musée du Quai Branly, and chronologically by the creation of the Musée d'Orsay and the Musée National d'Art Moderne.

As early as 1793, it became necessary to classify the exhibited works—an as yet disparate collection made up of the royal collections and revolutionary seizures but which, in spite of its gaps, already possessed considerable geographical and chronological breadth. The most obvious model of classification was that of an encyclopedia, distributing and classifying works into great articles, exalting the strong points, pointing up the gaps, and favoring cross-references (which, moreover, were debated at length), none of which is permitted by a *sensitive* form of hanging based on affinities.

DG: This necessity corresponds to a logic of *penser/classer* [thinking/sorting].

HL: Yes, exactly. When I used to be asked whether I regretted that the Louvre was structured by department, and within department by country, technique, or school, I would always answer that, no, this model inherited from the eighteenth century, the only one, in my view, appropriate to such a large collection, was always valid; the important thing was for it to be made visible and turned to good account.

This also implies a particular way of *using* the museum: an encyclopedic museum cannot be visited like a museum with a continuous viewing route. An encyclopedia is not read from A to Z. The articles, generally offering a system of cross-references to other articles, are leafed through. What the Louvre is lacking, moreover, are cross-references or links: each department is too isolated from the rest of the collections.

When Cézanne said, "The Louvre is the great book in which one learns to read," he was clearly thinking in these terms. He was talking about the encyclopedic museum, this reference book that he kept within reach at all times, just as we might keep a great dictionary to hand and consult it continually but without reading it from the first page to the last.

DG: So you don't agree with the idea of the encyclopedic museum being Anglo-American and the universal museum being French.

HL: No. The French model reverberated in the United States: look at the Metropolitan Museum, which is more universal than the Louvre (even if its collections are smaller), while nevertheless adopting an encyclopedic classification.

At the end of the eighteenth century there were some hesitations, with a collection suffering from considerable gaps (many departments did not yet exist), a collection not remotely what it is today. However, the supposedly *sensitive* hanging, that is to say an amateur, personal form of hanging based on affinity or supposed affinity, was swiftly rejected in favor of a far more rigorous system of classification inherited from the *Encyclopédie*, from the Enlightenment. This seemed both the right thing to do and, no doubt, the most conducive to any form of potential expansion. This classification showed what was there but at the same time underlined the gaps: the direction that needed to be taken was clear to see, and at the end of the eighteenth century, and above all in the nineteenth, the creation of what were properly called the *musées* was embarked upon, with, at the Louvre, the Musée Égyptien, the Musée Assyrien, the Musée Américain, etc.

DG: You distinguish between the ambition of the universal museum and the methodological character of the encyclopedic museum. What interaction is there between these two models? Is the encyclopedic museum often universal in intent?

HL: It is often universal. The idea of an encyclopedic museum with a collection like that of the Uffizi, for example, makes no sense: the Uffizi is a museum more or less dedicated to the Tuscan school, to the masters collected by the grand dukes of Tuscany. It's therefore a highly local collection and there's no other way but a chronological viewing. This can't be described as an encyclopedic museum.

From the moment you achieve a certain mass, like the Louvre, this profusion of works from every century and every point on the globe, you have to distribute them and think about a form of classification. When the collection is less profuse, when it is put together for the purposes of creating a viewing route, of putting in place a previously worked out scenario, you can achieve a different kind of museum format, which is not an encyclopedic museum. This is the case with the Louvre Abu Dhabi.

DG: The corollary of this question is that of hierarchy. What relationship do you think the encyclopedic model of museum has with the notion of hierarchy: hierarchy of objects, media, fields, civilizations?

HL: This is implied not by the encyclopedia but by the idea one forms of museums and collections. The encyclopedic classification has the virtue of classifying and enabling a reading of the collections, but it also draws attention to the gaps. From the moment you have this kind of claim to universality, this kind of ambition for a collection, the encyclopedic form of classification reveals more clearly and cruelly what isn't covered by this universality. And what isn't covered will affect fields, artists, and periods, but also certain genres, with the boundaries often unclear: between the *high* and the *low,* for example.

To return to the Louvre, for me it doesn't entirely satisfy its universal ambitions. In its current scope (from antiquity to the nineteenth century, from Europe to the borders of India and China) many areas are not covered. I soon realized that this was due more to disdain than to ignorance. If the Egyptian antiquities department didn't extend as far as the sources of the

Nile, this is no doubt to do with the political conditions, under which the Sudan was a British territory, but it was also to do with neglect of a civilization deemed peripheral to Egyptian civilization. For my part, I have always rejected this centrality and continually pushed into the margins.

One of the virtues of this system of classification is that it allows for a far fairer, more scrupulous, more measured reading of universality, highlighting the gaps, the limitations, and the dividing lines between what is considered the glory of a civilization and the more peripheral regions, or the minor arts. So the Egyptian antiquities department did not sail up the Nile toward its sources, and post-Renaissance, the decorative arts department, for its part, took a highly Francocentric point of view, regarding anything in the decorative arts field that was not as French as merely provincial. I remember some very strong reactions when I encouraged the director of the decorative arts department to introduce some Biedermeier furniture into the collection; many curators considered it unworthy of the Louvre.

DG: You talk about the need to update, but what meaning does this model have today?

HL: It has the same meaning that it had in the eighteenth century. One can question its validity, but this too, I believe, endures today. You can approach the problem from the other side: when you look at the Louvre's enormous collections, what form of presentation could be advocated if you abandoned that approach, even if you shuffled things up by hanging differently? What would the way in be? There aren't any others because any form of viewing circuit is out of the question. You'd end up with the Galerie du Temps at Louvre-Lens, based on an extremely limited number of works and a highly defined principle—in other words a strictly chronological reading of the works—but this would be impossible within the context of the Louvre. Lens was interesting for me because it was a project that turned things around and yielded a different reading of the Louvre collections that was not an encyclopedic one. But this was possible because we were dealing with a small number of works. It could have been thematic, but within the chronology one can read the emergence and continuity of a certain number of themes.

DG: In the encyclopedia there is the idea of a discourse or lesson. What does encyclopedism in the museum teach us?

HL: It's Péguy arriving at the Louvre: this poor young École Normale Supérieure student from the provinces, feeling a sense of rejection, who, at the Louvre, immediately felt a "promotion of the human essence" as a result of what he immediately became aware of in the density of the Louvre collections: "humanity's long and visible journey." It was there that he found both his origins and a sense of belonging.

This experience is fundamental to any visit to a museum like the Louvre. To carry this idea further, one encounters there "the faces of all those who have quested." This is something that can only be felt or grasped in a museum of this kind. Only the kind of classification that takes you from the Assyrians to the Romans, and many other civilizations, allows you to feel this very strong presence.

DG: Do you think this encyclopedic method allows a universality to be perceived?

HL: Yes, I think so. It has always struck me, at the Louvre, that the discerning eye, the eye of the connoisseur, notices even the gaps, what isn't there. There is a vision of humanity there, even if (and this was also apparent working on Abu Dhabi) it's seen from the point of view of Paris, of France; it's a French history too. Universality always adopts a point of view, that of the heritage of the collections, of the place where you live and how you consider—in every sense of the term—others. When one looks at the French national collections, which are France's real universal museum, incorporating the Louvre, the Orsay, the Musée National d'Art Moderne, the Quai Branly, yes, it's a form of universality, but it's also a typically French history.

What's interesting about our thinking on Abu Dhabi is that the world is seen in terms of an alternatively oriented map, one which takes Abu Dhabi as the center of the world and looks out at the world from there. This reveals a very different geography, bringing closer things that seem very distant to us, and meaning that India is just a couple of hours away. Relationships with the neighboring civilizations are quite different to when one is looking from Paris. This establishes a different geography.

DG: What do these different universalities, Abu Dhabi on the one hand, the major established museums on the other, have in common? Do they overlap anywhere?

HL: What they have in common is that they consider everything and neglect nothing: a full and comprehensive approach. This is also a way of tackling art history, based on the idea that nothing is central and nothing is marginal and that it's important to look as attentively at that which seems remote and sometimes hasn't been paid consideration over the course of time, at that which is the object of new research and new discoveries; an attentiveness to everything that might appear, be revealed, be reconsidered at every stage in the history of taste.

DG: The encyclopedic museum is not merely a museum of art; it's a museum whose objects serve a double purpose: as objects of aesthetic contemplation and objects of learning. How do you see these dual identities?

HL: They can indeed have this double status; it can coexist in them. I recall that when I was looking at the inscribed bricks in the department of Oriental antiquities, I regarded them as invaluable documents and enjoyed consulting the labels to see what they said, but I also looked upon them as fascinating and magnificent objects. These two readings are by no means contradictory.

Fundamentally, this raises more questions about the notion of masterpiece than it does about the notion of artwork or documentary piece. What's interesting about the encyclopedic museum is that the barriers between the masterpiece and the documentary piece are far less clear-cut than in museums that are more limited in scope, more focused on a given subject. I remember a discussion I had with the director of the Cleveland Museum, who said that what was striking about her museum was that it was a museum of masterpieces; but what was remarkable about the Louvre was that it set its masterpieces off against all that surrounds them, contextualizing its entire collection and causing its masterpieces to emerge against comparative works, as in art books that situate and contextualize works. Thus a virtue of the encyclopedic museum is to present and explain works in terms of the context to which they belong.

Contextualization is indeed the great challenge of the encyclopedic museum and the universal museum: the works have a wide range of vocations, provenances, and objectives; this piece was created as a work of art, that one was intended as a devotional or religious work, yet another as a utilitarian object, but all are, in a sense, bathed in the even light of the museum. There's a problem with the reading of these items, hence the importance of contextualization, the importance of showing that these works, despite the fact that we look at them, positioned side by side, within the precincts of the museum, did not originally have the same purpose. And this is all the more obvious in the Musée du Louvre because it finishes in 1850. The overwhelming proportion of its collections was therefore created before this date, and before the museum had become the natural target of every artist. The artists or practitioners who created the works did so for all sorts of reasons:

as an official commission, for a private collector, as a utilitarian object, as a devotional object, but certainly not with the museum in mind. Which was not the case after around 1820–30, when the museum was definitely on the artist's horizons. There was also a very significant change here in the way this notion of the universal museum was perceived: the vocation of the works it contains is not the same.

DG: To return to the much-discussed political stakes surrounding the encyclopedic museum: How do you see these?

HL: It's a fight *against* retreat into ourselves and *for* understanding of the Other. By looking, in a museum like the Louvre, at what yesterday was like, we can understand today and envisage the future. When Toni Morrison was invited to the Louvre, she did not know the museum well. What struck her as she made several visits was the thematic consistency throughout the collections. While viewing the collections in the departments of Oriental and Egyptian antiquities, it was above all about the parallel she was able to draw between certain objects, certain ensembles, and the situation today. From this contemplation, this visit to the Louvre, as its guest, emerged a theme Morrison had previously treated: of being a stranger in one's own land. Clearly this was the situation of African Americans in America, but it was also that of Israel in Egypt and of captivity in Babylon. All of a sudden, something emerged, reared up, that was of all time. What one learns in a museum is not simply specific information that can be conveyed about this or that work or artist, etc.; it's to do with gaining a better understanding of timeless, universal issues. And this is a reading that only the universal museum can foster.

DG: Can the encyclopedia therefore be seen as a way into the universal?

HL: It's a question of enabling people to see and understand. Encyclopedias allow for a very specific, personal path to be taken through them, one that takes the reader on numerous detours, with entries, words, and passages ignored. This favors discovery. And this is also the aim of the encyclopedic museum. From the moment visitors are liberated from the straightjacket of a viewing circuit, they can either lose themselves and let themselves drift or, in the case of the more attentive individuals, allow themselves to be guided from one word to another, from one civilization to another, from one artist to another. As soon as you use it in this way, the sense of wonder is considerable.

This model is now more than two hundred years old and has withstood the test of many changes and updates. But it is not made to bear enough fruit. A lot of people regard this encyclopedic classification as an opportunity rather than a handicap, something that encourages people to read and understand, but to which people haven't yet become sufficiently attached. I find there's a splendor in this model that needs explaining. It's our mission—by means of a system of intelligent cross-references, rather than circuits—to make everyone who visits and uses the museum, not just the art lover but also the visitor who has come to see the Venus de Milo and the *Mona Lisa*, want to return, and gain a greater understanding. (2017)

17

George Abungu

Former director general, National Museums of Kenya, Nairobi

Donatien Grau: Encyclopedic museums have been built from works of art acquired all around the world, some of them stolen, robbed, or bought at cheap price. Do you think these conditions of acquisition challenge their nature as encyclopedic, universal institutions?

George Abungu: Unfortunately, many of the major museums worldwide, including the so-called encyclopedic or universal museums, have had some skeletons in the closet. It is the nature of museums based on these aristocratic, elitist, and domineering foundations. Let us not forget that their very foundation as cabinets of curiosities was rooted in the need to show off one's ability to collect; the end justified the means, I suppose, and museums never moved away from this. These museums were not founded by poor people but by the very rich and powerful, who used their positions to acquire by all means necessary and possible, including as spoils of war and conquests. The very major museums in the West have in their possession spoils of war, domination, and colonization, and when war became an unpopular and unacceptable way of acquiring works, money replaced it. It is nothing but a continuation of Western economic and cultural imperialism: irregular buying, stealing, and looting where the source countries are not the beneficiaries but the victims became normal. So, yes, the condition of acquisition is a real challenge to the nature of the so-called encyclopedic or universal museum. And until they are willing to confront and deal with this in a respectful manner, they will always be haunted. And haunted institutions cannot be representative and universal.

DG: You have been dealing with the theft of major parts of African heritage. Do you still feel the restitution controversy is a major crux for encyclopedic museums?

GA: It is and will continue to be as long as they avoid dealing with their past mistakes and continue to engage in illegal acquisition, including those of sacred objects. I say this as a person who comes from a bleeding continent. The recent conflicts have led to a reemergence of looting of objects, and it is a one-directional traffic, south to north. Many of these institutions still have sacred objects that mean a lot to communities and they continue to collect them, for example, the *vigango* of the Mijikenda from the Kenyan coast. They are stolen, museumized, turned into pieces of art, curated, and openly displayed as tribal or ethnic art, and yet the source communities who consider them as ancestral representations suffer all the consequences. The West has a lust for heritage from elsewhere that can never be satisfied. And yet, what we call museum objects, pieces of art, or whatever name they may want to give them, means totally different things to the community, and their removal continues to cause irreparable damage to these very communities. As long as this relationship of inequality, exploitation, and lack of understanding for the other's human feelings and cultural integrity continue, the restitution controversy will remain a major crux for encyclopedic museums, and the few cultural exchanges, exhibitions, and training opportunities offered to the south will not compensate. Neither will time heal the wounds, if that is what some think will happen. Only true dialogue and correction of past and present mistakes will help.

DG: Do you think that encyclopedic museums are truly encyclopedic? If not, what do you think they could do to expand their encyclopedia?

GA: Well, they define themselves and so they may be what they say they are. It is a name. More so, I am not sure that I am the one to define what encyclopedic museums should be. However, as for the expansion of the encyclopedia, if this means being representative with a global outlook, then the first thing is the need to look at the world as one big family with many identities, feelings, and diversities and to respect each and every one of them with their norms and feelings. As one of the Native American sayings goes, "With all things and in all things, we are relatives." So yes, they can collect from all parts of the world, but with respect and consideration for the local feelings, traditions, and beliefs. Thus another saying: "Respect the giver and the gift." In many cases, they do not do this. They also have to retrospectively address the past injustices. Another saying that they can learn from the same source is: "Stolen food never satisfies hunger." They should avoid the trap of "money buys everything" and realize that injustice can only breed more injustice and conflicts.

DG: What is the encyclopedic museum's role? What do you think they bring to the world's cultures that other institutions do not bring?

GA: I am by blood a museum person and so do not just criticize for the sake of it. Each museum, including the so-called encyclopedic ones, does have many roles to play, including education, entertainment, cultural exchange, intellectual discussion, and stimulation. I think encyclopedic museums can be provocative and intellectually stimulating, leading to scholarly discussions that can enrich our world greatly. They can also be spaces of representation of many cultures and through art can demonstrate human creativity at its best over a long span of time in all parts of the world. In this age of migration, they can also be sources of comfort for those at home away from home.

DG: The encyclopedic museum is an institution that positions itself between the museum of cultures and the art museum. How do you think it should deal with its double identity—art being widely considered by critical thinking as a Western construct?

GA: Double identity is not a problem for me. There are few museums that do not have multiple identities unless they are very specialized. I do not know how one would qualify the National Museums of Kenya, the Nairobi National Museum with its great archaeological and paleontological collections and exhibitions, or the remarkable zoological, ornithological, and ethnographic exhibitions and collections, with the main Nairobi Gallery for art. So for me, art and culture are not opposed, as art is possibly just part of culture. Of course, art as a Western construct may be true observation, but only on the basis that it is used by the West to elevate its status among regions and peoples. However, if we start from the premise that art is human and humans are everywhere and so art is everywhere, then there is no problem. The encyclopedic museums can be more relevant if they do not use art to divide but to unite, and look at it through the lens of humanity rather than as a Western invention. Equality is the issue here. If that is the case, then cultures and art as represented in museums are bedfellows.

DG: Objects in encyclopedic museums have been extracted from their original situation. How can they be displayed in a way that would make sense in a broader narrative and would pay justice to their nature?

GA: All museums have their objects extracted from their original situations, not only encyclopedic museums. This is the nature of the museum. What they can do is to control the damage of the absence of the original situation, all while creating excitement. In this case, I can say that encyclopedic museums should only exhibit material with proven provenance and, where possible, provide multiple contexts simulating both the original situation and the current exhibition practices. By this I do not mean that there should be dioramas everywhere as of old but that the visitor should be provided with original context, including the meanings of objects and their uses in the context of the cultures in which they were produced, as museums also strive to keep up with new exhibition techniques. I do not know whether that is possible.

DG: How do you think that encyclopedic museums should engage with their past as institutions?

GA: Here again I want to borrow from the rich and enlightening Native American proverbs. One says: "Truth does not happen, it just is." They have to be truthful and not hide under the guise of the inheritance of injustices. As custodians of at times suspect material objects, they are responsible. And they also need to reevaluate the narratives of the past that portray others as less human and stop to promoting some of the same narratives of power, domination, discrimination, and stereotyping. They need to come to terms with the past unjust and cruel practices of collecting and to correct their equally unacceptable current collecting practices that do not respect the source societies' cultures and norms. They need to come out in the light so that they can be seen and engage with the daunting issues of the past. There is no need for mass restitution of materials from the museums to source communities; however, there is a need for engagement and acceptance of wrongs. Bad practices of the past must also stop, and curators cannot hide behind intellectual freedom when they know some of their collections are stolen. As the saying goes, "He who is present at wrongdoing and does not lift a hand to prevent it is just as guilty as the wrongdoer."

DG: There are no encyclopedic museums in Africa. Do you think it is possible for an encyclopedic museum to be created outside of the Western world? According to which rules?

GA: African museums, especially the ones founded during the colonial times, are equally not innocent and do in some instances have skeletons in their closets. Thus some museums still have human remains of former freedom fighters that were donated by the colonialists and some have material that belonged to their neighbors because they were located in privileged and "safe" colonies. Some of them have even acted as collection points for illicit trafficking of cultural material from other countries. Nobody talks about them and there is a general and collective amnesia as today they champion the cause of communities. However, they can see the wrong in others and not in themselves. At some stage they will also have to deal with what is wrong in them. I think there is a possibility of an encyclopedic museum to be created outside the Western world. It would probably take an informed billionaire in Africa with resources to spare, in order to start something of the same. It is not impossible. The only problem is that most museums in Africa, especially national ones, are funded by the exchequer and they have to serve or show that they serve communities. They are therefore responsible and partly answerable to the state and communities. Encyclopedic museums are mostly answerable to themselves, and their positions are often assured and given without having to prove their worth, if I am right. That would possibly be the only hurdle. According to which rule? They would simply copy what is in the West were there to be any, I suppose.

DG: You served as the director general of the National Museums of Kenya. The encyclopedic museum stands at the opposite side of the national museum. How do you think the encyclopedic museum and the national museum can interact?

GA: I do not think the two are opposed to each other. They are all museums, they have their issues, and they collect and exhibit and also carry out public programs. They can cooperate in all these areas. They can share their common as well as different experiences to build and reinforce one another's activities. The encyclopedic museums can also reach local and source communities through the national museums, selling their changed strategies and ways of doing things and reconciling with their past. The national museums can benefit from the resources of the encyclopedic museums through exchanges and capacity building, and some are already cooperating.

DG: The encyclopedic museum is telling a story of many of the world's pasts. How do you think these stories are to be told? Especially if the sources are of different natures and availability?

GA: I would just reiterate that each area and group should be given opportunity to tell his or her story. Museums for so long have been used to promote the narrative of the powerful and the dominant. This cannot continue. As noted above, "truth does not happen, it just is." Let us tell it how it is from those who own it. The idea that curators know it all cannot suffice, especially a curator in the north constructing stories of the south. Thus, if museums in the north want to deal with the inherent biases, they have to be able to invite the curators from the south to lead the construction of exhibitions about the south. (2016–17)

18

Hamady Bocoum

Director, Musée des Civilisations Noires, Dakar

Donatien Grau: What are your thoughts regarding the European model of the encyclopedic museum? Did you position yourselves toward it at the Musée des Civilisations Noires?

Hamady Bocoum: We have elaborated a polysemic model for a museum, since the world has to be polysemic. Today certain voices are almost speechless, because of information, of communication. We have to leave room for alternative voices.

DG: Did this model for a museum—that aims to bring all cultures together in one place, whether it is in Paris, New York, London—have historical relevance in your project?

HB: I don't know what you mean by "all cultures." We are developing a museum of black cultures in our world. What we decided to do was somehow to break with the development of museums in Africa. We observed that almost no one was visiting them. Their staff was very limited. We drew a map of what was wrong with our museums. What was wrong was that they were ethnographic museums. Ethnography is the idea of the Other, of the culture of the Other, of colonial otherness. How do you want people to like their own otherness and the discourse that comes with it? We gave up on the ethnographic museum. We gave up on the anthropological museum, because, in the name of anthropology, many inhumane deeds have harmed black people. We also decided we did not want to be a chromatic museum: it is not a "museum of the Black." The black person here is not essentialized, but historicized. It is the history of black cultures, in the long run, from Toumai, the common ancestor shared by all of us, who does not have anything chromatic, up to contemporary creativity. Finally, we decided we did not want to make a subaltern museum, in the sense that we were not going to copy any other museum in the world. We worked toward doing things our own way, with all the risks it entails. We also worked toward having a discourse, a discourse that would not be one of rupture but of coherence, in relation to the observations we were able to draw from the evolution of the African cultures of the diaspora. We saw that the red thread of this whole evolution was the constant celebration of humankind. Humankind means all of us. Being African, we are a universal museum. Which also means that we are one of the few museums in which there is no discrimination on the ticket fare to get into the museum: everybody pays the same thing, and strictly so. That is what we have tried to build.

DG: In what you have tried to build, how do you position yourselves in relation to the art museum?

HB: We do art too. When I say "from Toumai, our common ancestor, to today, to contemporary creativity," it does mean that we include art. Today we have a room, one of the most beautiful ones, dedicated to contemporary creativity.

DG: In museums as they have emerged in Europe, categories are separate: ethnological, anthropological, art museum, history museum. I am under the impression that you lifted all those categories.

HB: We are not in the business of separating things from one another; we are in the business of polysemy. In our museum, there is a bit of all that. We carefully avoided entering any category. By the way, we decided not to have a permanent display: you cannot present black cultures in a credible way through a continuous display. We are constantly moving. This world moves very quickly, and we are trying to be in the time of this world so that we could also remediate the lack of collections.

DG: What place is left to collections, when they are lacking?

HB: We have collections but we are not dependent on, nor prisoners of, these collections. Some museums have huge collections, of which they are prisoners. We have very light collections, which meet extremely precise aesthetic choices. As the museum will progress forward, we will constitute collections, but it is not a constraint.

DG: What is the status of the collection in the museum, if you are not prisoners of it? Is it a starting point?

HB: It is not a starting point. Collections of museums were constituted in conditions that were extremely blurry, to say the least—conditions of spoliation and violence. They are prisoners of them. We are not. The collections we are about to constitute will be constituted following our needs. These needs are linked to our curatorial choices. If we'd like to show Coca-Cola bottles, we'll do it.

DG: The museum is basically a book written in the present tense.

HB: Absolutely. We are not a museum rooted in the anecdotes of nostalgia. The young people of Africa need knowledge and perspective. We go from Toumai to today: following that path, we present the cultures of continental Africa, as well as the contributions of Africa to sciences and crafts. We also engage with encounters: everything started from Africa and went to the whole world. But things come back too, therefore creating new encounters: among others, religions. A room is devoted to African religions, Abrahamic religions. We discuss the globalization of blackness with terrifying episodes, when colonization was slaving people in their own homes. We do not essentialize any of this. We discuss contemporary creativity, which has a lot of following. Spaces are dedicated to dialogues of masks, in which we bring masks from all over the world in dialogue with each other. The dialogue is fascinating, since, whether they come from Africa, from Oceania, from China or elsewhere, masks often say the same thing but do not say it the same way. This discourse of representation as well as of encounter is the one we seek to develop. In our museum, we deal with everything.

DG: We are under the impression that large-scale Western museums have their collections as starting points, and then now have to create narratives. It seems to me that your process is exactly the opposite.

HB: Most of our colleagues inherited immense collections; these collections are a burden. At the same time, in thinking about the museum, everybody is trying to move away from the ethnography museum. Today, we say we are poor, we have no collections, but we have ideas, we have a brain. What do we do? We are reflecting on the context? These reflections are not exclusively Negro. These are professional reflections. We build our discourses, our scenario, and we see how to implement them: if we have two valuable objects, we display them, if we have twenty, we display them.

This is why ideas are extremely important in the model of museum we are working on.

DG: How do you bring together ideas and works—the art museum and the post-ethnographic museum?

HB: Objects illustrate narratives. The functional relationship between objects and narratives is self-evident. It is true that I would have wished, unlikely example, to show the *Mona Lisa*. We are preparing a Leonardo da Vinci exhibition in 2020: I know I won't display a single original work. But young people from Africa have a right to know. With digital means, and with the authorization of the owners, we can create a scenario. The discourse is here. We have no pressure on our shoulders.

DG: You mentioned the post-ethnographic museum. Can you tell me about that?

HB: Ethnographic collections have been constituted in a context of domination, of violence. We should not forget that ethnography, at its beginning, is the discourse on the Other. Who is the Other? The person who has been colonized, discovered, who is controlled. It is totally exotic. When you see the commentaries on the labels of ethnographic objects, this is exactly what you see. This discourse may have been interesting for imperial Europe, which organized colonial exhibitions to present people "as they were." It is an extremely dangerous discourse, and we are now aware of that. There are several methods now to get things moving: one of the simplest means is the restitution of works. There is also interpretation, intellectual matters. There is circulation. Each of those museums tries to move away from the traditional ethnographic exhibition, which does not interest anyone anymore. You need to have those objects speak otherwise: to revisit them, to recontextualize them. It would be a very bad idea for a museum of black cultures to try to go into traditional ethnography.

DG: I am under the impression that you are a museum of knowledge. What knowledge does it transmit?

HB: For us, museums as you know them in Europe, and as we have known them here, by the way, are a dead end. That does not mean that we do not have conservation habits. We do have conservation habits, but works were not exposed, with the exception of the exhibition of specific ceremonies, and then they returned to our storage. We began thinking about those questions already a while back: Alpha Oumar Konaré, the president of Mali, took the plunge when he said that you had to kill the African model of museums. It did not fit. People did not visit them. We at the MCN said that concepts were the most important thing, since a thing that has been studied well is easier to realize. While building the museum—and I don't know if many museums have done this—we decided not to stay between colleagues but to open our thinking in a very broad way. Conversations were tense sometimes, but we reached a consensus on which we built the discourse. I think we have been faithful to what we were asked to do.

DG: The museum is based on the present.
HB: We are in the present.

DG: When you say you deal with everything, what do you mean by that? What is your relation to large-scale European museums, which aim to deal with everything?

HB: For a long time the Louvre was not willing to accept in its walls what is known as African art. How can they pretend to deal with everything? They don't. The Louvre has an immense collection of classical antiquities; that is its DNA. Our DNA is a mutating one. We think that our society, our community, our humanity move very quickly. If you want to be in the time of the world, you have to be in these shifts, and contextualize them.

DG: How do you realize this project?

HB: Today we live in a rapid time, in the time of artificial intelligence. We think that the future is happening with the digital. We are aware of our weaknesses in that field, but we know what to do. We think that with digital we can participate—even the people described as "illiterate," people who can't read. Let's just look at the outstanding penetration of mobile phones in Africa. We are cultures of the spoken word, and digital allows for all that. While being connected to our digital platforms, visitors will be able to choose their language, which will include, among others, an African language.

DG: Speaking of artificial intelligence and digital, how do you see their roles in relation to the works you display?

HB: They are essential. There are many works to which, at this point, we do not have access. Maybe in a hundred years. But for the moment, digital allows our audience to see the *Mona Lisa* better than the real one. What we cannot have at hand, we can show our audience via digital. Let's take a simple example: our kids are all glued on TV networks, on Cartoon Network, they know all the mangas. It is their language. If we do not share things using the language of the time, which is digital, we can't be fully active. Shifts are needed today. Digital is transforming the spoken word. The spoken word, oral cultures, were being lost, and that was such a shame. Today we can put a spoken word between parentheses and share it with the whole world. You have to push those categories and leave room for preserving oral cultures.

DG: The museum is therefore a platform.

HB: Absolutely. The museum of black cultures has been built on duality: we have traditional galleries, which you can find in every museum in the world. But our galleries are open spaces; they do not relate to fixed discourses; and they are extremely flexible. In our open spaces we can talk about everyone and we can put on, face to face, very different cultural performances.

DG: You are setting the idea of the museum as a political place, a public place, back in motion.

HB: Political—I don't know. Intellectuals have the leadership here, even if politicians support us. But a public place, yes.

DG: You were talking about the *Mona Lisa*. As a museum of black cultures, you do not essentialize what a black culture would be, but you create a museography of relations.

HB: In our thinking, we gathered that Africa is mostly cultures of encounter. In spite of the difficulties it has experienced, Africa has always encountered, assimilated, and observed. Generally, museums in Africa only speak about themselves. They are only focused on themselves. But African youths yearn to discover something else! Next year we are going to have an exhibition on Leonardo da Vinci, and then Picasso. We are looked at from elsewhere, sometimes we are looked down on, but we want to look positively at others. What is positive is fertile.

DG: You are an archaeologist yourself. How do you write this history of black cultures, on long time periods?

HB: It is natural. When you are an archaeologist, you work on long time periods. When you work on long time periods, you situate yourself much more in synchrony than in diachrony. Of course we can focus on a sequence, if we want to share a message on something, but, more globally, we are in synchrony. Archaeology is not only a knowledge of very old things. It has become, especially today, a science of the living with urban archaeology, etc. I am very at ease with long time periods.

DG: Isn't it also a way to rethink categories?

HB: When you are working on long time periods, you are amused to see rivalries—you put them into perspective. When you work on very long time periods, you get closer to what is constant in our humankind—evolution, constant renewal—and that is what is interesting to observe.

DG: Is this still a narrative of progress?

HB: Yes, of course. What I am about to tell you is a very personal point of view, maybe a utopian one, but I think the world has never been as close to its unity as it is now. It comes across as being extremely divided, apparently, but we are in fact very close to an achievement that will make our humankind something very joyful.

DG: I am under the impression that the museum of black cultures is a sort of laboratory for the unity of human lives.

HB: It is a laboratory to question the most complex questions, the most dreamlike as well. We have to dream. Humankind is a dream. If we dream, there is no problem anymore. We have to think, to raise questions, to always question our humankind, which is what museums do. Museums, as I see them, are laboratories dedicated exactly to that, to channeling generous ideas carried by our humankind.

DG: What image of humankind does this museum give?

HB: This is the idea we are very modestly trying to give: that our humankind is something wonderful. When we start with our common ancestor Toumai, who was the weakest of his contemporaries, he survived because he was smart. We also think he survived because he was generous, because he was able to constitute a group for himself, to evolve amid others. The whole history of humankind has the trace of this. There are moments of fire, of violence, but it is the founding principle of history, and therefore of this museum, to think of this evolution.

DG: In the museum thought you are developing, the old anthropological separation between nature and culture exists no longer.

HB: This separation is meaningless. All categories of this kind are obsolete. We now know there is no black race. Let's work on the positive, not on conceptions from the past.

DG: I am very interested in the idea of programming according to encounters, which is the opposite of European museums, which are traditionally structured around schools.

HB: European museums were mostly museums of identity. Art museums, even with the word "art," which is an essentialization, start with an identity of the concept of art. We are against any essentialization, including the one of "the black." When you say "a museum of black cultures," people think they are doing a black museum, a "museum of the Negro." That is not the case. For me, black cultures, since the Festival Mondial des Arts Nègres [begun in 1966], which was an important historical event, cannot be thought in this essentialized fashion. Globalization is cruel, [Léopold] Senghor spoke about it. We are always in the utopia of the encounter. In Senghor's view, the universal is the encounter between giving and getting. We give and we get, we are constantly in between both.

DG: The large-scale Western museums conceived themselves as encyclopedic museums, aiming to include everything, but not including everything. It seems to me that in front of this model, you are standing for a form of fluidity.

HB: We had no choice. When you look at the collections of these magnificent institutions, which have dedicated such effort to collecting and displaying, we are aware that their goal is never met. Fighting to try to compete with them means being three centuries late. We do not want that. This is not our ambition. We say, let's make discourses, let's create the institution. Everyone conceived their own method, and our advantage lies in not being prisoners of any collection; it is our mobility, our freedom. Many large-scale museums are recycling models and discourses that have existed for centuries. We are giving ourselves the possibility of being free, of thinking in a carefree but respectful manner. You can agree or disagree with it, but disagreeing is also a human quality. (2019)

19

Amit Sood

Director, Google Arts & Culture, Mountain View, California

Donatien Grau: It is often said that Google is as close as anything to being an encyclopedia. Would you agree?

Amit Sood: Google's mission is to organize the world's information and make it universally accessible and useful. Since the beginning, our goal has been to develop services that significantly improve the lives of as many people as possible. Giving access to knowledge and information is essential to this mission, but Google is not an encyclopedia, that would not be my main association. I always have thought of an encyclopedia as deeper research-oriented information. Whereas what I get from Google is right to the point. Exactly what I want. Done. That's Google, the search engine. Google Arts & Culture is our effort to give access to cultural stories online and be an innovation partner for the cultural sector. We strive to be more than just a place where people can find artworks online; we want to offer a platform for museums to tell stories and help people connect with cultural experiences.

DG: When the structure of going through information and looking for information is used to deal with art, how does one reach the point of putting together an encyclopedia of art?

AS: This is the problem but also the opportunity I see: as society moves toward a model of everything being instant, condensed, and summarized, it raises the question of the role a cultural encyclopedic website or institutional platform has.

Currently, people tend to divide the public in two groups: those who say they are interested in art and culture and those who say "it's not for me." One of the reasons why that has happened might be that museums have led themselves to become encyclopedic—information and research driven. You have to understand the context behind a painting. You need to understand what the artist intended. Maybe we have forgotten a little bit about the pleasure of just enjoying an artwork. I think about the group that considers they don't know art, that they don't know museums. But in fact they know a lot about art and museums. They just don't say it in that way, and we have to foster their enjoyment toward more information.

My mother, who lives in India, has always been conflicted about the career choice I have made. In her opinion, this is a waste of time. She was worried I would go into museums. As is often the case in India, my mother wanted me to be a doctor or an engineer. I was an engineer, but I deviated. I used to work in Android. I had what you could traditionally call a very strong job in that area. Now, I am dealing with art and culture. What I have explained to my mother is that she might think visiting a museum is just something you do when you're on holiday, or that it's just boring.

During the first two years, I had no chance of convincing her, regardless of how much I spoke to her. Then I realized: let's try a different approach. My mother loves gold. She's a big fan of gold jewelry, and she likes to look at very, very old gold jewelry. As museums around the world kept publishing new content on Google Arts & Culture, we gathered a phenomenal collection of gold from around sixty museums across the world. One day I was looking at the site, and I told my mother, "Do you like this kind of design?" She said, "What is this website?" I said, "This is the project I am working on," and she instantly asked: "So you have gold jewelry?" I said, "Yes, Mom, that also exists in museums, you know?" She answered: "Oh, really? Let's get into this." She doesn't know how to operate a computer, so now, every time I go home, she sits with me and she says, "Show me stuff on this or on that." I realized it has created this hook that allows her to feel that actually the stuff is very interesting.

One of the things I feel is that the role of a museum, or what it will be in the future, is to bridge this divide that has taken place over the last two or three hundred years since museums have come into being. Different people might have different opinions on what a cultural institution is. For most cultural institutions, from what I learned, the primary mission is education, a public-serving mission. What we focus on is what technology can do to help people build a deeper relationship with the institution. That is all possible if we can have multiple ways of engaging with different audiences.

DG: Such a structure for a cultural institution has an impact on its very definition. Some would call it a museum of a new kind. Would you agree with that? Does it seem relevant at all?

AS: Eventually it comes down to this: Do I have an asset with an important story to tell to people? If I do, then I should be able to find new ways of doing the storytelling to get people engaged in it and then to see how it reflects upon all paths of life.

Is what I am describing a shift in attitude for museums? Is it a new kind of museum? I do not think so. I wish I had gone to the British Museum when it first opened to see what exactly it was like! Of course, all objects come from different countries, from different cultural contexts, but I think this notion of curiosity-led exploration has always been core to museums. Not a narrative imposed on you, but the possibility to establish multiple entries for people who want to explore. That's what we are seeing happening on different platforms now.

You have to do demographic research on museum visitors to see what is happening. If you remove the tourists, which is very seasonal, and just look at the regular museum-going population, this is a much older demographic. The people museums need to go after are consuming content on very different platforms. This issue of the public—a public that is curious and who uses a whole new set of different platforms to find what they are looking for—is at the center of this: allowing people to create different narratives, different approaches, different ways to explore cultural content that matters to them. For that, you need to put your trust in the public.

DG: The encyclopedic museums tell stories. Do you want to tell a story with Google Arts & Culture?

AS: Google Arts & Culture is Google's effort to give access to culture and help the cultural sector make the most of the latest technologies. What we want to do is core to Google's mission: improve access to information. In our case, it's cultural information. The more niche certain cultural verticals are, the more challenging it will be to do this.

We are creating the base layer, which is just access to information. Contextual narratives only come on top of that. The story that we want to tell is this: you need access to content, but you need access to content with context, with participation and with engagement—all three being equally important. Some museums have done some very good things with open data: they just put up all their assets. That is a good first step, but it does not mean your digital strategy is done. That is literally the first thing you needed to do. There is a fundamental problem for a museum director or someone who is running a museum. Where do you put your resources?

Our approach is this: first, let's give people access to the information. Let's organize it, let's contextualize it, let's get people engaged. Our aim is to take care of the technology and let museums focus on what they do really well: acquisitions, curation, exhibitions, and storytelling.

Can we—and I mean not just Google, but the Internet companies, and anyone who's up for it—help the cultural sector succeed in an era when digital and technology in general offers immense opportunities? Some museums have embarked on pretty ambitious technical and digital projects. Is that a good thing? I don't really know, because if I had to choose between acquiring a very important piece and putting a couple of million dollars into a website, I'm not sure what the right priority would be.

DG: Do you think that this technical element relates to telling a story? Because you said the moment would come to tell a story.

AS: It is coming already. When Google Arts & Culture started, maybe because of the fact that I had no knowledge about the world of museums and the world of art at the time, I did not have a very clear plan. I consider that actually a strength, because I learned. I went around asking people. I asked people in museums, "Is this right? Is this wrong? Just help me out." Then I asked the people at Google, "Why are we doing this?"

What I realized is that the first one or two years were about convincing museums to share. Then about sharing, and sharing together. We achieved the first, we achieved the second, we are still trying to achieve more. Now our goal is about: "OK, you are sharing collaboratively, but now how about creating a form of storytelling from all this information?"

In the last one and a half years, it has been a big priority for us to essentially push curators to embrace digital tools for storytelling. Because the storytelling can happen two ways: it can happen from users, who just jump on it and tell their own stories, their own personal feelings, their emotional relationships, which is good. I am not too worried about that, because there are enough social sites out on the web where that can happen.

What I am most interested in is getting curators who have been studying and researching these topics for years and years to embrace new ways of publishing content. That is happening now. We have created an exhibition platform—so simple that in one hour a curator without any technical knowledge could publish an entire digital exhibition—professional, properly done.

When we started, we had maybe around thirty of them. On 31 July 2015 there were 1,600 professionally curated exhibitions. Compare those to another feature on our platform, which is users coming and telling their stories: we have 1,600 professionally curated exhibitions, and we have over 400,000 user-generated ones. This is what I tell the curators: there is a demand. People want to hear your stories. But it is going to be a little bit touch-and-go because we still do not have the right formats. It is just very early days in all of this.

DG: Google Arts & Culture is based on access, but an access that takes place without the object itself. The information is the object. What is the nature of access to information that is not the real thing, as one would have in a museum?

AS: It is based on access to the information, but also on access to a slightly non-quantifiable magical feeling. The only reason we insist on ultra high-resolution zooms is that we want people to travel into the paintings. Quality is a big bar for us. If we were just providing metadata, it would be very basic access.

We are trying to get people excited with access: feel a little bit of joy when they zoom into *The Starry Night*. We want them to feel something. The reason we want them to feel something is because that is going to drive them to actually physically want to see the work. No one talks about it anymore, thankfully, but when we launched the initial idea in 2011, everyone was saying, "Oh my God, people are not going to go to museums anymore!" It does not work like that. If I see a beautiful image of something online, I am not stupid. I understand that it is not the real thing. I want to then have the opportunity to go see it.

But we also have to understand that more than half the world's population is not traveling around the world visiting museums. For them, this is level-one access. For those who can go every day, who live next to MoMA and can see *Starry Night* in all its glorious beauty every single day, there is no need to go to this website at all.

DG: You referred to the other half of the world. How can this access platform avoid the usual criticism launched at the notion of encyclopedia in the museum, namely, that objects are not treated as equal and that there is a hierarchy?

AS: The way I deal with the hierarchal problem is this: on the site, all museums and all objects are equal. This is the first platform on the web where you can go to the British Museum, then just suddenly find your way into a museum that maybe you had never heard of, that you might never have had any plans of visiting. But from a hierarchical standpoint, they are exactly the same. The British Museum does not have a bigger logo; it is an equal platform, which then trickles down to the object as well.

One of the most interesting experiments we launched was very simple: we told ourselves, "If we can bring this content to the people without their actually asking for it, we can surprise them." We can do that on the platform, of course. But the way we have done it is that every time you open a tab in your home browser, we will show you a completely different artwork. We did user testing and users said: "That is phenomenal! I didn't even know that painting was there." I think that is when the hierarchy just gets thrown out of the window: J. M. W. Turner, Emily Brown, Henri Rousseau. When would we think of them together, on the same hierarchical level, in a museum?

Their hierarchies are also due to physical constraints: you can only show so much. Museums cannot show their whole collections. What we say is: "Then use the web." It will come slowly, though, because people will be wary about, "Oh, shall I do it or shall I have Google do it or shall I do it to myself?" It does not matter who does it. If the museums had just gotten together, hired some clever engineers and collaborated with them, built such a platform, there would have been no need for the Google Art Project, which turned into Google Arts & Culture.

DG: Museums are often limited by national structures. Google Arts & Culture by nature goes beyond frontiers. Are they still relevant or do you think Google's platform points toward a boundless way of looking at art?

AS: It is definitely a boundless way because one of the most interesting things we are doing is mixing different genres of culture: we have got a history channel now, a World Wonders channel, we have art, and then we have photography, street art. This is where I think it really gets interesting. We can create connections with no limitation whatsoever. We can ask ourselves: What is the relationship between ballet and street art?

On this website now, you can actually go through the archives of ballet and of street art and find such a connection. We are not going to do it for you; we will try in some ways, but we are looking for people to do it. You are breaking down this preconceived division of the status. Are you a national museum? Are you a foundation? Are you a historical archive? It is not a problem for us.

It comes down to this little question I always answer with when people ask me, "How can we join?" I say, "Very simple. A. Are you nonprofit? Google Arts & Culture is open only for noncommercial partners. B. Do you actually own the rights to make the artworks, artifacts, and information you have available? C. Are you willing to put it up online?" This is as simple as it gets, and people are shocked; they ask: "Can I be on the same platform as the Ministry of Culture's number three museum in Italy?" I answer, "Yes, you can."

DG: Encyclopedic museums, and museums in general, are seen as institutions of authority—the authority of the nation, the authority of the canon. Do you think they can be democratized?

AS: We have not thought of what we do in terms of a museum that has a responsibility and an authority to tell certain stories. This is always going to happen. Museums are going to keep doing it. We need that, and it does need us. Boundaries need to be broken. Online, there are no boundaries. I can jump from one place to another. For one second, I can be seeing the National Museum in Afghanistan and then another minute I can be with the National Museum in Bogota. We can have an extraordinary, boundless experience.

We have to allow for people to feel that experience of culture. Sometimes it might also be enjoyable to explore art from a point of view that is not nationalistic—even though I understand that people can be proud of the culture their country has created. I say to people in national museums: "Yes, of course, you should be proud of yourself and of your culture. But it is also great just to explore the content without thinking whether it belongs to one country versus another." From mid-February 2016 we uploaded this very interesting visualization of art from all over the world, with all boundaries removed; the world will be organized by art and not by territory.

Governments and nations will always have both the responsibility as well as the authority to protect, conserve, and fund. This is the role from the government side. Removing boundaries online does not mean that you will not still need governments to support culture.

DG: Then the question becomes: What is the impact of that online experience on the real world?

AS: I think we need to differentiate the story from the art itself. If an object merits physical attention, the experience of art online is certainly not going to be the end of it all—rather the beginning. You are always going to want that physical attraction. Someone has to actually have a building where you can go, see it, experience it. That is always going to be there, but it is true that for stories, narratives, information, there are opportunities online for giving users more content than they would ever be able to access in a museum. You can have all that information, without negating the need for physical experiences. They complete each other.

DG: Google Arts & Culture as an encyclopedic museum is the closest to being a complete encyclopedia. What would the complete encyclopedia of art—an impossible book—mean?

AS: It will never be complete. But it is always going to be my goal to try to make it as comprehensive as possible, and we will never stop. We will never ever stop.

Where are we? We are at the very beginning. Half of the objects of the world are in hidden places: they are invisible. They have not even reached museums. Once we manage to be closer to encyclopedic we can be—that is, comprehensive in coverage—I think it will be one of the most exciting research tools. The uses are numerous: from traveling, to fun, to education. When you get real comprehensiveness, that is where, I think, you can have really interesting insights and data work. We are now starting to look into correlations, cultural relationships.

Can I very quickly understand Van Gogh's use of color through his life? Without having to read a major research paper, can I get a glimpse visually? Now you can actually do that and then be able to organize it better. You are going to be able to actually look at different color patterns. You go beyond the level of passive experience of the image. We uploaded a letter of Van Gogh to Gauguin making a sketch of his room in Arles; and we have the two versions of the painting online. Anyone can compare; anyone can think; and that is what you get with comprehensiveness: more information, more knowledge. (2016)

Methodologies and Potentials of the Encyclopedic Museum

3

20

James Cuno

President and CEO, The J. Paul Getty Trust, Los Angeles

Donatien Grau: Why is it that the encyclopedic museum matters today? Should we be content with the way it is, or should we try to improve it, update it?

James Cuno: Encyclopedic museums collect, preserve, exhibit, and research representative examples of the world's many cultures. Like encyclopedias themselves, they present evidence about the world and encourage investigation and interpretations. They encourage curiosity about the world. In this respect, encyclopedic museums should be encouraged where they don't exist today. The more encyclopedic museums there are, the more distributed—and safer—the world's cultural heritage will be.

As museums, encyclopedic museums serve a broad, general public. Unlike universities, they don't examine their visitors before they allow them entry and they don't test them when they leave. Given that, by definition, encyclopedic museum collections comprise examples of cultural difference, visitors to such museums confront cultural differences in their galleries and have their view of the world enlarged and enhanced in the process. Of course we acknowledge that regional distinctions do exist and that artists from the same region of the world often make things similarly and make things that look similar. But that's a matter of habit and convention rather than of nature or national spirit. Artists, like the rest of us, are victims of the limitations of their experiences. And encyclopedic museums argue against an essentialist view of culture.

DG: How do museums make sense of the range of cultural forms in their collections? How do they not confuse their visitors when emphasizing diversity and difference?

JC: Encyclopedic museums present works of art on two registers. One register is the permanent collection, and the other the temporary exhibition. The permanent exhibition register is played out by installations in sequences of rooms. The experience of a room, of the objects in a room, creates a form of coherence. People necessarily, as they pass from one room to the other, experience a kind of coherent narrative. Encyclopedic museums can complicate this experience, breaking up the long march of single-themed gallery exhibitions with alternative and complementary themes in neighboring galleries.

Human beings have moved about the world from the beginning, taking different routes and confronting new things and experiences. We don't experience the world in single, tidy narratives. That's what we impose upon the world. The world is messier than that. We should provide opportunities in our galleries to allow our visitors a break from chronological, iconographic, or material clarity of our narratives' similarities and let them explore this messiness of life, the many cultural and material differences the world is made of. Our visitors should be given the opportunity to experience our collections contrapuntally at times.

Galleries can function differently. At the very least, permanent collection galleries can offer one kind of narrative, and temporary exhibition galleries another, a different kind of narrative, even one that argues against the one presented in the permanent collection galleries. We should be bold and confident. And we should recognize that however clever we think our gallery installations are, we can't predict how our visitors will experience them. Gallery visitors roam through galleries as they wish, from one object that catches their eye to another. Sometimes they seek the path of least resistance and go where it is less crowded. We shouldn't try to be too clever. Museum galleries are for discoveries, not arguments.

In any case, encyclopedic museums of the future, and increasingly of the present, are not going to be limited to presenting one kind of experience. There will be the experience of the museum itself, of objects in galleries, and then the complementary experience of the museum's collections, archive materials, library, online experience. The curation of that experience is going to be left up to the individual online. In an even more expansive way, museums will provide their visitors opportunities to explore their collections as they wish.

DG: The question of online presence is really important. Is a museum online still a museum? If you think a museum is about the experience of things, what is the status of online data?

JC: Things can be experienced in different ways, as physical objects or as digital representations. The latter can provide different truths about an object, even about its materiality, that an object in a gallery cannot. Digital images can be touched—we called it "pinched"—and enlarged, turned, and looked at in different ways. They can break down the materiality of an object by allowing its examination to penetrate the object's surface. Anything that allows and provokes greater curiosity about works of art is good. This empowers our visitors. Our job is to provide our visitors information for them to propose and test different truths about what they are seeing. This is what encyclopedias do. They provide information and encourage their readers to interpret meanings.

This information expands to labels, to available publications, or to online information, which they can download there in the museum; they can link to other information about the subject or the material or the artist, or the period in which it was made, whenever it might be, download all that into their own personal device, and then go home and increase, amplify that by gathering other information elsewhere in the Internet, where they wish. We do not control any of that.

DG: You seem to suggest the idea of a form of hybrid narrative beyond national narratives. There is a slight tension there, because the good thing about national narratives is that they are readable. And there seems to be a form of tension between altering the traditional narrative a little bit, and yet bringing it to the public.

JC: We have to acknowledge that works of art have different meanings, just as we have multiple identities. Museums are limited spatially. We can only present a few kinds of meaning at any one time, in any one kind of installation. That's why complementary interpretative materials, online and in print, are so important.

DG: Today you deal with a very different audience, which of course is global, and who may not be as well informed, yet wants to experience. However, knowledge is one of the key elements of the encyclopedic museum. How do you deal with it? How is this audience to be treated?

JC: Respectfully. We have to trust the agency of our different audiences. We can't presume they have no agency, and that they have to rely entirely on us, on the professional's point of view, to experience the museum. We have to trust that these are curious people. After all, they have made a decision to come to the museum. They have already demonstrated their agency by coming to the museum. This is profound, it seems to me. People who have never been to museums live perfectly good lives. But people who go to museums have sought to enhance their lives. They are in search of something, some kind of new experience, something out of the ordinary. And that experience is going to be provoked and maybe even defined by the things they see in the museum. Our job is to put our collections on view in ways that attract the attention of our visitors. We should provide information about our collections, for sure. But we must at the very least present them in ways that draw our visitors to them.

Once again, I think that information cannot be limited to what they just see in the label as provided. We have to amplify that information virtually, so they can take that experience home with them and amplify it with other, online information.

We can't underestimate the ability or willingness of people to be curious about the world. And we need to respect that. There was a period of time in the 1980s and '90s, and it lingers a bit, when there was a dominant theoretical position that museums have an explicit narrative that reinforces the hegemony of a particular segment of society, and a particular political view of the world, and that the people who come into the museum are influenced by that narrative. They become part of that narrative. They are made to feel either part of it or become dominated by it, as if they have no agency to break from it. I just do not think people are that stupid; I do not think that ideology is that totalizing and so controlling. I don't think museums are so controlling. Neither are they neutral institutions, of course. At any given time, museums are limited by their history and perspectives, by the quality of their staff, and by their financial resources. But the people who come to the museum are able to see beyond that. The same is true of universities, of course. I always find it interesting that university-based "institution critics" don't turn their critical gaze back on their own institutions. Perhaps because they if they did, they would be implicated in their own kind of hegemonic ideological control regime. It's easier to criticize others than to criticize oneself.

DG: One could argue that the encyclopedic museum is, strangely enough, the ideology of the day, with the idea of hybridity, the idea of global culture. A global culture that would be about connectedness, which is also very much one of the great ideologies of today.

JC: The encyclopedic museum is a creation of the Enlightenment. The Enlightenment view of the world was one based on regard for the inquiring mind, to find truths about the world from things in the world. These truths could be multiple, conflicting—they could be scientific, or cultural, or historical. Whatever these truths are, if you bring enough evidence together representative of the world, you can get a sense of the world. And then that particular sense of the world can be critiqued or enhanced. The world is bigger, richer, and more varied than a single interpretation will allow.

Some people, typically university-based scholars, criticize encyclopedic museums as institutions of empire, not of science. If they are, so too are universities, of course. My view is that encyclopedic museums are witnesses to empire and give evidence to empire rather than being instruments of empire. If one is looking for evidence of empire in the encyclopedic museum, it's going to be almost everywhere. The empire has been around for a long time, in many different parts of the globe. It is not a creation of the Enlightenment.

Encyclopedic museums are Enlightenment institutions: the Enlightenment has left its mark. If we value freedom of speech, human rights, critical inquiry, and human agency, we value the Enlightenment. And by valuing the Enlightenment, we necessarily critique it. We should encourage encyclopedic museums everywhere. They are empowering institutions.

The question is how to do this. The future of the encyclopedic museum is about building relationships throughout the world, relationships of exchange and sharing objects, artifacts, staff, and expertise. It is crucial to build these relationships between institutions and individuals in order to propagate a curiosity about the world.

DG: But there is a crux here: there is almost no encyclopedic museum outside of the West.

JC: I think that is because encyclopedic museums are related to the Enlightenment, which was mainly a European movement. To me, it is one of the great tragedies of the British imperial experience in India that among all the institutions that it left to independent India, including universities, a robust legal system, democracy, scientific inquiry, and political systems—with very few exceptions, it did not leave the example of encyclopedic museums.

One great exception is the CSMVS museum in Mumbai—the former Prince of Wales Museum. It is truly an encyclopedic museum built by the citizens of Bombay for the benefit of all who live in or visit Bombay, now of course, Mumbai. Encyclopedic museums everywhere have got to partner to build additional encyclopedic museums. If we value encyclopedic museums for what they are, we should value them everywhere.

DG: Do you think that geopolitics have to be accepted in order for the encyclopedic museum to move ahead?

JC: Geopolitics is a reality. One must work through them and respect their stubbornness and know that their feature dynamics will change over time.

I think there is tremendous potential for the encyclopedic museum, and great hope for its future. That said, we can't be blind to the difficulties of propagated encyclopedic museums in the world. War and iconoclasm are not things of the past. Current tragedies in Iraq and Syria, not to mention Mali, Yemen, and Myanmar, are evidence to that truth. But times will change. And until then, we must protect the world's culture for the world. And only encyclopedic museums are dedicated to that proposition. (2014)

21

Jean Nouvel

Architect

Donatien Grau: Do you think the encyclopedic museum is too ambitious an idea?

Jean Nouvel: I think the more you try to do things at the same time, the more difficult it is. Edgar Morin described noology as a science to be developed as quickly as possible—this science that enables us to draw up a hierarchy of knowledge and organize the best transversalities and complementarities. Wanting to create a museum that would gather everything together, that would aim to include everything, would be too ambitious and is not desirable.

An encyclopedia is always interesting if you can dip into it. To go and dip into a museum is something we already often do, but is a museum always the most appropriate place for this form of consumption? Do we need to be confronted by this method? Wouldn't an encyclopedic museum entail gathering together all information? Yet this is something computer science is getting better and better at. Now we go and look at something online first and only then in the museum.

However, an encyclopedic museum as a unit in terms of place and presence—I don't really believe in it. One often drowns in a museum as it is. "Encyclopedic" would mean that everything that is known is brought together there, and that's impossible!

If there is an encyclopedic museum, it therefore exists in the dialogue between collections, which are necessarily fragmentary and piecemeal, and online resources, image- and text-based resources, which are, by definition, far more extensive.

DG: You prefer the term *museum of civilizations* to the term *encyclopedic museum*. Why?

JN: The museum of civilizations speaks of civilizations with a small *c:* it doesn't claim to give a comprehensive reading of the world. It speaks, in its own way, of civilizations that are either still there or no longer there, even if it is more about civilizations that have disappeared or have left their mark on history.

In the museum of civilizations, there's the idea of exploring the meaning of these civilizations through witnesses, through objects, which, by force of circumstance, provide an elliptical testimony. In every case, the principle is to present evidence that these civilizations have actually existed. It's a way of getting them to talk, of putting them into context within a very long historical perspective, within a global perspective that leads to an evaluation, comparison, or opinion that one might form upon seeing the witnesses of these different civilizations.

It's difficult to form an idea of civilizations; that's why I have a problem with the *encyclopedic* logic. The only evidence of a physical kind that remains to us relates to eroded architecture, traces that are difficult to interpret, or rare and precious objects. And to texts, when they exist, or, from the early days of writing, undeciphered plaques.

The presentation of civilizations in a museum is a way of making something that is illegible self-evident again, of replacing within their historical context the characteristics of each of these civilizations. These civilizations often stood alone, that is to say, they were completely isolated from one another. They weren't on the same continent. And often, they didn't express themselves during the same eras.

There's a dimension here of dizzying exploration as you become aware that cities existed and have disappeared. It dawns on you that these civilizations that existed were mortal. This, I believe, is the most fascinating and moving thing: to adopt this historical perspective and realize all over again how unimportant we are.

DG: Today there's a lot of talk about museums of civilizations, encyclopedic museums, universal museums. Why is this so important? What is it that gives this conversation about civilizations its meaning?

JN: It comes down to asking oneself what History is for and why History is important. This is History with a capital *H*, and this History with a capital *H* is not over yet. The exploration is not finished. We're probably going to discover other civilizations. We're engaged in an exploration of time, of the limits of time, of what has managed to develop behind our backs, so to speak. It's difficult to grasp the significance of all this.

We're often astonished by the lifestyles, the beliefs, the customs, and the horrors, too. It's like a journey, in the same way that a novel is. We say to ourselves: "They did things like that, they used objects like that, they had those rites, they were in that country, that forest, or wherever." It's astonishing! The museum of civilizations transmits this knowledge to us through the objects: it takes us back to these reflections in order to feed our thinking in the present.

A question that then arises is: From what point do we stop talking about civilizations and start talking about contemporary history, about recent history? Today there's an almost global civilization. There's such an osmosis, such conformity, such a blurring and such interaction, that it's extremely difficult, today, unlike a few centuries, a few millennia ago, to isolate entities of thought, territories of thought, practices that were highly specific. We're experiencing a hybridization associated with this permeability. It's for this reason that the museum of civilizations, with its differences and parallels, is particularly important.

DG: One hears the term *museum of art and civilizations*. What's the relationship between art and civilization in such a museum?

JN: Every civilization has its evidence of an artistic kind: it has created forms, objects, texts. This is often what has survived and has come down to us. It's through these objects, which have a strong emotional and plastic dimension, very strong formal characteristics (styles, colors), that these civilizations are known to us and symbolized for us.

DG: You talk of civilizations in the plural, and reject the concept of the encyclopedic museum. Do you think the museum of civilizations can be a universal museum?

JN: Universality is a deep and broad concept. It doesn't merely stem from the—no doubt illusory—representativeness of the world's civilizations; it's transversal in terms of its sense of humanity. What tells us that a museum is a universal museum is its reading and interpretation of these civilizations, because it's talking to us about common questions. There's a complementary dimension here, which is not at all the same thing, to do with being of relevance to each and everybody. But this is already a curatorial option and I'm not going to give a verdict on it here.

However, it's worth underlining that many civilizations were highly specific and had customs and characteristics that one could say today were not universal but corresponded to nothing but themselves, that they formed a universe in themselves. They are therefore universal in the sense that they constitute a universe but not necessarily in the sense understood by *universal museum.*

Surely everyone has their own view of a universal museum. A universal museum—this is an enormous ambition. I think a museum with a message whose scope touches humanity already has a kind of universality. It's highly ambitious to try to achieve this objective through the exhibits. It's therefore an elaborate strategy.

DG: How do you show different civilizations within one and the same museum?

JN: There are several ways. In the Louvre Abu Dhabi project, it's based on an approach that's strictly chronological and directly comparative, involving a juxtaposition of the objects. It's also very interesting to see the similarities and differences between civilizations that weren't known to each other but were often talking about the same thing.

There's certainly a very interesting dimension to this but it's not the only way of going about it. It could, by contrast, be done by going into each of the civilizations in depth, but then you need all the material that will enable you to talk about each one of them. By its very nature, a presentation of this kind is so large that it often demands a lot of time deciphering, reading, interpreting. It's extremely difficult to tackle a lot of civilizations together unless accurate didactic information has been prepared.

DG: What's the starting point from which, in terms of collections, the museum can think about being able to offer a discourse?

JN: It depends on what your idea of a museum is. You can have a museum based on a single piece. The Rosetta Stone is enough to justify a museum by itself. There's no predetermined notion of what a museum is.

However, if the objective is to give an account of the dialogue between civilizations, you can't start a discourse on the basis of two pieces: it's not enough. In the case of world civilizations, there are also issues of scenography: often, the works on display require their own space. No picturesque treatment. I'm fundamentally against a form of museography like that of the des Sessions at the Louvre, in which African, Oceanian, or American works have been placed on a plinth underneath four spotlights. This is completely meaningless. If the same thing were done in an African hut with a quattrocento painting placed on the ground, everyone would object, and rightly so. In both cases there is a lack of respect shown to the original spirit.

It's very important to be aware that these works are the victims of a form of abduction, whether legal or illegal. Having said that, it's okay to try to preserve a part of the emotion that might have accompanied their discovery, or that of the presence of these works under different lighting conditions, on other scales, or in other colors. If this is done in a stupid way, the results will be equally stupid. It seems particularly pertinent and important to me that it be done in a poetic, subtle way.

DG: The problem of the encyclopedic museum stems from the fact that it is also a big museum. Is a big museum the best way of approaching civilizations and knowledge?

JN: What we're up against here is the problem of collections. Today something of interest has to enter the museum; as a result, a sort of accumulation is created of which, at any given time only, a tiny percentage can be shown and so a degree of rotation is instigated. Museum workers all know how impressive the collections are and that there's a sort of hidden world that no longer belongs to the art lovers: a kind of enormous library accessible to the curators alone. I don't think this situation is right. As a matter of principle the museum should, with its public spaces, whether inside or outside, be life. And the works of art should, by and large, be in living places. The museum should thus be living.

My notion of the museum follows the Greek model: a place to visit and revisit, where things change and where thoughts are displayed on the walls so that it's not merely a place of conservation. Obviously, I'm in favor of conservation. There are places whose works are so precious to humanity that their conservation needs to be guaranteed. This is one of the key functions of the museum. It's for this reason that over here the people who look after them are essentially conservators. This role isn't something to be challenged, but for me there's a kind of contradiction in the idea of a crowd that communes with art by consuming it, with a total impossibility of experiencing successive emotions.

People normally go to a museum with a desire to see what they have an idea of finding there. So the museum becomes a place of consumption. They're going to see five hundred masterpieces in succession. There's something Pantagruelian about this, which means there are going to be problems digesting it all, followed by the inevitable amnesia. And all the more so as museums are becoming bigger and more impressive. I therefore believe that the function of the work of art is to be located in a living space. On this basis, the museum's ambition is to become a living space, a space in which you feel good, in which you linger, rather than a space for temporary consumption after enduring impossible queues.

I don't reject an ideology of communion, but I think the major museums, other than the less-visited ones, are museums of consumption and storage, which does not in any way detract from what's there. The big museum, whether we call it a museum of civilizations, an encyclopedic museum, or a universal museum, is at the heart of these reflections. (2015)

22

Bénédicte Savoy

Professor, Technische Universität, Berlin,
and Collège de France, Paris

Donatien Grau: What do you think today, in 2019, about museums' encyclopedic claims?

Bénédicte Savoy: Rather than claims, I see their encyclopedic past as a historical fact, a legacy, a given. From the German point of view, I think more work needs to be done on this very important historical fact than has so far been the case. I'd like to stress that when I talk about it here, it's from the German point of view, which is the most familiar to me because I've been living in Berlin for the past twenty-five years.

I know that in France, for example, it's somewhat different: the Louvre has put its history on show. During its years under Pierre Rosenberg, one could learn something of the history of the Louvre in the Louvre itself, but here in Germany you learn nothing of the history of the museums, of their former encyclopedic visions, of their former universalist fantasies. You have the feeling, even today, that the museums are ahistorical, that the objects arrived by helicopter one night, that they fell out of the sky. The visitor has no awareness of their historicity, of these encyclopedic claims that, precisely, form a part of their historicity.

DG: You've drawn a parallel between the terms *encyclopedic* and *universalist*, and the relationship between these two ideas is one of the most difficult to clarify. Do you think it's possible to distinguish between the two, and if so, where does the distinction lie?

BS: When I was at the Collège de France, I dedicated a course to the year 1815, pondering the origins of the term *universal museum*. Contrary to what one might expect, it doesn't appear in contemporary sources in the 1800s.

During this time, the Louvre was often described as the most beautiful museum in the universe. The universe is brought into conjunction with the museum, but the combination "universal museum" was not common around 1800. In reality, it seems to me that "universal museum" made its appearance far later, possibly around the early 2000s, at the time the 2002 declaration on the universal museum was made public.

Neither does the expression "encyclopedic museum" appear in French sources around 1800. One finds an insatiable desire to have everything, to fill the display cases, but not under the banners "encyclopedic" or "universal." Hence my suspicion that within the European context these terms are political constructions contrived at a precise moment in history in order to defend this kind of museum, which until then had not required a label. This is what museums were, and that's all there was to it.

As far as I'm concerned, I would therefore see these as two terms constructed by the museums, which felt themselves under threat—perhaps because they saw looming on the horizon the issue of restitutions, which had already appeared in the 1970s and 1980s.

What interests me far more than the self-professed universalism of the museums is the issue of their historicity and the way in which it can be presented to the visitors. This is the big issue that preoccupies museums and is set to preoccupy them in the future, too: their own historicity and how to present it. It's not easy, but they certainly won't get there by simply erasing this historicity. Here, in Berlin, certain museums have been destroyed and the buildings rehabilitated. If you go to the Gemäldegalerie, the very architecture is ahistorical and you learn nothing about the history of the collections. You enter a temple, which is one interpretation of the museum—though a largely inadequate one today.

It's here that the question about encyclopedism might be asked. No longer would it be a label that legitimatizes a certain type of bulimic museum; it would be applied to objects as repositories of different kinds of knowledge: aesthetic, material, historical; of knowledges in the plural, and of plurality in general.

DG: How do you see this archaeology of objects?

BS: Not of objects alone but of the collection as a whole. The historicity of the museum is a history of the collections. How can it be rendered visible and intelligible as a point of access to the cultural history of Europe, if we are talking about the European point of view?

Take the bust of Nefertiti and a dinosaur, both of which are conserved in the Berlin museums. One of these two objects is seventy million years old; the other dates from 1400 BCE. Each of the objects has a temporality of its own, but the two arrived in Berlin at the same time, just before the First World War. If I visit the museum, this is extremely valuable supplementary information that helps me to understand why they're here. They couldn't have arrived after the First World War because Germany no longer had any colonies in Tanzania, and thus the dinosaur wouldn't have come to Germany. Similarly, in the 1930s, a find such as the bust of Nefertiti would have remained in Cairo.

Knowing this gives the museum a density and a degree of interest that far exceeds the individual poetry of the objects, which is already present. It pays heed to their narrative, which is particularly necessary for the younger generations, who are generally highly attentive to the provenance of things, wanting to know where things come from, when they came, and how they came.

It can be seen as a form of political correctness. Even more than our generation, the younger generations are used to thinking about the origins of their consumer products—including the products of cultural consumption. They want to know where their coffee or their steak comes from, where their clothes, furniture, and so on come from. When you visit galleries or museums with them, they undoubtedly experience an intense, primordial emotion in front of works of art, these things that are poignant to behold in their real dimensions and real colors, these objects that one has to physically move oneself in order to set them in motion. But very soon they come around to the question of conditions: when, how, the price of the work. For these young people, who inhabit the world of social media, the question of source is key: Is it real? Is it fake? Am I being fooled? Who's talking to me at the museum?

It's almost a question of respect, faced with these young generations and indeed faced with all the visitors, to make this history available to them. Instead of rejecting this curiosity, one could take advantage of it in order to make the museums even more interesting than they already are.

DG: You could say that in such museums the objects have discovered a kind of fluidity: between artistic and anthropological status; between information and contemplation. What do you think about this fluidity achieved by the objects?

BS: It seems to me that they always had a fluidity. What's happening is a growing awareness of the fact that these unique objects come from somewhere and are now absent from this somewhere. It's the double game of their presence in the British Museum, the Louvre, and Berlin, and their absence elsewhere. It's a gain: they're already in three dimensions, but they're acquiring an additional dimension: that of the time passed here, in their display cases, in relation to the time passed elsewhere, before, in the sand of Egypt or the earth of Nigeria. Moreover, some are not objects but subjects, etc. They're capable, outside their vitrines, in cultures other than ours, of having a different power, a different agency.

In *Black Panther* there's a key museum scene: the museum director is asked about an object by a young African-American man. She possesses the "dry" knowledge of the specialist, a knowledge of the geography and the dates, but she doesn't have the knowledge that the young man, who potentiates the object, has.

DG: In the report you authored with Felwine Sarr on the restitution of African works of art, you describe the need to return works to the continent of Africa. Isn't this the very opposite of representing the world in its entirety to the world, which is the principle of the encyclopedic museum?

BS: Representing the world to the world is a European, Western vision, which opposes the good universal, in which we find ourselves, to the bad local, where the others are.

Quite simply, in the case of these objects, of which there's often only one in existence, this is where the original set of data is, and once it's in London or Paris, or some other Western capital, it's impossible to have access to it anywhere else, notably in the place where it was created. It's a "universal" without universal access.

But let's be clear: it's not a question of returning five thousand, ten thousand, fifty thousand objects all of a sudden. It's more about allowing these objects, and the societies to which they're connected, to experience a universalism that would be seen from a point of view other than the Western, European one. It's not at all about preventing the European museums, with their long history and long love of the objects, from representing the world to the world, it's simply about saying that with this kind of representation a very large part of the world is de facto excluded.

Just recently, I've spent a lot of time delving into the discovery of antecedents of this debate on restitutions, which was thought to have been something new. The young Emmanuel Macron was believed to have had a new idea in a flash of inspiration. In the archives, however, we realized that everything had been said and thought at the latest by between 1970 and 1980. Pierre Quoniam, former director of the Louvre, former director of the Bardo Museum in Tunis during the colonial period, and inspector general of museums in France, submitted a report. Quoniam was a distinguished museum man, not an anarchic academic. At the beginning of the 1980s, he came to the conclusion that the restitution to Africa of a significant portion of the relevant museum holdings would be an act of solidarity, of "fairness," as he puts it in the report.

I came across sources of this kind in both France and Germany. In 1982, Hildegard Hamm-Brücher, a senior figure in the German liberal party in the 1980s, announced restitutions planned for 1984, the centenary of the Berlin conference on the partition of Africa. Then the government changed, Hildegard Hamm-Brücher left the government, and the restitutions were never made.

While working in the archives, I realized that the fine and legitimate project, which no one denies, of representing the world to the world, was, as early as the 1960s and beginning of the 1970s, confronted by the legitimate thirst of young African nations to connect with their own cultural heritage. In the archives there's a letter of 1972 from Ekpo Eyo, director of the Nigerian National Museum, to the Berlin museums. In it he requests the loan of one or two objects for the museum in Lagos. The response from the Berlin museums was a flat refusal on the basis that it was an encyclopedic museum: if a fragment of it was loaned, the encyclopedia would no longer be complete.

It's somewhat perverse to use this encyclopedic, universal, world-representing character as a reason to reject the very modest claims of young nations. And with an arrogance exemplified by the following statement: "Let the Africans come to us and be happy to see all that over here.' This created an extremely strong sense of frustration.

We need to be able to conceive of a representation of the world in a place that is not Paris or London or New York, but elsewhere, in Dakar or Lagos. This is starting to happen. What we now need to do is to see universals in the plural. Felwine Sarr and I have been accused of "populism" for supposedly wanting to relocate the arts to "their" nationality, in "their" country. This is clearly not what it's about. It's about us, as Europeans, understanding that representing the world to the world is not a Western prerogative, that others can want to do this, and indeed do it very well.

DG: I was coming to that. What place do you give the nations on the one hand and the local element on the other, in this mechanism of restitution?

BS: In the report, the question of nation becomes an operational matter from the moment we raise the concrete issue of proceeding with restitutions.

We were accompanied in this initiative by an inspector general of the fine arts, Isabelle Maréchal, via various ministries, agencies, and groups. One of the questions that arose, and which we therefore put to the French ministry of foreign affairs, was: How had the requests for restitution been recorded by the administration? What needs to be done in order to set a procedure in motion? The answer was that a request was required from state to state.

So in reality, we don't really raise the question of nation, we start from a formula of the ministry of foreign affairs in France, which receives only state-to-state requests. Naturally, we don't talk in terms of sovereign nations and the idea that cultural heritage would promote national affirmation. This is not at all what it's about. We talk far more in terms of regions, and even place of origin, which can also be a mythical place. And we prioritize in our thinking the issue of a new quality of relationship between the African and European countries.

For example, we were in discussion with colleagues in Benin, where the voodoo religion is omnipresent. In one particular place, certain objects that subsequently went into Western museums had been set aside and were no longer used because they weren't active anymore. When the ethnologists found them, they had already been set aside, and there was therefore no problem about them being in Europe. In this precise case, without interesting the religious communities, their value might be that they enable historians of this place to study the history of styles. This thinking in terms of place is not the same as thinking in terms of the local, as place includes the different voices connected with it.

Moreover, if restitutions are made to different places of origin that have become nations, states associated with these places, this does not mean that in these places there will be an exclusive focus on this cultural heritage alone. The Museum of Black Civilizations in Dakar, for example, has a project of representing the world to the world, but from a pan-African point of view, a point of view that is not that of the dominant European narratives.

DG: One also sees an expectation for museums to tell a story, which is not merely the story of art. This narrative is political.

BS: The political character of the museums has always been there. If you look at the history of the French museums after 1800, you see that the Louvre was called the Musée Napoléon. And then the Musée Charles X, and then the Musée Napoléon III. The museums were all linked to geopolitical contexts that favored the accession of works into their collections. The arrival of the Winged Victory of Samothrace took place in a precise context; the excavation of the Pergamon Altar took place within the context of the relationship between Germany and the Ottoman Empire. The link between provenance, history, politics, geopolitics, and diplomacy was more conscious than today.

But what's new is perhaps that the museums have become places of negotiation. The days when they had a monopoly on conferring meaning are over. The young generations have understood that the museum is not a neutral place and that they can no longer be told exactly what to think about each work without this being challenged by them. They want to recover their own ability to attribute meaning. The museums are in the process of losing their monopoly as the conferrers of meaning on the objects. If the collections are fully online, if they're available in the form of open data, anyone in any part of the world can draw whatever meaning they like from a particular moment in a work's history, and perhaps even share their emotions or knowledge—cultural, philosophical, anthropological, technological—about each work.

This brings to mind the question of the relationship between the library and the museum: in a library, the librarian doesn't claim to read all the books before lending them to the readers. There are catalogs, you go to borrow a book, and the librarian simply places it at your disposal. In museums, objects are often still being read for people; visitors are being given an object pre-read. They're being told: "This is what you need to know and think about this object." Increasingly, however, visitors want to *read* the object on the basis of their own knowledge and horizons.

DG: Which leads to: What's visible and what's not?

BS: Absolutely—the visibility and invisibility of a large part of the collections, of the choices made. What do we show? What don't we show?

I like to talk of the three timeframes of the museum. There's the time of the objects, an antique or ancestral time. These objects are encountered at the museum in a second timeframe, which is that of the visitor. You can go to the Museum of Islamic Art and see intact pieces from Aleppo from before its destruction. This is not the same thing as seeing them ten years ago. The third timeframe is really the invisible time of when the collection was formed. In the Berlin museums there are whole crates of works that arrived from the colonies at the end of the nineteenth and beginning of the twentieth centuries and have never been opened. They had arrived en masse and there had never been time to open them. And they still remain closed to their future. All this is invisible. If the encyclopedic claim really is to be taken seriously, it's important to see it as a source of information about this invisible time.

DG: Another question facing the museums today is the separation of nature and culture, of the world of anthropology or ethnology and the world of art, and essentially the issue is also about the status of these multiple objects.

BS: And about their epistemologies, which are linked, and the categories that will have been applied at a particular time. All of this being connected to the history of the sciences, the history of art being a science just as paleontology is. The boundaries between disciplines have become far more fluid in the universities, but this has not percolated—or has only a little—into the museums, at any rate here in Germany.

DG: Doesn't your method entail the risk of fragmenting the museum? The museum becomes a multiplicity of objects, each with its history, each with its power, each with meaning. But in this situation how can it even be possible to envisage the whole?

BS: When we talk of our public collections, the bulk of their history occurred between 1880 and 1930. You might say there's a risk of fragmentation, but historically, the reality of the museum was played out in four, five, six decades in Europe and the United States. This was the period that made the museums what they are today—the mania for collecting between 1880 and the Second World War.

The encyclopedic museums started a little earlier and stopped a little later. But these were their glory years too. Seen from this point of view, there's no fragmentation; on the contrary, there's a complete coherence in terms of collection type—and a national rivalry—among Paris, Berlin, London, and the United States.

Thanks to this coherence, whether you're in London, at the Louvre, on Berlin's Museum Island, or in Vienna, you'll find configurations and collections that bear an enormous resemblance to each other. This reading of mine is not remotely an activist reading: it's European, and it highlights the common basis of what we do, what Valéry calls "Europe's capacity for absorption." The museums are monuments to this capacity at a time when Europe is no longer alone in playing the role of orchestral conductor to the world.

DG: Doesn't this idea of a museum forever holding up a mirror to itself risk calling into question the immediacy of experience of a work of art?

BS: The collection history needn't necessarily assume a dominant role, but it should be integrated into the experience of the whole. It won't negate the visitor's emotion before the object, but without it the museum is depriving itself of a particular dimension. I don't see why aesthetic emotion should have to be separated from historical emotion, from an understanding of the historical plinth on which we rest, in Europe for example.

The museum needs to accept that it should show its wrinkles. You see a face, and if that face is all artificial intelligence inside a rubber mask, then it's highly abstract. What I'm talking about is the opposite of a rejection of emotion; it's a recognition of the quality of lived experience, the lived experience of the museums, the lived experience of the institutions, which are like the lived experience of a person. The face of the museum takes many forms—the display rooms, etc. And if a face is capable of telling its story through its appearance, the emotion will only be greater, faced with this engaging honesty in telling its own story. Many still clam up on this history, but it's not a taboo subject.

To hide behind a kind of formalism or atemporality is an aestheticism that excludes many potential visitors who feel there's something not quite right. The challenge for museums is to update without obliterating. A museum's display cases are changed every ten years, which is a shame. Nineteenth-century vitrines could be shown alongside those of the GDR and contemporary ones. The history of the museum would be told at the same time that the objects were made visible.

The museum is an agglomeration of periods, of ensembles. This can be seen at the Louvre, which is an accumulation of strata, or at the British Museum, which still has rooms—possessing a great poetry—that date from the 1970s. The museum is like a medieval town whose different strata all co-exist, and it needs to be able to bring itself up to date without rubbing itself out. (2019)

23

Kavita Singh

Jawarhlal Nehru University, New Delhi

Donatien Grau: How do you see the relation between the encyclopedic museum as a project and the national museum as a project? Do you think they contradict each other? Complete each other?

Kavita Singh: Far from being its polar opposite, the national museum is the mirror image of the encyclopedic museum. Both kinds of museums come into being through a state's power and authority that allows it to extract artifacts and even entire monuments and arrogate these to itself while suggesting that they are doing this for the good of the monuments themselves, the disciplinary fields through which they are studied, and the cultures that produced them and from which they have been now taken away. Both kinds of museums place objects within a disciplinary framework of history and/or art, in which they are presented as objects of study or aesthetic contemplation. Overtly, the suggestion is that the artifacts have been moved out of a plane of affect into a plane of cerebral, disinterested study, but of course this declaration of disengagement is a ruse, for museums place the objects in service of a power structure to which many members of their audience are passionately devoted: try suggesting a repatriation from an encyclopedic museum to the source country or from the national museum to a province or community of origin and see how quickly emotions are aroused.

The national museum uses things created by diverse cultures, places, times, and for a range of uses, and stitches them into a "national" narrative that is—allegedly—supra-regional, supra-ethnic, supra-religious—addressing an uber-community that is formed through the dissolution of other, communitarian bonds. This uber-community is the fictive national community. The encyclopedic museum lifts things out of their diverse cultural, geographic, historical contexts and stitches them into a "universal" narrative that is—allegedly—supra-regional, supra-ethnic, supra-religious. To my mind, both these kinds of museums are engaged in projects that are very close to each other. The encyclopedic museum's antithesis is not the national museum; this antithetical role is performed by the source community that demands that the museum has no right to take away, categorize, and construct explanations about their things. That assertion of exclusive rights over cultural property by those who are connected with its origin; that attitude which will not brook another's right to an imaginative relationship with them; that refusal to submit them to the control of academic disciplines; the disallowing of the secularization of objects and the demand that objects be seen exclusively through the lens of the uses for which they were first made; *these* are the attitudes that precisely refute and refuse the premises on which museums, encyclopedic and national, were built.

DG: You mentioned the fact that its principles can be sacrilegious and hurtful. How do you think it should deal with that?

KS: Although I can see many sides of the same story, and sometimes my sympathy is stretched in two opposite directions at the same time, my own commitment is to an Enlightenment-inspired modernity. There is no other option; under no other political philosophy could I, as a woman of color, from a minority community and a low caste, imagine gaining the education and the opportunities I have had. Traditional religious communities are not just the oppressed minorities of today, they are and have been societal structures that oppress their own members in many ways.

We cannot really afford to turn our backs on Enlightenment values and the goals of political modernity because these are the philosophical systems that have grappled with the idea of universal equality, and its consequence, universal rights. Indeed, if we look carefully at the liberal or left-wing critiques of the Enlightenment and its values, we see that what is being critiqued is not the ideal of the Enlightenment but the way its benefits have not flowed equally to all. Rather than rejecting the Enlightenment, what we must be alert to is the gap that always exists between the promise and the practice of a system that promises equal opportunities and universal rights. So, if a museum claims that it holds artifacts in the name of the people—all the people—we must see how it can actually live up to the noble promise that it makes.

When museums were built in the nineteenth century, the noble rhetoric of the museum-makers was hollow. We understand now that museums were imbricated in imperialism, capitalism, and so on, systems that gained advantage through the maintenance of gross inequalities. Many museum collections were built through transactions that were extremely unequal. Rather than dismantling the museum today, however, I prefer a pattern of truth and reconciliation, where the museum acknowledges its history and tries to use its possessions in an intelligent and ethical way in the here and now. This is a way of moving forward, rather than trying to undo the past—a tactic that tends to blow up in our faces with disturbing regularity.

I am concerned about the place of feelings in politics today, where those who can make the loudest claim to hurt feelings become the purest representatives of a supposedly traditional community. Much of the hurt feelings and accusations of sacrilege come not from some noble victims but from astute political figures who are not following tradition but are using it in order to create disturbance based on a claim of feelings hurt. What is the way forward? To my mind, the best way to deal with the situation we have inherited is to own it, and to go ahead, together, from there. The demand to send things back—to a ritual context, to deny outsiders the right to see, learn about, or enjoy these things or to believe that these things are part of a shared heritage—is not necessarily a forward movement.

DG: The notion of an encyclopedic museum is programmatic: it conveys a certain idea of the museum, a certain idea of humanity, a certain idea of art. Do you think a museum can be programmatic to that point?

KS: I would ask whether this proposition is really true—even for a nineteenth-century white European museum director, surely the project he embarked on looked very different depending on whether he was in Dresden or London, Athens or Stockholm. That said, even if we accept the proposition, museums have never been programmatic in that sense: there are as many museums as there are visitors, just as there are as many books as there are readers. Each visitor makes and unmakes the museum in his or her own way. In colonial India, we see accounts written by museum directors who are puzzled, exasperated, and sometimes defeated by their audiences, who seem to demonstrate a robust immunity to the museum's pedagogic lessons even as they arrive in huge numbers to enjoy its gardens and wander through its imposing halls. In 1908 the keeper of the Madras Museum boasted that the visitorship to his museum was larger than the visitorship of the British Museum that year. But the visitors who came to the museum had no interest in what the keeper sought to show in his careful arrangement of natural history specimens brought from afar. Instead, they rushed through the galleries until they came upon something familiar to them—a stuffed bird, a clay model of fruit they ate. The museum hoped to teach them about strange things, but they only stopped to see what was familiar, thrilled to recognize themselves within its lofty walls.

DG: You have discussed the Western museum's passion for objects. How do you see their status in the encyclopedic museum? Is such a museum mainly a collection of objects? Or isn't its purpose the very fact of going beyond the materiality of objects?

KS: The art museum, the museum of civilizations and cultures, is a dated thing that has its own birth, life, and death. The kind of collecting that gave rise to the major Western museums was only possible at a certain point in history: the colonial period. Colonialism produced the need to study and understand the world, to take cognitive control over a vast range of human productions. And colonialism provided the enabling circumstance for the enormous collections to be made. So much of what is in "new" museums—in American museums set up after World War I, in global museums being set up in China or Singapore or the Persian Gulf now—depended on secondary sales out of the primary collections made in the late eighteenth and nineteenth centuries.

Eventually, as we move to other kinds of museums—to virtual museums, or indeed to museums dedicated to something other than things—these object-rich museums will begin to look quaint to us, and the institutions will eventually themselves become the artifacts of another age. They will not appear to us so much as treasure houses filled with precious relics, as they will seem to be giant repositories burdened with the responsibilities of caring for far too many fragile, decaying, demanding things. Those who have not invested in such museums will be grateful that the opportunity passed them by.

But the museums that have a large number of objects will have to find ways to make their objects count, to be interesting or desirable. I imagine franchises, loans, exchanges, and a looser understanding of ownership in the future of museums. That said, the object-rich—or object-burdened—museums will continue to keep their objects, and representations of them, at the heart of their identity. I don't agree that these museums are concerned with going beyond the materiality of their objects. If we look at the knowledge production—the websites, the publications, and the research sponsored by these institutions, which do go beyond the physical object—the knowledge production is still inspired by and circumscribed by the objects the museum possesses.

DG: Do you think the encyclopedic museum only makes sense in the late-imperial locations where such museums are located today, or do you think there could be other encyclopedic museums elsewhere?

KS: An important phenomenon relating to the encyclopedic museum in the twenty-first century is the way it is desired, or at least was desired—before the recession, when these economies were more buoyant—in certain new locations. The Gulf projects and some of the projects in China, Singapore, and Japan are cases in point. In all these locations, there was the sense of an "arrival" on the global economic scene coupled with the need to rebrand a place—for tourism, perhaps, but more often to upgrade it as a "world-class" city that could be fully competitive in the global economy. Museums were one of the several things needed to make these cities places where multinational businesses could function and offer their employees and their families the kinds of infrastructure, schools, and cultural life that they were used to.

If we see encyclopedism as an intellectual ambition, expressed through a curiosity about other places rather than as a function of institutional heft and collection size—if we can see a Manchester Museum or a Stuttgart Museum as also being encyclopedic because they have some Egyptian and Indian and African collections along with European ones—then we will find that there have been many locations that have had encyclopedic museums, small and modest examples of the genre as these may have been. But in our remembering of the history of museums, these institutions—often in provincial locations, made by elites within colonial societies—have slipped between the cracks and have been forgotten.

DG: You have placed the museum in relation with the temple, and with today's rise of religious revivalism. What is the role of the encyclopedic museum at this moment?

KS: I think the temple and the encyclopedic museum are enemies.

DG: Do you feel the encyclopedic museum can a play in role in today's world politics?

KS: It already does play a role. This was very clearly articulated by Neil MacGregor in the British Museum, and is much debated in relation to the Humboldt Forum or to the Louvre Abu Dhabi—two quite different yet closely interrelated sets of contexts for "new" encyclopedic museums that have sparked much discussion and disagreement. But these encyclopedic museums are really national museums in that they are about the pride, the leadership role played by Britain and Germany, and anticipated by the United Arab Emerites. The next phase will come when the large museums, burdened by their collections, will start monetizing them in various ways, leading eventually to a rhizomatic structure like a multinational corporation.

DG: It seems like a rather dire approach to its potential. What do you make of the idea that the encyclopedic museum would expand cultural dialogue and allow for a broader vision of the world?

KS: I have to ask you whether "broader vision" and the "cultural dialogue" that you speak of are not simply cosmopolitan privilege of those who are fortunate enough to have middle-class lives in the world's great metropolises. The universal museum starts having another meaning and another purpose when it tests new ground and begins to travel to new locations.

When I suggest that museums will become rhizomatic like multinational corporations, why do you see it as a dire vision? The fact that I in India and you in the United States can buy the same antibiotic when our children fall ill is a result of the rhizomatic spread of multinational corporations and their products. That is not a bad thing, is it? It's certainly better than antibiotics being made unavailable to me because these medicines are not part of my traditional culture. When I invoke corporations, I'm not pressing a button marked "bad." And I am definitely not pressing a button marked "good" when I invoke "national" or "universal" spheres.

Let's pursue the metaphor of museum-as-multinational-corporation a bit further. There is a knowledge and infrastructure framework here that transforms raw materials (objects) into goods (art). There is an establishment cost (maintaining and running the museum, paying employees, supporting activities like conservation, research, publications, exhibitions, educational programs). There is a resource (expertise) and a stock (art objects). There is a supply, but where is the demand? When local demand is not sufficient to support the establishment costs, inevitably museums will look afield for new "markets" and regions that can generate demand that would be met through satellite museums and franchises, long-term loans, sister museum agreements, and traveling exhibitions.

I could describe this trajectory that the encyclopedic museum is likely to take by using a different set of words and the scenario would immediately feel more acceptable. I could say "international cooperation," "knowledge-sharing," "cultural dialogue," and "fostering links across the globe." That's UNESCO-speak and it's fine too; this language outlines the loftier goals that inspire museums and cultural work, just as the goal of health and well-being inspires the pharmaceutical industry. But if we speak of a set of operations only in the loftiest terms, we will obscure certain other conditions that deeply affect the field and its spread and expansion. International cooperation requires airfares. Knowledge sharing means consultancy fees and training costs. Cultural dialogue means investment in infrastructure. It's immediately clear who can and who cannot be part of this growing club. We can have a Louvre in Abu Dhabi but not in Senegal.

Money is an important limiting factor, of course, but it is not the only one. There are political conditions and localized cultural conditions that include, among other things, different kinds of bureaucracy. I thought the exhibition *Picasso in Palestine* (2011), which brought one Picasso painting from the Van Abbemuseum to the IAAP [International Academy of Art Palestine] in Ramallah, and the film that documented the complications en route and the strained conditions under which the exhibit was seen, very sharply showed the uneven terrain we occupy. Speaking blandly of cultural dialogue and mutual understanding as though the possibility exists universally for us all, is an absurdity in today's world. (2017)

24

Kwame Anthony Appiah

Professor, New York University

Donatien Grau: The encyclopedic museum is meant to be a space where all cultures converse? Do you think it makes sense at all?

Kwame Anthony Appiah: I am profoundly pluralistic about museums. I think of a museum, in essence, as a place where you allow curators to show you something. If a curator wants to have a dialogue of civilizations, a dialogue of cultures, I am interested, and I do not see why anyone should not be interested: I would love to go and see something like that. The most interesting museums imply or make arguments by the way they display things and locate them in relation to one another. It makes sense to have a museum that features the idea of dialogue, but it would also make sense to have an encyclopedic museum that resists the idea of dialogue.

What defines the encyclopedic museum—the kind of encyclopedic museum that was invented in the Enlightenment—is the ambition to have material from the widest possible range of cultures.

DG: What you are saying relates to the issue of art. How can an encyclopedic museum be an encyclopedic museum of art?

KAA: Once you engage in the path of being an encyclopedic museum, you cannot be just an art museum, because art is a local cultural concept. I do not mean that there aren't universal forms of aesthetic response; maybe there are. But the idea of art is very specific.

As I said, I am a pluralist: if people want to take spectacles and present them as art, that is fine with me. I might find it interesting, I might not, but I don't think there is any reason why I should try to stop them. I do not object. I'm on the board of the Smithsonian's National Museum of African Art. Most of the material there was produced by cultures that did not have a concept of art; it was not produced as art. That emphatically does not mean we can't receive it as art. It does not make much sense to organize your response to a very wide range of human cultures through the concept of art alone, because, as I say, not only is it a local concept geographically, it is also historically local.

Think about the ancient world in the West, the Greek world, and the way in which they considered these things: some of the Muses relate to things we do not think of as belonging to the arts at all. Clio is the muse of history. History can be well or badly written, but we do not think of it as one of the arts anymore. We do not think of it as one of the things that the Muses do. Poetry has a huge place in the Greek notion of what the Muses do, of the things that the Muses are muses of. It does not play that role anymore for us. On the other hand, it is just a great experience to wander through spaces where you move from objects from one cultural zone to those of another. It is also interesting when they are presented side by side.

DG: How would you see the function of the encyclopedic museum in today's world?

KAA: Museums do not just show things. They are sites of research, and they are places where objects are cared for. They are preserved and made secure so that future people can have access to them. Assembling all of those functions in the same place means that you are not just collecting objects, you are also collecting kinds of expertise—material expertise in terms of knowing how to look after stone, metal, canvas, wood, and bone, and all of the things that you've got. I think that is a very important part of the function of the encyclopedic museum: to be a site for conservation and scholarship.

I consider ridiculous the Enlightenment ambition to have a piece of everything. Of course, you cannot have something of everything. There are too many cultures, too many civilizations, too many societies, too many kinds of objects. But you *can* have things from many representative times and places. In the British Museum, they have things made by our human ancestors a hundred thousand years ago. Scratched with bone.

To sense the depth of the history of the things that people have done with objects—in making them, shaping them, looking after them, caring about them, and worshiping them—to sense the range of ways in which that has been done across space as well, is a really important resource for thinking about who we humans are. For the museum to help us do that, it has to have people who know what they are talking about. I do not mind people putting together objects, where the connections between the objects were in the mind of the person making the connection. In a responsible museum, you try not to make such connections. Not because there is not another role for people who could do that, but because encyclopedic museums have a place in the economy of knowledge as well as in the maintenance of the object.

You have to be serious. You have to be scholarly. This does not mean that the ways curators will think about objects are going to be necessarily the same as the ways in which art historians, ethnographers, or historians will want to think about these objects. Eventually, the fundamental obligation is to get it right.

As a result, there is a role for something very old-fashioned and unfashionable, which is connoisseurship: knowing what things are, knowing how to tell what things are, knowing how to identify, to the extent that we can, the processes and the people that are behind the object that we are looking at. You can do all kinds of interesting interpretive things, but in the end, it seems to me, it is best if they are tied to truths about the object. That is one of the things that you expect to find in an encyclopedic museum: it is going to provide you with the basis for any interpretative argument. There you want people who know, who can say as much as one can find out about Baule masks, Chinese pottery, Indian gods, and nineteenth-century French painting.

People who go to museums often are unaware of the work that the museum is doing. Maybe museums should do more to let people know that so much is going on outside the collection. On the one hand, they do very scholarly catalogs, and on the other, they open up to the public. For most people, often it is just going to be standing in front of the object and not necessarily even looking at the label. Unless you are going to be very authoritarian in a way that would mean that you would drive people away, people will put things together in their own way. Even if you put them in different rooms, if they march from one room to the other, they will make connections. Those connections may or may not have anything to do with the objective, historical relations between the objects.

Quite obviously, it makes the museum a space of extreme relevance and outstanding opportunities, where there are lots of things to be doing.

DG: Where do you stand on the debate on origins and the relation of encyclopedic museums to their past?

KAA: It is certainly useful to have a wide range of cultures and times represented in one place. The possibility of assembling such a collection, in the first instance, depended upon the context of empire, and the fact that Lord Elgin could negotiate with the Ottomans about objects that did not belong to either of them, and the fact that Napoleon could collect things out of Egypt. The great German collectors could travel through African villages assembling things. You cannot do that anymore, for cultural and political reasons, to quite the same extent.

In the contemporary world, of course, almost anything can be done if you have an infinite amount of money. If you go to the Museum of Islamic Art in Doha, Qatar—that is a new, beautiful, modern building. They have lots of money and have been able to make a collection limited to the Muslim world. That means it can only go from Morocco to Indonesia, which is a lot of the planet. It is a very interesting museum, and all the things they hold there have in common the fact of having been produced by Muslim societies. It is essentially a slice through the universal museum, though they do not yet have, in their collections, the depth of spectacular objects that the Metropolitan Museum of Art has in its Muslim collections.

Even with lots of oil money, it is really hard to assemble the kind of collections that already exist in the British Museum, and the Metropolitan Museum, the Louvre, the Hermitage, the Berlin museums. Which is sad, because it means that, for large parts of the population of the planet, they will never be near one. I like the fact that, for example, the British Museum has assembled interesting representative collections of objects and sent them to Beijing, and Nairobi, to share them.

The big political question about the encyclopedic museum, because of the imperial context of the assemblage of the objects, is the question of ownership—cultural ownership, which I myself think is a really boring topic. I think the interesting questions have to do with giving people access to the objects. The legal question of who holds the title to an object in a public museum is really uninteresting. It is just a matter of doing what you need to do in order to secure a rational system of access and preservation and research and so on. In the period since the Enlightenment the modern conception of culture as a national project has grown considerably.

Those conversations are very fraught: people think it's ours in some sense, and very often they want it back. I would like to hope that we can resist that. Though, I think, the questions about how to, not so much democratize but globalize access are really important. The British Museum has been on the forefront of thinking about those questions.

I think it is good, but I do not think the solution is to spread the objects back all over the planet. Because, as I said, I think there is something profoundly interesting that happens when you spend a bit of time looking over the range.

DG: Encyclopedic museums come from empires and states, and as such they represent moments in the history of the world.

KAA: The argument we make about encyclopedic museums can be made about any form of cultural project: it is certain that the collections of the encyclopedic museums were brought together in the context of an ethically impermissible process. But they are not the only ones. The pyramids were produced by an ethically impermissible process.

It is quite certain, today, that you are not allowed to use slaves to create monuments for fantastically powerful and rich people. But what are we supposed to do? Take them down? One of the things you learn from an encyclopedic museum is that people who are doing things that we now think of as barbarous could nevertheless produce things that we still value profoundly.

Aristotle, too, was wrong about slavery: there are no natural slaves. There were people in is own time, and in his own society, who were right about it. That does not mean we can't read the *Nicomachean Ethics* and value it.

Part of the interest of, especially, older objects is to get a sense of their passage through space. How did they get here? Many of these things that have lived underground for a long time are to be found in the archaeological sections. It is certainly part of the job of the museum to allow us to learn the history of the object, to the extent that it can be uncovered. The museum itself has a history, and this complex history goes far beyond the limitations of an imperial history.

Many bad things occurred in the process of the development of the declaration of the rights of man, many bad things happened in the American Revolution, and many bad things happened in the lead-up to the democratic extension of suffrage in Britain in the mid-nineteenth century. None of those bad things means that everything that happened was bad and we are the heirs to what happened. I think we should look at it honestly and thoughtfully, but I don't think that anything about its history rules out maintaining the collections.

I went to the opening of the Quai Branly, and I sat in on a seminar about questions of repatriation in relation to the Pacific. It was very interesting listening to the representatives of the Pacific countries saying: "We do not really want to have the objects, we want to be able to use them." And, "If you'll give us the plane tickets we are happy to use them here, because you can look after them better than we can." In other words, different people have different relations even to the most sacred of objects.

The ground of our relation to those objects should not be in terms of ownership or ideas about property, or in ethical ideas about the relations between institutions and societies. If it is really true that this totem is something that you have a use for in your current religious life, it would be a decent thing to do to give it to you, not because you own it—suppose your ancestors sold it, or exchanged it, or lost it in battle—but because that is the decent thing to do. I do not think that the idea of property or the idea that it belongs to a culture is going to help anybody deal with those things.

The history of the museum is a small part of the history of empire, but it is a place in which we can think about that history in an interesting way, because the history of the empire is not the only history it includes.

The encyclopedic museum allows us to think about how extraordinary it is, really, that societies where many people were living close to subsistence nevertheless devoted huge amounts of social energy and resources to making things we still want to look at. That itself is a puzzle.

We learn a lot from looking at things produced by people whose level of material technological sophistication was not very high. They are essentially, and again this is an old-fashioned way of putting it, thoughts about what it means to be human. They give you responsibility.

You have a good sense of the range of what human beings have done. That is what you get in the great encyclopedic museum. You get to think about the relationship between the material objects and symbolic life over the full range.

DG: In that sense it positions itself against a limited conception of the national ideal.

KAA: The national ideal as such is a recent phenomenon: it really grew to be much more than it ever had been at the beginning of the nineteenth century. Great British museums are not national: they are called the British Museum or the National Gallery, but they are not British or national per se.

If you wanted to make a museum of French art, German art, or British art, I am not sure what that would mean: it would never have occurred to the people who made the works that what they were doing had no connection with what was being done in all the other places where people were painting. In the 1770s, they made their Grand Tours. They went to look at the objects in other places, of which you cannot make sense if you draw the boundaries; this is true in all the arts. It is true in the literary arts as well: imagine trying to take all the foreign bits out of Shakespeare. There's no *Coriolanus*, no *Julius Caesar*, no *Hamlet*. Hamlet's a foreigner, he's a Dane. No sonnets: it's an Italian form stolen from Petrarch. This is one of the things that, even if you organize galleries in national forms, an intelligent viewer will immediately grasp.

The encyclopedic museum refutes such theories just without the labels. You can see both that something about an object came from somewhere else and that it has local connections. That, of course, is what the real research reveals.

DG: What would you see as the particular character of the encyclopedic museum?

KAA: The strength of the encyclopedic museum is that it plays to both sides of what a museum is: the Benjaminian idea of the aura still works. When I am in the Louvre, in front of the *Mona Lisa*, I am truly in front of something Leonardo made. Not a photograph, the thing itself. I feel the same thing about the goldweights (they are brass, made for weighing gold) from Ghana. Somebody around where I grew up made them a couple of hundred years ago. I know a little bit about how they did it. I feel a connection to those people whose names and histories I do not know.

The aura does make a lot of sense to most of us. But what is needed as well is the more objective story. I think that sense of magic is important because it is one of the reasons why people are willing to support the expensive project of maintaining these objects in a museum. If it was just their meanings, we could get rid of the objects and just write down the meanings—photograph them and throw them away.

There is a good research reason why we do not do that, which is that we have no idea what we will be able to learn about the object in the future when technology changes. If we had thrown away the Greek vases before carbon dating, on the grounds that we have very good drawings of them all, we would not have been able to do the research on dating that we have been able to do since.

We do not know what the future holds for the possibility of interpreting these objects. Maybe we will believe less in them, and we will know more about them. That's a discursive reason for holding on to the actual object, even though the reason people actually want to be in the room with it has to do with this strange sense of magic that we have.

It is relevant that I picked Leonardo: known or unknown, and in the case of much African art it is going to be unknown, we have this sense that they were made by a genius, that you just could not have made this thing that strikes us if you didn't have some very special capacity.

Nowadays, in museums of African art when objects can be assigned to the same studio or place of production, even though we do not know the names, we say, as we say in European art, "from the master of..." We want to see them made as by a single mind. This is, in a way, preposterous. There is no doubt that, in the most literal of senses, Leonardo was a genius, but what he did depended upon the background of many, many people and things. That's true of all the geniuses. It's true of Beethoven; it's true of Shakespeare. Encyclopedic museums enable us to go back and forth between the individual and the community he belonged to.

DG: You mentioned earlier that most people do not know what encyclopedic museums actually do. How would you change that?

KAA: I think part of the task is to bring children and young people in as part of their education, and not just show them the painting. Show them the conservation room, show them that there are people here who can tell you that this would have looked a different color when it was made, because it was made of such and such and the colors fade. In other words, show them that what the connoisseurs know is interesting and valuable.

There is a profound contrast between the relations of the Metropolitan Museum to the city, and the relations of the National Museum of Ghana, in Accra, to the city. The Ghanaian National Museum is mostly an object for foreigners and tourists to come and look at. Even though there are things in it made by their ancestors—sometimes not very long ago, sometimes their living ancestors—people from schools do not come in much. If they do, nobody says anything or gives them a really good story about what was going on.

Part of these educational relations has a political function. It is not simply an educational function, though it has to be a primarily educational function because otherwise it will not serve the political function. Namely, to create a constituency, to create the museum's public: citizens who understand what it is doing. That's true whether museums are private or public. The Metropolitan Museum of Art is not a public museum in the sense that it belongs to a state. It is a public museum in the sense that it is a trust, legally speaking, and that the obligation of the board of the museum is to serve certain public functions. The state is supposed to guarantee the promises made to the project.

Whether you are technically public or technically private, you need a constituency, you need a relation to a public. You can cheat: you can get the public to love you by doing blockbuster shows and not telling them what the real work of the museum is; or you can tell the truth as well.

You can say: Look, we are a home to these astonishingly learned people who are learned in ways that mean we can preserve the objects. They are conservators, they are the people who know that if that happens to the painting, here's what we have to do to stabilize it. These learned people can say: "We are pretty certain that that is 1647. We are pretty certain that the name is this. That it is part of this body of work. In our catalog, we have photographs of other work in other museums by this person; you can think about it." I think it is really important to make it public.

Though the museum is universal, it has a local location. It has a place. It's in New York, or London, or Paris, or Berlin. It needs to have a strong relation to that civic life. Not necessarily to a national life, but to the lives of the city. They are part of the lives of great cosmopolitan cities. There is no great cosmopolitan city that doesn't have a great museum.

DG: You mentioned earlier that you didn't believe that new encyclopedic museums could be founded. Why?

KAA: I do not mean the project does not make sense anymore. Yes, the project makes sense, but there are two obstacles. One is money. The other is UNESCO. To put it bluntly, it is a way of thinking about art and culture that has become, I think, too nationalistic, too nationalized. Take the story of the attempts to save the national museum in Kabul: in the end, that collection was saved by the curators there because they buried the works to protect them from the Taliban. The Taliban said these things are haram. "They are Islamically impermissible so we're going to destroy them because they are idols." Fortunately, there was a sufficiently trained group of curators there who were horrified by this. They basically concealed it.

There had been a plan, from a museum, to haul those objects away for safe keeping. Many people think, as I do, that the plan was stopped because

UNESCO said it was not allowed: "It's Afghan art, it has to stay in Afghanistan." Notice what that means: it has to stay in Afghanistan even if the Afghans are going to destroy it. Even if they are going to do what they did to the Buddhas in Bamiyan. The point is, it was not Afghan in the sense of the modern state of Afghanistan. The Gandhara figures are not Afghan in any sense except that they were made in what is now Afghanistan. There was no Afghan state when they were made. There was a Gandhara state. Part of why they are interesting is because they show strong signs of Hellenistic influence, a consequence of the travels of Alexander the Great, who was famously not an Afghan. He was a Macedonian. That is the point.

My own preference is to say, "Art is always on a national territory. That nation state has the responsibilities of trusteeship in relation to it." It is the common possession of mankind. Because it is the common possession of mankind, states are trustees for what is on their territory, including what comes from other places.

We cannot create, just for reasons of resource, too many places like the Metropolitan Museum. What we can do is create opportunities for people around the planet to see significant collections, not organized in national ways but across a wide range. The Met, the British Museum, the Louvre are all trustees for the world. What the Louvre, the British Museum, and the Guggenheim are doing in the Emirates, I consider to be part of their job. It is part of their mandate to make objects available, because it is the common property of mankind.

Access is more important than ownership, as I have already said. You are successful if you can give access to a new lot of people in a new place, making sure that you are preserving the objects and conserving them—you cannot send them to places where they will be destroyed; you cannot send them to places where they do not have air conditioning. There are constraints on what you can do.

In a way, I would say my vision is singular: we should move toward *one* encyclopedic museum, whose collections are temporarily in Paris, London, New York, Pittsburgh, Accra, Beijing, and Delhi. In this one museum, the objects, a significant proportion and a wide range of them, circulate consistently with a concern for the preservation of the objects and the knowledge of human culture that is embedded in them, which we would lose if we destroyed them by plane crashes and all the things that might happen if you travel. There is a balance.

That is a future in which all these objects that are legally owned by trusts and governments, people and institutions, are seen more generally to be the common property of humankind. Just apply this in a practical way: What should we say about the Parthenon marbles, or the Elgin marbles, depending on what you want to call them? I think we should say that, at least some of the time, it would be very apt for them to be in Athens, but at least some of the time it is very apt for them to be somewhere else. More people—and different people—are going to see them in London than in Athens, for various reasons.

There is a tradeoff between different kinds of access. The Greeks are people too, and they should be entitled to have access to the whole thing, or to more of the whole thing, for a period. You cannot get to that solution if you think of these things as owned by nations; you would then see them as properly residing in the nations that own them. That is what I mean by the UNESCO problem.

I also have the impression that there are younger people than me who think of the Internet as a great encyclopedic museum. While if you gave them a ticket and said you could go see the Leonardo in the Louvre, they would go, they are pretty excited to see the Leonardo on their laptop. They like the fact that, with the Leonardo on the laptop, they can click through a bunch of links and discover answers to all their questions, or discover that there are not answers to the questions they have about it. They can place it on their screen alongside anything they like.

They can look at it at the same time as a Chinese scroll or a Hittite stele. We want them to do that. That great assemblage of images on the web is a huge tool that I do value for investigating objects, and for learning about them. The web naturally presents itself as one thing to which there are seven and a half billion different relationships, going on eight billion now.

The contrast, between how I find myself relating to the objects on the web and the objects when I am in the space, is part of what one needs to think about, if one is trying to understand the aesthetic.

One has to think that it is not true that there are virtual objects on one side and actual objects on the other side. It is not, nor should it be, an opposition. They should complete each other. There certainly is an experience that requires the object. In that sense, for people like me anyway, the museum is never going to be obsolete. And the great encyclopedia of art is never going to move away from the objects themselves. (2015–17)

25

Homi K. Bhabha

Professor, Harvard University, Cambridge, Massachusetts

Donatien Grau: As we are talking in terms of the encyclopedic museum, what would be the nature of its narrative? One narrative, a plurality of narratives, or even an impossibility of narrativity?

Homi K. Bhabha: Most curatorial categories, even those that seem plainly classificatory, are informed by narratives that trace developments in the nature of materials, or the evolution of forms and ideas, or the history of genres and periods. And for this reason alone, it is difficult to conceive of an encyclopedic museum constructed around one narrative, however "universal" that narrative may claim to be. I don't quite understand what it means to talk of the "impossibility of narrative" because even the most disjunctive or disorienting curatorial practices are subject to the passage of time that it takes the viewer to progress through the arrangement of works on display. Where temporality mediates the making of meaning—whether it is in the space of the gallery or contained within the covers of a book—there is always a kind of narrative, even if it transgresses the duration of beginning-middle-end. So we are left with the plurality of narratives. Is plurality a way of allowing any one narrative to exist in the midst of several other narratives in the celebration of difference or inclusion? Is plurality a way of provoking the viewer into making comparisons and establishing connections that create an "encyclopedic" understanding of art making?

Plurality is only meaningful when inclusion is accompanied by intervention, and comparison comes with critique. Encyclopedic collections are often the result of conquest, violence, and expropriation; equally, on the positive side, they are collaborative achievements of archaeology, scholarship, and conservation and preservation. The diversity of encyclopedic collections become the preserve of wonder and connoisseurship; historical harms and the vagaries of time are aestheticized as "ruins" and relegated to academic annotation. The encyclopedic narrative must make graphically present, in the gallery or across the museum, the relation between cultural creation and cultural destruction. Walter Benjamin's dictum, "There is no document of civilization which is not at the same time a document of barbarism" is in the spirit of my remarks. As an institution of cultural memory, the encyclopedic museum must enact the iterative irony of remembering and forgetting—and this should not be seen as the special responsibility of the Holocaust Museum or the African American Museum or whatever.

Doesn't the power of the great encyclopedic museum lie in its civic cosmopolitanism rather than its national mission or its universalist disposition? The scale of the encyclopedic museum is frequently attributed to its comprehensive coverage of works, which provide unparalleled opportunities for comparative intercultural conversations over large time periods. The reputation of the encyclopedic museum as a global institution, dedicated to pleasure and pedagogy, is based on this expansive potential for comparison and cross-reference. However, civic cosmopolitanism reminds us that scale is also a function of location and movement. The density and intensity of the encyclopedic museum is grounded in the city—in the ideals of *civitas*—and its identity is civic rather than national or world-historical. When you think of the British Museum, London comes to mind, not the British Isles; the Prado signifies Madrid, not Spain; the Louvre conjures up Paris, not France; MoMA and the Met evoke New York, not the United States. The museum is embedded in the melee of the city and its motley gathering of visitors—citizens, scholars, tourists, flaneurs—who enter the museum as civic cosmopolitans rather than national citizens. Museums are increasingly seeing themselves as urban passageways—gathering spaces for civic discourse—which makes them spaces of public "presence" similar to the piazza, the square, the arcades.

You could say, after Benjamin, that the museum is engaged in a kind of *Passagenwerk*, to borrow the title—and concept—of Benjamin's Arcades Project. We tend to think of the museum as a space of quiet contemplation and reflection, of concentration and stillness. But like all public institutions it is also a space of the urban traffic of peoples and things, negotiating their way between art, lectures, restaurants, and retail outlets. And there is, increasingly, a traffic of objects and ideas between cities and countries that manifests itself in projects such as the current show at the Shivaji Museum in Mumbai—*India and the World: A History in Nine Stories* [November 2017-February 2018]—which is a collaboration between the British Museum, the Getty, and the Tata Charitable Trusts, with curators from different institutions working in concert with the director of the Shivaji Museum. This cultural traffic creates civic constellations distinct from the model of museum outposts such as the Louvre in Abu Dhabi.

If you read the museum principally in terms of its "objects"—the great treasures of its collections—then the institution is august, but in danger of becoming strangely inert. The museum then becomes an exclusive haven for scholars and connoisseurs. Museums are, however, increasingly engaged in "outreach" or "public education" aimed at drawing in new audiences that reflect both demographic diversity and minoritarian imperatives. In my view, many museums have gone beyond anodyne paradigms of liberal pluralism—the neutrality of an equal playing field—and have striven to transform curatorial practices in an effort to redistribute the "symbolic value" of cultural goods. The aim of attracting a diverse and plural audience has developed into a curatorial commitment to enhance "cultural citizenship"—a term I often use in explaining my directorial ambitions for the Mahindra Humanities Center at Harvard.

If you see the museum from the angle of civic cosmopolitanism, then you notice a subtle shift of emphasis from the world of collected objects to the life-world of civic subjects. This practice of subject formation is often called cultural citizenship. But what aspects of citizenship relate specifically to cultural institutions and identifications? What rights and responsibilities does cultural citizenship inculcate? What, indeed, is cultural citizenship? This is too large a question to take on in this discussion, but it is worth providing a passable definition in order to avoid the vagaries that frequently afflict suggestive concepts.

The most obvious aspects of cultural citizenship are easy to fathom. As citizens we should be committed to protecting cultural rights and seeing them as integral to our commitment to civil rights and human rights; we should pressure the state to provide social and political opportunities that establish infrastructural frameworks for the support and protection of cultural institutions in the public good; as citizens we should contribute to cultural philanthropy and encourage public-private partnerships. So much is obvious, and it sits well with our legal and political responsibilities as citizens.

What makes cultural citizenship distinctive is its ethical emphasis on civility as a practice closely related to the idea of civic cosmopolitanism. According to one definition in the *OED*, civility is "a branch of the liberal arts; a division of culture." And an early illustration of the use of the word is explicitly cosmopolitan: "This Cyclopadia hath beene observed to runne from East, to West: Thus have most Civilities and Sciences come from the Indian Gymnosophists, into Egypt; from thence into Greece, so into Italy." (Henry Blount, *A Voyage into the Levant*, 1636, 85).

Civility extends a neighborly hand of hospitality to the representation of cultural differences—differences of race, identity, belief, sexuality, generation, status, power. Civility is a disposition that emerges in the practices of social discourse—however difficult the negotiation, however oppositional your position—and refuses to violate the dignity of the person addressed or the public standing of the community represented. Civility is not the formality of polite manners that metes out cautious measures of tolerance. Civility is an ethical disposition that seeks to establish equitable frames of reference and representation for those subjects or objects that might appear to be foreign or marginal, although they exist in the interstices of our existence or participate in the intimate weave of our everyday lives. Civility is an open invitation to interlocution, interpretation, and intervention. It is the embrace of civility, as an ethical expression of civic cosmopolitanism, that increasingly places the museum at the front lines of cultural debates and contestations such as the current controversies around the concept of appropriation. Civility isn't quiescent; it can be mobilized in the cause of resistance and opposition, but it protects the right to interpretation as the deep structure of democratic dialogue and productive debate in the public sphere. And the museum is an active agent in the shaping of civil society, just as it is crucial to the architecture of urban life.

DG: What is the role of the museum?

HKB: I prefer to talk about the museum's jurisdiction rather than its role. Jurisdiction has two components: *juris* is the spatial demarcation of a territory; *dictio* is a mode of narrative representation—language, visual culture, social discourse, narrative—that defines the territory, the *juris*, and gives it the authority of voice and place. The jurisdiction of the museum—virtual and material—is a territory of civic relations, aesthetic education, and critical thinking. Each museum has a distinct institutional history and a specific geopolitical context, but collectively they symbolize a spirit of civic cosmopolitanism rather than cultural nationalism. The jurisdictions of the museum is rather like the network of galleries that is marked by thresholds and passageways that bridge countries, communities, and diverse creative media. "Cosmopolitanism," one scholar suggests, "is a series of fluid and shifting locations of a 'self' that places itself in a multiplicity of relationships to various traditions."

Civic cosmopolitanism takes us further. It emerges from the museum's urban jurisdiction—its sense of *civitas*—and, at its best, has the capacity to track the contours and crises that shape "turning points" in practices of visual culture and histories of critical thought. In such encounters, narratives became deeply intersectional and hybrid. Counternarratives that reverse the prevailing order of cultural norms and aesthetic values are instructive, but they are never as innovative as curatorial and critical practices.

The scale of the encyclopedic museum is more properly represented by narrative strategies that intersect and intervene while creating networks of assemblages. The museum is not a total institution of universal dimensions; it is an institution built around the dialectic of civilization and barbarism—creation and destruction—in art as in history. It is because the authority of museums is engaged in this powerful yet precarious dialectic that the museum is so often embroiled in controversies that arise from the representations of historical memory or the contestation of identities and interests. Civic cosmopolitanism emphasizes the close relationship between the museum and civil society. And it is through that relationship that the profile of the museum's public becomes a project of inclusion.

DG: There seem to be strong moral issues in the definition of the encyclopedic museum: where it comes from, where the objects come from.

HKB: I assume you are referring to the repatriation debate? This is closely related to my suggestion that the museum's rich collection may itself be a sign of history's poverty. Civilization and barbarism, creation and destruction, this dialectic are the ethical foundation of most encyclopedic collections. How is one to work this dialectic in the interests of the dispossessed? What are the claims of the past on the present? There are complex legal and contractual issues involved that I won't rehearse here, because it is the moral issues that most concern you.

What are the degrees of moral distinction between expropriating an object and paying a paltry price for it in conditions of inequality? Is the "heritage" of those who were dispossessed the same as the "heritage" of those who claim the right of return? Should the nature of the prevailing political regime influence our decision? Should we heed the demands of totalitarian governments? And should we return objects of great value to countries that do not have the facility to conserve and preserve them? This cluster of questions suggests that there is no escaping a casuistic approach, case by case, in dealing with moral issues.

A rough rule of thumb might be that a claim for the return of an object that plays a significant symbolic or practical role in holding together a community, providing it with a reflective and representational sense of the past (whatever that may be) to empower a productive and progressive sense of agency in the present, should be sympathetically and fairly considered. I am being careful about my formulation because it could well turn out that an iconic object is reclaimed by a regime to foster a hierarchical and hegemonic cultural imaginary that would discriminate against minoritarian rights to a shared life of cultural dignity and political freedom.

DG: Is there not a tension between the encyclopedic and the global?

HKB: Yes, tension is the right word here, because the encyclopedic is as fraught with tension as is the global. The tension lies primarily within each category and, only secondarily, between them. The encyclopedic museum, as I understand it, is an institution with an imperial or national history that aspires toward a transcendent universalism or comparativism as a way of narrating its diverse collections. What would a global museum be? Let's think imaginatively or virtually for a moment. I suppose you could think of a museum of global Islam, for instance, which focuses on acquiring Islamic artifacts from every corner of the umma and ends up with a global collection of Islamic art on an international scale. Is this a form of encyclopedic globalism? I wonder. And then one could really think outside the box and suggest that the global museum is an iterative and impermanent structure that has a diasporic trajectory rather than a territorial location. Is the biennial the global museum of the future? As it circulates from city to city, does the biennial embody the spirit of *civitas* and civil society? Is this civic humanism on a local scale—Venice, Berlin, São Paulo, Havana, Johannesburg, Shanghai—that tracks art movements and cultural practices in the process of movement across regions, nations, and communities? Perhaps the biennial is a kind of global museum—a virtual space of objects, meanings, curators, and audiences as they circulate between cities. This is not a plug for the biennials, which have their own limitations and constraints; I am only proposing a thought experiment about how we might deploy the concept of the global. Perhaps the global museum—whatever that might mean—is a curation of convergences rather than collections.

DG: There seems to be a reality of the museum, which is a collection, and there is a purpose of it, which is slightly mythical.

HKB: All archives are mythical. And the museum is an archive of artistic and historical memory. What makes a collection mythical? The museum's myth exceeds its iconic artworks that have become popular cultural myths—the *Mona Lisa,* for instance. What gives the reality of the museum a mythical aura is similar to what makes myths mythical. And that is their powers of repetition, which are acts of renewal: the very process of iteration (or reiteration) is an act of narration or performance that makes the myth contemporary. It is the temporality of repetition—even more than the content or context of the myth—that gives the myth a power of presencing. The myth renews itself—and through its narration we renew ourselves—as it is being performed. Museums, like myths, are archives of the afterlife of objects, images, ideas, materials. The myth of the collection emerges from acts of curatorial reinvention that displace objects from the conventional order of things. The myth of the collection lies in this institutional imminence—the collection as it is about to reimagine itself, the collection made yet again in the re-collection of the archive as a form of remembrance that restructures the institutional memory.

DG: This emphasis on the works of art leads me to ask you about the status of the collected objects: Are they artworks? Are they documents? How do you think the artwork and the object coincide?

HKB: They are archives, as I have suggested. They can be artworks, documents, models, working sketches, notebooks, maps—you name it. The archive has a sense of infinite potential and mutability. Its materials are less important than its powers of mediation. In my view, it is less a collection and more a *combinatoire.*

DG: Today encyclopedic museums are somehow instruments of cultural diplomacy or power. How do you stand toward the fact that they are instruments of global power?

HKB: All cultural institutions are instruments of power, if they play a significant role. Nothing wrong with that. The issue is who wields power and for what purpose. And, moreover, how can we deploy those symbolic powers to redistribute cultural authority? [Washington's] National Museum of African American History and Culture and the United States Holocaust Memorial Museum are attempts at the redistribution of cultural authority and symbolic power. The danger lies in using cultural institutions for the purposes of soft power. It certainly has its uses in fostering negotiation and avoiding perils of hard power. But soft power often veils the workings of hegemonic power. During the Cold War, the CIA mastered the art of soft power—the uses of art and culture to further the legitimation of political power and influence—and the Soviet Union did the same in a more shambolic way. Cultural diplomacy for just causes is more transparent and effective than the great game of seduce and abandon that characterizes global diplomacy as it is exercised through the secret state in many regions of the world today. (2015–18)

26

Camille Henrot

Artist

Donatien Grau: The encyclopedic museum, such as it is defined today, is based on a dream of bringing together all civilizations under one roof. Does this ideal seem relevant to you?

Camille Henrot: Let's clarify the terms of the question: Is it relevant to do it today or is it relevant to continue to do it? Fundamentally, the idea of the encyclopedic museum belongs to an era that began with colonization and functioned within a colonial context. It's difficult to dissociate the idea of the encyclopedic museum from the project of French eighteenth-century Enlightenment, which was to gather the world under one roof and then claim dominance over it. There's a certain arrogance in this project; there's also the fact that the objects of other civilizations were often seized within the context of violent confrontations with these other cultures. The process of forming these collections has therefore been problematic.

It seems to me that if we ask ourselves how we would envisage an encyclopedic museum today, my reply would be rather different. What would be interesting today would be for those encyclopedic museums that already exist to work on what ought to be their culpability, on their relationship with the context and the way in which the idea of the encyclopedic museum came into being, the reasons that led to the creation of an encyclopedic museum, how its creation benefits a culture, and in what circumstances the objects were taken.

What should we think about this today, with the deeper reflection on the ontological nature of objects that has come with speculative materialism?

There's much discussion, in the contemporary art world, on this strand of thought. But it has been understood for a long time that perhaps these objects possessed thought, or at any rate a power. The restitution of objects is not a subject the museums like to think about; it's something of a taboo for most of the directors of major encyclopedic museums. I believe this question needs to be taken into account far more clearly, both in the public presentation of the works and politically.

This, then, is what the encyclopedic museum should do; it should take the initiative to confront these issues clearly. The Metropolitan Museum of Art in New York, in partnership with the Musée du Quai Branly and the Nelson-Atkins Museum of Art in Kansas City, organized an exhibition called *The Plains Indians* in 2015. I sensed a concern in the museum's wall texts to slightly tone down the dramatization and to avoid the term *genocide*. I felt that there was something of a normalization of the tragedy, as if it had simply been a natural stage; as if it had already, today, been atoned for. Nearby I heard a father saying to his daughter as he pointed out the costumes used for the Ghost Dance, "Look, this is Pocahontas's dress, look how fashionable Pocahontas was." The information about the political meaning of the Ghost Dance was in the wall text, but I couldn't help wondering how to prevent that kind of erasure in terms of the audience's engagement with politics. There is a need for representation of these cultures but also the need to hear the history of the land from an indigenous perspective. For now, what seems the priority is learning to hear the history from another point of view—one that is not pretending to be neutral. These objects carry so much pain and tragedy it seems that it would require a different format than the wall texts to share it with an audience. Despite my initial impressions, I was personally excited to see this exhibition and had great expectations for it—I'm sure these questions will continue to be addressed.

DG: The question you pose comes down to asking: How can the fact that these objects come from a particular place be guaranteed, while at the same time enjoying the benefit of having them all in one place?

CH: I don't think that the solution has to be binary. It is a complex history and different everywhere, also with different implications and consequences, depending on what groups are involved. It's not "We need to return all the objects" on the one hand or "We keep all the objects" on the other. What seems important to me is to reflect on it and to bring people together to see different perspectives and be aware there is no neutral point of view: what is an appropriate form of communication to accompany, for example, the presentation of Dogon objects or Plains Indians objects? What's fair, what are the difficulties, why do we have problems? An exhibition like this one at the Met and the Quai Branly is an important exhibition, and it's important that it exists. Shows like this enable us to see that there's a knot here, but it's important for this knot to be communicated to the public, too, and not avoided. It's a problem that hasn't really been resolved—to make public the questions that one is asking oneself. It's always better than to continually say, "This is the way it is"; better than to be in a state of truth, of certitude, of some sort. The encyclopedic museum can't have any meaning if it has no doubts: it has the responsibility to voice its own contradictions, mistakes, and doubts.

DG: In this case, one could perhaps say that of all museums, the encyclopedic museum is the one most open to questions.

CH: Yes, of course. At any rate, the encyclopedic museum, in itself, is the very archetype of a museum. It's the ideal of a museum, the utopian museum, a kind of synthesis, Noah's Ark. It gathers together all the animals. It's the ultimate house. It's ideal in being a place in which everything is contained and which therefore defines itself as an autonomous space.

The ambition to have a sort of general theory—to bring a natural history collection into contact with an art collection, or to bring together collections of different cultures—is something that should continue to exist. The intercultural dialogue is what's most interesting to me; the idea of "partial connections" posed by anthropologist Marilyn Strathern. Cultures are not defined only by their points of rupture but also by their points of contacts.

DG: When we reflect on the geography of the different forms of museum, there's the art museum, in which we look at art and where we're expected to have a sort of contemplative reaction, one of veneration, admiration. There's the museum of ethnography, where we're supposed to see objects as documents, and there's the encyclopedic museum, which casts a bridge between the two. This is perhaps where its problem and its interest lies, that is to say, in the ambiguity of the discourse it conveys, which is simultaneously artistic and political.

CH: It is not like the artistic and the political are two totally different things. I've often wondered about the approach an artist can take within an ethical and political discourse. Is it possible? Is it interesting artistically? And what is "right" from an ethical point of view? There are two types of artistic pitfalls: works in which the art is instrumentalized by an ideology, and which are too heavy and fail to provoke reflection, and works that are too light, for example peddling received ideas or failing to take sufficiently subtle account of the sensitivities of the subject, or even ignore them completely. I think these are the same dangers that the director of an encyclopedic museum needs to think about.

My feeling is that the solution lies in trying not to restrict the image the viewer might form of a subject, but instead to preserve ambiguities and contradictions. What needs to be attempted is to provide a series of information and images, while at the same time maintaining that none of these images represents a general truth. Yes, it's difficult. But the fact that this problem is complicated and thorny doesn't mean there's no need to confront it.

DG: How can we react to this question of origin? How do we negotiate with what is described as art, and to which, in general, we attribute value?

CH: In 2010, I attended a conference at the Musée du Quai Branly, entitled "La restitution anthropologique: Comment et pour qui?" [Anthropological restitution: how and for whom?], organized by the Anthropologie de la Perception and the Laboratoire d'Anthropologie Sociale and the GDRI [International Research Network] group on anthropology and the history of the art—Anthropologie et histoire des arts. Marie Mauzé—director of the CNRS/LAS—presented her research under the topic "Ceremonial heritage and restitution: what are the challenges for the community of origin? The case of the Kwakwaka'wakw in British Columbia." She recounted the difficulties of two communities that had come together in Canada for a potlatch, a ceremonial event wherein gifts and possessions are presented as symbols of social status and prestige; also considered the primary economic and governmental system of the community. At the time, potlatches were prohibited by the Canadian government. The police arrived, seized all the objects, and put the two leaders in prison. A court case ensued in which the two nations eventually succeeded in obtaining the release of their leaders and the restitution of not all but a large part of their objects. The condition for the restitution of these objects was that they should be exhibited in a museum. Each of the two nations therefore reflected on what form their museum might take. One created a museum about the prohibition of the potlatches, including photographs of the arrest, a museum therefore highly focused on the events and the story of this potlatch. The other nation created a museum with these objects, but conceived of the museum as something entirely living, in which the objects could be replaced from time to time. After a while, an object disappeared and was replaced by another because they considered a different object to be worthy of conservation. This was therefore a completely flexible and fluid museum.

DG: The encyclopedic museum enables the very nature of the work of art to be questioned, along with its status as a work of art. In addition to the romantic ideal of contemplation, the work of art can also be considered as an element of knowledge.

CH: Of course. There seems to be a gulf between museums such as the natural history museum that collect objects intended to communicate knowledge, the art museum, and the ethnographical museum, a place of questioning that is uncertain which direction it should take—to move closer to the art museum or closer to the scientific museum. In truth, it is doing a bit of both. One senses this a little when visiting the Smithsonian: the National Museum of Natural History and the National Museum of the American Indian, then the Smithsonian American Art Museum, and then the National Museum of American History. Each of these museums takes a completely different approach to its collection and the status of its objects. The scenography provides a perfect example of this: the more the object is held to be an object of knowledge, the more it's accompanied by a form of scenography that uses extensive texts and the more the question of the authenticity of the object disappears. There are a lot of facsimiles and items fabricated by the scenographer. There are fewer and fewer real, and therefore potentially fetishistic, objects.

What happens in such cases? There's a miniature of the rocket and then a dummy disguised as an astronaut in a stage setting. The whole thing is made up of representations constructed in order to tell a story via the staged objects. It's the same principle as the diorama, as the Christmas window.

Similarly, I would say that an ethnographic exhibition that's excessively scientific, that's overly staged and surrounded by texts and accompanying items, also results in a loss of the mystery, of some of the magic of these objects. It's not necessarily important to know everything. In reality, there's no radical solution.

DG: The encyclopedic museum is the one that poses these problems most clearly, possibly more so even than the museum of ethnography, as it is genuinely, at the same time, a museum that presents art objects and a museum of civilization.

CH: Yes, but does the encyclopedic museum also contain nature? If there had to be an encyclopedic museum today, it would need to take account of the way the history of nature and the history of objects are intertwined and also how little the history of culture is compared to the history of nature.

Which museum brings these two things together? Strangely enough, it's the science museum, which occasionally shows a bird's nest, for example, and explains how architecture has been able to take inspiration from the way it's constructed. Or the way engineers have been inspired by spiders or the honeycomb of bees. Or how honeycomb is a form that allows for maximum-capacity storage and has provided a model for this. This relationship between nature and technology is presented in a clear manner in a lot of science museums. It would be nice to have an art museum that did something of the same but that would integrate the artists' proposals, too. A museum that showed us, a little like Archipenko with his archives, an image of a shell and an image of a Le Corbusier staircase and highlight the connection between them. It's more than a formal relationship because a formal relationship would obviously be very easy to establish. An exhibition about aggression would be interesting, comprising a study of animal behavior, notably reproductive competition, and the way in which this issue is represented in human culture. It would be fascinating to get a museum curator and a behaviorist to work together.

DG: The great limit of the encyclopedic museum would therefore be the disparity between, on the one hand, the institutions that present reasonably focused collections and, on the other, what could be a truly inclusive encyclopedic museum, which is a completely different matter and, as you were saying, idealist. This connects with the question of universality. The principle of the encyclopedic museum, or at any rate of its ideal, is that it's a universal museum, a museum that shows everything. Quite simply, does this make sense? And in what way could it do that?

CH: The encyclopedic museum is the type of museum that looks most closely at the question of how museums benefit us and why we need museums. What function does a museum have from an ethical point of view? Where are human desires tending and how do these desires and fears translate into actions and objects? The encyclopedic museum is the museum with the greatest possibility of addressing these questions and establishing a dialogue between the different disciplines. I dream of ambitious programs, of seminars at which psychoanalysts would be talking to biologists, philosophers, art historians, artists.

The reason this does not happen very often is that there's a problem of place, but also, most importantly, of language. The authority of each discipline is based on the possibility of having a language of its own, a vocabulary of its own. The more you use the words that belong to a particular field, the more of an authority you are. It's a way of signaling to those both inside and outside that you're a member of a professional community and have mastered your field. Paradoxically, this is also what makes it difficult to have a dialogue with other disciplines. Apart from the university, the encyclopedic museum is the only place in which it's possible for these barriers to be, if not lifted then questioned, and for this questioning to be embodied by the objects, and therefore rendered clearly visible and perceptible.

An encyclopedic museum has four key roles: to conserve, to disseminate knowledge, to give pleasure, and to ask questions, to show the unresolved problems of ethics and history. It's the balance between these different dynamics that enables the museum to adopt a position that's simultaneously stimulating for the mind and the eye, and establishes that an ethical image that visitors can use as a basis for the construction of their own opinions and reflections and political thinking.

DG: The encyclopedic museum would therefore be the place of dialogue par excellence between ethics and aesthetics.

CH: Aesthetics has always included political and ethical questions. From the moment the aesthetic field has to do with representation, questions of responsibility arise. The field of art should be an interrogative space. Are the works moral? Probably not. Do they lead us to question our moral position? Definitely.

When everything is good, good will no longer exist. A Zen adage goes: "The beautiful cannot be beautiful unless it is ugly." Good cannot be a given: the question of good and of ethics needs to be lived out on the level of the individual. Individuals can only ponder ethical questions if they've had to face questions or problems. The question of what I should do, what I should think, can only arise if I'm confronted by something that's not given from the outset. This is why it's so important to ask these questions and to ask them in a way that shows that they haven't yet been resolved.

DG: The Internet has made everyone part of a globalized culture that the encyclopedic museum, with its differentiations, is challenging. The museum offers two things the Internet doesn't: a connection with the objects—in other words a materiality—and selection.

CH: A selection that's also a vision, a discourse. On the Internet, there's a multiplicity of discourses, whereas the museum can propose a selection and lay claim to a certain truth based on scientific criteria, which are its specialty. This claim to a certain truth, to a *solidity* of the story the museum tells, can become highly problematic in the context of the encyclopedic museum; and yet, this is also why it counts for so much. In a certain sense, it needs to be a bit like a teacher who has the courage to elaborate his teaching but who also reveals himself capable of admitting his doubts. (2015-20)

27

Massimiliano Gioni

Artistic director, New Museum, New York;
curator, 2013 Venice Biennale

Donatien Grau: I would like to start by asking about your point of view on the encyclopedic museum. In an encyclopedic museum, obviously, you deal with the past, whereas you are noted for your work with contemporary art. How do you think this pattern of encyclopedic museum is relevant for the present, in the contemporary art world?

Massimiliano Gioni: I don't know if I believe in the encyclopedic museum as a valuable form. But I believe in it as a tool to keep contemporary art museums from being the way they are.

More than encyclopedic museums, I think what interests me as a contemporary art curator is the idea of a museum where you look at visual manifestations of culture. To simplify brutally, today, you have contemporary art museums, or modern art museums, which more or less voluntarily propose an idea of art that I often find self-referential, self-enclosed, and eventually sterile.

Let us use the most obvious and canonical example: the Museum of Modern Art—and I do not mean to join the legions of MoMA bashers, but the example here is relevant. The Museum of Modern Art proposes an idea of art as a self-referential game, where art objects can, at the most, be beautiful masterpieces.

To this model one could oppose the model of the Metropolitan Museum of Art, and particularly the sections not devoted to contemporary art. If you look at the collections of the Met, or if you look at the collection of any museum founded on an ethnographic, encyclopedic model, you realize that in those contexts artworks function in a variety of ways: as tools to understand and describe different cultures, or different aspects of a culture; as relics of a distant past; as religious objects.

More importantly, within encyclopedic museums, art appears to be only one aspect of a much more complex and richer narrative, in which different manifestations of culture—material, visual, ritual, etc.—can be displayed. In this sense, encyclopedic museums appear to me to be less hierarchical and as such perhaps more complete or certainly more complex. More broadly, you could say that in the encyclopedic museum objects are looked at and interpreted in order to understand something about the culture from which they come.

That is a simple distinction—and again I'm brutally simplifying, from a methodological point of view—between the way in which objects are used in the encyclopedic museum and the way in which artworks are used in modern art museums. In modern art museums, we are meant to simply look at objects and be stupefied by their beauty. The interesting thing with places like the Met—let's use the Met as a reference point—is that there is a sort of horizontality between media and between provenance of objects, particularly when you look back at prehistory, Roman history, or any sort of distant past.

In a way, the polemical position that was articulated in my exhibition *The Encyclopedic Palace* for the 2013 Venice Biennale is: Can we imagine a museum of the future in which any expression and manifestation of visual culture can be treated equally? We can do away with the distinction between art and non-art, with the distinction between high art and low art. What happens, then, to the objects in this museum? What stories do they tell us? What can they allow us to understand in visual culture, differently, and, I believe, more deeply?

The provocation for me is: Does the encyclopedic museum teach us to use art, and contemporary art in particular, differently? Can it teach us to understand visual culture more than other museums in which art is treated as a sort of self-enclosed system that admits no dialogue with visual culture or culture at large?

DG: There seems to be a relationship between art and visual culture. The encyclopedic museum would position itself differently, outside of the fact that "high art" is a Western construct.

MG: I think the moment you stop worrying about constructing a hierarchy among artworks or among types of art or different visual expressions, a new productive questioning of these realities can happen. I am not going to say that the encyclopedic museum solves all the problems in the world of museology, but it helps us to do away with a few definitions that I find limiting.

It helps us to do away with certain realities that have become sterile: for example, it can help us understand that artworks are not opaque objects; they are also transparent or transitive; they tell us something about the place where they come from and the way they were made or used. It helps us understand that artworks were born, not in a vacuum, but within a cultural system. It helps us break away from an idea of art as a masterpiece that too often overlaps with a celebration of economic value.

I think what happens in many museums of art is that people are encouraged to be stupefied and respectful of certain works in a rather passive manner: the public is implicitly told that certain works are great expressions of the human mind. In a way, I think that kind of passive reception of artworks is not too dissimilar from the same ideological values that auction houses seem to spread: it is as though the only legitimate feeling in front of artworks should be a kind of stupor, a wow-moment in which the public is stupefied by the beauty, grandiosity, and price of the artwork.

In encyclopedic museums instead there is a much more blurred distinction between the minor and the major. That is perhaps the key. That is what makes encyclopedic museums a much more versatile tool for understanding and presenting art: in encyclopedic museums, every object seems to be treated as minor, as a document rather than as some mysterious beautiful artwork. Paradoxically, I believe that approaching artworks and other artifacts on an even level, on the same playing field, actually allows us to understand more about the culture from which those objects come. And in this juxtaposition of different types of artifacts, different intensities emerge.

DG: You seem to position the encyclopedic museum against the model of the modern art museum, and oppose them on the issue of the canon.

MG: Yes. Obviously, the model of the encyclopedic museum is built on colonialist impulses. The first encyclopedic museum, the one created by Athanasius Kircher, was the direct emanation of the Jesuits' missions. And in encyclopedic museums the ways in which identities are constructed is often far from unproblematic. I do not want to be naïve about the model of the encyclopedic, but I think it is a more porous concept and much more attuned to complexity. In that sense, it is more contemporary and possibly has more potential to be renewed and transformed. If anything, it can allow for a variety of scales and a variety of rhythms. Encyclopedic museums rarely seem to be preoccupied with establishing a canon. The problem with traditional modern art museums is that they seem to be solely interested in establishing canons. My ideal museum would be a museum in which canons are not established, but are constantly questioned or reconfigured.

Encyclopedic museums allow for more flexibility. They are built on a sort of confusion of status that I think is quite productive: every object in the encyclopedic museum is at the same time a document, a relic, an artwork. Every object is included for a variety of reasons and not simply because it is an important artwork. This confusion allows for many interesting ideas to emerge and many different ways of looking at art to work simultaneously. What I try to do in some of the exhibitions I put together is precisely that: Can you look at contemporary art or contemporary images not just as artworks, but also as documents, as relics, as traces of existential adventures, as many things at the same time? What happens when you do so?

DG: Eventually, there is the issue of universalism: everything that ends in the museum is human, and the accumulation of objects creates a sense of universality.

MG: I do not know if I am comfortable with the idea of universalism The idea that, by seeing all these different expressions, you see recurring patterns across cultures makes me a little nervous because I do not believe in it.

The question of universalism is perhaps one of the most problematic shortfalls of the encyclopedic model. The universal can be a terribly regressive concept, often violently so. It is in the name of presumed universal values that horrible things can be done. I actually believe that a contemporary version of the encyclopedic museum should struggle to be absolutely relativistic, or anyway more skeptical about notions of universality.

Encyclopedic museums are based on the idea that you look at objects to understand cultures. And as such, they should show us the diversity of cultures and not try to prove that all humans are the same. That is a really frightening position.

DG: The current interest in the encyclopedic museum has to do with the fact that the world is more global than it ever was.

MG: If we find a way of freeing the encyclopedic museum from its colonial undertones, then yes, it will become a model more attuned to global culture. Perhaps the way to go would be by having a plurality of voices, which can be in the form of several different experts working together on the same topic, and bringing together these different approaches on one subject. The other is to deal with the history of the objects: their provenance in the encyclopedic museum is not often fully revealed. It is revealed in the caption, but not in all its complexity. One could say that the work of an artist like Danh Vo is somehow playing with the model of the encyclopedic museum, but revealing its colonial undertones. And he does it mostly through techniques of display, as well as through the history of the objects and through their descriptions.

DG: It seems that your idea would be that the encyclopedic museum offers a possibility for discourse, as opposed to the astonishment of the modern art museum.

MG: What I like about certain encyclopedic museums is how they deal with the problem of narrative. In museums, narration is crucial, whether it is explicitly addressed or simply implied by the kind of history they are telling, and by the tools with which they are telling it. Encyclopedic museums do not tend to have an all-encompassing narrative. At the Museum of Modern Art in New York, particularly as it was envisioned in the past, there used to be one narrative, which was the development of modernism. At the Metropolitan Museum, you cannot even try to grasp a single narrative, and this multiplicity of viewpoints and stories makes it immediately more contemporary. Of course at the core of many encyclopedic museums is the perhaps misguided belief that they could contain all the knowledge of the world in one place. This assumption is problematic and absolutely unrealistic at this point, but once you get rid of that assumption, then I think encyclopedic museums paradoxically tend to refuse grand narratives. They are built on multiple narratives, on digressions, on interruptions. I am more fascinated by museums that are constructed on this more clouded or plural logic, that are archipelagos rather than monoliths.

Today, we have so many forces at work in the art world, or in some sectors of the art world. Particularly mainstream culture, the museums, and the auction houses seem to attract the attention of the public. To me, both traditional museums and auction houses suggest a view of art as a series of grandiose, major gestures. Perhaps involuntarily, they promote an idea of the sublime that is very close to the idea of the spectacle, and to the reality of the market—an art of big numbers and big gestures, of masterpieces and major artworks, all of them to be consumed and accepted passively.

In encyclopedic museums I found a model that seems to suggest the opposite: it immediately offers an antidote to the so-called grand narrative, which I think is no longer useable.

DG: How does it relate to the status of the artwork, then?

MG: Don't get me wrong; I love beautiful artworks. I love the wow effect as much as any other person, and I guess you can say that as a curator I am often guilty of that type of spectacular approach. But at the same time I believe it is important we contextualize art in a dialogue with visual culture and with culture at large. We live in a visual culture that has become so aggressive, so prominent, that it is important we provide tools with which to try and understand it. If we leave art to be understood and experienced on its own, in its own ivory tower, then it is the end of art. And this also means simultaneously consigning visual culture to marketing experts only.

If we do succeed in freeing ourselves and artworks from the passive consumption of masterpieces, if we are able to integrate them in a larger cultural debate, I think the following question should be: "Can we find a way to re-enchant those artifacts?" On one hand, I believe we have to do away with the notion of high, major art, and treat all objects of different provenance as equal. On the other hand, we also need to find a way to re-enchant these objects, so that they can give us access to another kind of sublime, another kind of intensity. And maybe that is the sublime of knowledge, the sense of facing at once the vastness of knowledge, the vastness of diversity, and ultimately of our own ignorance.

DG: This idea of equalizing art and visual culture raises the issue of the relation between the encyclopedic museum and the ethnographic museum. How do you see the relation between the two?

MG: I think the ethnographic and the encyclopedic museums—not that they are the same in their origin—are quite similar in their visual expressions and in their techniques of display. The Met is an ethnographic museum.

The problem arises when only certain cultures within these types of museums are allowed to have high art—which happens in almost all of these museums. Think, for example, of the Metropolitan Museum, where it is quite apparent that all the cultures of the past, and the non-Western cultures, are analyzed from their artifacts, without any distinction between high art and low art, between practical objects and objects to be contemplated, between ritual objects and artworks. When it comes to modern Western art, we immediately distinguish high art from any other expression. You have the galleries of the impressionists or you go to the contemporary section and you have only a very specific certain type of "great" art on the walls; all the other visual expressions are kicked out.

I think it would be interesting to treat our own culture in the same ways we treat others—exhibiting artifacts of different provenance and function, of different quality and importance, all next to each other. That would give us a more complete understanding of the culture in which the artworks and the other objects were born. Can't we understand more about the historical avant-garde, say, about Surrealism, if we do not just look at the paintings? What if we look at the paintings, but also at the movies, the literature, the documents and manifestos, at both the masterpieces and the minor findings? It strikes me, for example, that in many visual arts museums, you would never know what artists were reading at the time, what other pictures they were looking at, what the cities in which they lived looked like. I think that looking at art in dialogue with other forms of creativity does not diminish its power but, on the contrary, enhances it and also enhances the significance of supposedly minor types of expressions and manifestations of culture.

DG: You could characterize an important part of modern and late modern art as being also an evolution or a displacement of the notion of the object. You could say that the encyclopedic museum is a way to refocus or re-engage with the object.

MG: Yes. That's a very interesting question. Supposedly the fashionable "speculative realists" invite us to rethink how objects question the place of humans in the world. For me the potential of the encyclopedic museum is to ask: Can different histories be told with objects of different values?

By including more objects or objects of different status in our museums, we could question the accepted values of the masterpieces. In the encyclopedic museum, the discourse has to be incarnated in physical manifestations.

I think another crucial element, which I keep in my head every day, is how language and narration enter into an exhibition. For a few years now, I have been thinking that texts are fundamental tools in the organization of an exhibition, to the point that in some of my recent shows—such as *The Encyclopedic Palace* or *The Great Mother*—the experience of the exhibition is very much tied to reading thousands and thousands of words in wall labels and accompanying texts. Perhaps I have gone even a little too far, but for me this explosion of text in the exhibition functions as an antidote against a quick consumption of the artworks and the objects on view. It's also a way to force the viewers to slow down, to experience a kind of time that is not the same as the one they can experience in a mall or in the world beyond the museum. Museums should be places of learning and experience, but one should not simply overshadow the other.

Umberto Eco wrote a beautiful short essay about his ideal museum. The concept of the encyclopedia is crucial in Eco's philosophical system, and for him the encyclopedia is something quite different from just a repository of knowledge. It is a much more dynamic entity: it is the set of information and knowledge and experiences that compose a culture and the interpretative horizon of an individual. For Eco the ideal museum would be one in which we have only one artwork, but all around this artwork the viewer would find hundreds of objects and images and materials that help the viewer reconstruct the knowledge—the encyclopedia—that was necessary and required for that specific artwork to be looked at, understood, or interpreted in the particular moment in history in which it was made.

Can you imagine, for example, Botticelli's *The Birth of Venus* being the only artwork in a museum, and all around were all the books and religious experiences and music and illustrations and so on that could help you understand not just the eye of the Florentine viewer in the quattrocento but also the encyclopedia of the viewer in the quattrocento in Florence?

Could we have a museum like that, not just for an artwork but for many artworks? That would be the encyclopedic museum of the future. (2015)

28

Bachir Souleymane Diagne

Professor and director, Institute of African Studies,
Columbia University, New York

Donatien Grau: You write about the notion of universalism as a political concept as opposed to the universal. I was wondering if, in the museums that we see as encyclopedic museums, you think that this notion of universalism as a stance of a museum that would pretend to describe the world to the world is politically motivated, and if so, if it is today problematic?

Bachir Souleymane Diagne: First of all, let me explain very quickly the distinction I'm making between universalism and the universal. Universalism, as I understand it, is a unique way in which Europe, at one point, claimed to be the very incarnation of the universal. Universalism was the way in which Europe projected itself to the rest of the world as being the model to be imitated. The only location of the universal was supposed to be Europe, as opposed, now, to what I call "the universal," which is a quest and a task. When you live in a decolonized world where there is no reason to put Europe at the center of that world and to consider it the incarnation of the universal, then universality or the universal becomes the pursuit of all cultures and languages on equal footing. That is, very quickly explained, the difference I'm establishing between universalism as an imperial way of thinking of the universal and the pursuit of the universal, which is something we should do.

Now, let me translate that in terms of museums. There is this idea that there are certain museums that are considered to be universal or the location of the universal. Again, these museums are to be found in Europe or North America. At one point, for example, in the current debate about the restitution of African art to African countries that have been spoiled, it was said that, actually, these objects became art when they were on display in these universal museums. Again, you find in the language of museums the same discourse about a particular and unique European location of the universal. These objects became universal objects because they were in these museums.

As opposed, now, to what I would call the pursuit of the universal, where in the same museums, you will have art objects coming from different parts of the world, speaking different classic or visual languages, and talking to each other. In that case, what I would understand to be a truly encyclopedic museum—which is not to say that there is a particular location of the universal and everything has to come to that project, to that place, in order to be considered of universal value—this museum would be a place where many different objects would be talking to each other—the way, actually, they did historically. Because African art objects, as you know well, had big conversations with the creativity of European artists in the beginning of the twentieth century, when Picasso created a dialogue between his own research and the African forms that he was witnessing in his own collection—because he was an art collector himself—and the objects that he went to see at the collections at the Trocadéro. That is the kind of artistic gesture he made. It should be introduced for me by this encyclopedic museum.

DG: I would be interested in considering this issue from the point of view of the one and the multiple, which is something you have given a lot of thought to. There are two views on this sort of museums: one is to say that they are universal, which is the French way of phrasing it, *le musée universel*, the other is a more American way of phrasing it, which is to say they are encyclopedic. Obviously, when you think of an encyclopedia, you think of many different articles or entries, whereas if you think of a universal museum you think of a sense of totality. What do you think of those two paralleling ways of addressing the same institution, encyclopedic or universal?

BSD: I'm afraid that when you talk about a universal museum, one is assuming that the museum itself is the location of the universal and, therefore, is making the objects in it universal, in a way, while encyclopedic seems to me more welcoming of plurality and pluralism. In a sense, to call yourself a universal museum means that you are somehow formatting everything that comes in. You are giving to them your own label because of who you are and what your location is.

The encyclopedic museum is built on pluralism. Its point of departure is plurality. Therefore, universality becomes a horizon, or a goal, or something that is going to come out of the very presence of these different objects coming from different places. The universal seems to mean, "Here I am, this universal location. I'm going to grant you some form of universality by welcoming you in my own place."

Of course, I'm simplifying somehow and exaggerating the opposition between the two, but if that is the case and if I had to choose, I would rather go to the encyclopedic understanding of universality in art.

DG: Which also raises another issue because, I think, obviously, most of these museums we now call encyclopedic or universal are located in Europe and North America. Do you think that there is a legitimacy to these museums presenting a vision of the world as being complete, even though it is from their own point of view? If it isn't legitimate, then what can be done, since they are there and they have all those holdings?

BSD: This is the de facto situation. It doesn't say anything about the de jure side of it. It is a de facto situation where museums were invented in Europe. Big, renowned museums are now in Europe and North America. Given that, what does it mean to pretend that you are going to reflect the whole world and not just this specific viewpoint? Encyclopedic museums seem to be negating that universality comes from the location of the museum in Europe or North America.

To call yourself a universal museum is another way of just thinking that the very stage of universal history is naturally Europe or North America. To come back to the previous question we were discussing, at least the encyclopedic museum in its very name of being an encyclopedia assumes that there are many entries into the universal. An encyclopedia is made of different entries. Each entry is actually a legitimate entry. That is what I call respecting pluralism and assuming that universality should be built upon the foundation of pluralism and not something to be granted from above by a location calling itself universal. In other words, again, that de facto situation of the great museums being located in Europe or North America is taken for a de jure right as well in the universal museum—in the very phrase *universal museum*. While when you call a museum an encyclopedic museum, it is considered to be a simple fact, and the location of it could be everywhere else.

DG: You were talking about the pluralism of the institution and the building the universal. How do you do it in a museum like that? Do you think that the current way of organizing geographically by schools, or by country sometimes, or even by continent, is relevant? At the Met, you have African cultures on one side, Egyptian on the other side, which is not included in African. You have Italian, Dutch, etc. Do you think that it is still right to do it, or do you think there are different ways of building the universal in a museum?

BSD: I would say that you have different ways. In other words, of course, chronology imposes itself, and schools also impose themselves: that is the history of the museum, and history itself. Given that, you also have to look at the way in which these objects in the museum talk to each other.

I gave you, for example, the case of Picasso talking to African art, which was quite improbable. It was not something that you would have expected. After the fact, of course, you see how evident this was, but this was not really something that was supposed to happen when he was looking for the faces of *Les Demoiselles d'Avignon*.

The moment when he decided to put African masks on their faces, this kind of gesture was a huge leap. Afterward, this became something revolutionary and opened a new path. Maybe you would, of course, look at Picasso, putting him and other artists in their particular school, the European school. But somehow you would have another face of his work turned toward African art objects. You would try, and that is the challenge in this case, to have chronology respected, schools respected, but also make sure that you create, or you put on display, the conversation that happened in that crossed the boundaries.

In other words, the challenge is to, at the same time, make the borders between schools and periods felt, and also cross those same borders by establishing a conversation between different objects that could be from very distant cultures or distant periods.

DG: This emphasis on the conversation between objects can be considered as a breaking down of what would be the grand story of humanity, presented through objects. Is there still a grand narrative to be had from an encyclopedic museum, and what would the narrative be? Especially if you're breaking it down, creating these conversations, can there still be a grand narrative in such a museum?

BSD: I think so, if you do not think of a grand narrative as something unilinear, which is what had been the case, unfortunately. The simplest way to have a grand narrative is to have something unilinear. The way, for example, we enrich the history of, let's say, creation or the Spirit—we use a capital *S*—that has been told for a long time as originating in Greece and being transmuted to Europe.

You had this unilinear path, leading from Athens to Rome, and from Rome to London, Paris, or Heidelberg, or all the European capitals. That was the way in which a grand narrative was conceived. Everything else was just at the periphery. In that framework, you consider that everything else in the periphery are curiosities. In a way, you just have one single, unilinear narrative, and everything else outside of it is a curiosity, something that you should be visiting to be curious about. Not something that is a narrative, or belongs to a narrative of itself.

Complicating the path, routes, tours, and detours of human creativity and human spirit is still a way of creating meaning. You do not abandon the idea of having a narrative. You are just having a much more complicated narrative, looking at the way in which narratives are maybe here and there as well.

They belong to the bigger flow, and you have derivations here and there, but you can still have a picture of the great adventure of human creativity in general. If you give yourself that picture, if you think of humanity as a totality, and you think that your grand narrative is going to be a braid of narratives and history—if you accept the challenge of a more complicated picture like that—you do not need to abandon the idea of having a narrative at all. It is going to be more complicated. Let's say that instead of being a very simple, straightforward novel, you are going to have the type of Russian novel—or these world novels that we have now, the kind of world novel that Edouard Glissant was calling for—where you try to put the "tout-monde" as he called it, or the "chaos-monde," in the form of a novel.

The trajectory that has been followed by modern novels would be the trajectory to be followed by museums, in the way in which they are trying to tell the story of humanity. Taking humanity as a subject, not just one grand narrative, and considering that the rest of humanity has to organize itself at the periphery of that narrative. That is the picture you have to change.

DG: In your philosophical work, you have made a very important contribution in thinking about what African art and African philosophy could be, and showing that the limitations in those terms to establish them as Western was quite arbitrary and chronologically dated. In a way, the whole notion of the encyclopedic museum is that it's a museum in which objects have at least double citizenship. They are artworks, they are cultural items, and they are not either/or, they are both.

BSD: It recently occurred to me that art objects should be called "mutant." That is, they are at once, as you say, it is not either/or, but they are at once many different things. This is why I like the word *mutant*, because in French, *mutant*, as you know, is a present participle. In other words, the metamorphosis is continuously happening to those objects. Their very presence in an encyclopedic museum, or, for that matter, a universal museum—here, the distinction might not be that important—means that they are, by just being there, still acquiring or displaying new possibilities and new meaning. I would be happy to work toward that direction of exploring further what I tried to say by calling these objects "mutant."

DG: Which also is interesting because it is shifting them out of what is a very limited vision that is maybe 140 to 150 years old, and in the oldest case, a 300-year-old term of being in these museums. It's basically bringing back their life and a form of instability, as well.

BSD: Exactly, absolutely. I like both words. Life, in the first place, because it captures what I tried to say by calling them "mutant." Also, instability, which is the way in which they are oscillating, so to speak, among their many meanings, and trying to show them all at once, in a way.

DG: How can you do that? This is the practical question. How could you ever show all these meanings at once?

BSD: That is the billion-dollar question, obviously. The scenography, as you know much, much better than I, is trying to translate visually a concept that you have. Exploring the concept as we have been doing in our operation is probably the easiest part of it.

Then how do you translate it in the visual language? Here, I have to confess my own incompetence.

I would say, sorry for being direct and personal, but someone like yourself, who would have a foot on the conceptual field, and also be very attentive to the visual translation, is the one who is always more able to answer that kind of question.

DG: I'm going to move onto another billion-dollar question. We have these institutions—the Met, the British Museum, the Louvre, Berlin's Museum Island, and a lot of American institutions—which were actually founded as encyclopedic. Each of them has their own distinctions, and this includes a lot of American museums, actually.

They are the institutions that we call encyclopedic museums or universal museums. Do you think that the notion, like this, can apply outside of these museums? Do you think that there can be an encyclopedicization of the museums? In other words, do you think other encyclopedic museums could be founded, or is it just a historical notion that belongs to a given moment, and that it still exists?

BSD: I think that the idea is such that it should be reproduced globally. This notion has to become global for two reasons. The first reason is that, de facto, you have a form of globalization of different models. The way in which, for example, the Arab Emirates are reproducing—mimicking, really—European museums shows that there is the idea of a global model, but mimicking is probably not the best way to go.

The encyclopedic museum is, by its very nature, a way of questioning the universe, aiming at the universal, but not taking it for granted. Therefore I think that, in its very essence, it is meant to be globalized. Obviously, the context, the locations, are going to be important factors, as well. You cannot just duplicate something in Dakar the way it is at the Met. At the same time, you can try, and here is where a concept that is very important in my work can be very useful: the concept of translation. For something to become global, because of its own intrinsic interest and what it itself is, means being translated and appropriated in different locations and in different languages. My answer would be that this is obviously something I want to see become global, and that you still see it become translated in many different vernaculars.

DG: Let us speak about the collections: most of the holdings are in Paris, New York, London, Saint Petersburg, Berlin, etc. Would you build these new museums without the collections? Would part of those collections need to be repatriated? Would you find another way? How do you see that unfolding?

BSD: This is also where circulation becomes a very important notion. It seems to me that a museum cannot seriously call itself encyclopedic if it is not also a place of transit, where objects come and go. This is where the whole notion of restitution comes into play.

I am among the people who say: yes, restitution should be taken seriously, because first of all, when a president says "restitution," a presidential word has to be taken seriously. There needs to be restitution. You cannot have the totally asymmetrical situation where collections are owned in the

West and are not present in the rest. This is where it is important to have circulation.

When it comes to the collections as wholes, of cores, every museum has to have a kind of stable core, but things have to be put in circulation. For a long time, there were requirements, due to important factors such as the security of the objects and so on. When you try to have objects circulate from the north to the global south, you have all these questions about insurance, questions of security. How secure will objects be when they go here and there? Those are the problems to be solved, and they are being solved. You have more and more very secure and good museums in the global south.

Let me take the example of my own country, Senegal. Senegal has, now, a big, very secure wonderful museum, built by us in partnership with China. Many African countries, for example, are catching up in terms of the museums that they have in the capital city.

Working on the circulation of objects is also another way of working on the very concept of an encyclopedic museum. An encyclopedic museum, in a way, is a museum without a particular location, at the same time as it is beyond every location.

Obviously, there is the Met, or the Louvre, but at the same time, the objects it contains are meant to travel—are meant to be *mutant*, as I said earlier. The simplest way for an object of being mutant is to travel.

I read about the exhibition of the young Picasso's work in China, the biggest to date. I don't know all the detail, but that amount of Picasso paintings and works, traveling to China, was a huge headache for the insurers, who actually demanded that these works travel in seven different planes.

They are going as far as thinking, "OK, we don't want everything to be on one single plane. What happens to that plane?" At the same time, we have here an example of what it means, what the challenges would be, if we have to put forward this concept of circulation. Why have it go to China and not to other places in the south? Collections, yes. Stable core, yes. But the museum which is truly authentically encyclopedic, or universal, means also that it is always delocalizing itself, and that means making the objects travel.

DG: In a way, what you seem to be leading toward is not thinking of one encyclopedic museum that would be the Louvre or the Met, but that would be a network of all those museums.

BSD: Exactly. I'm thinking in terms of a web of museums. The way in which a museum is going to aim at the totality and to aim at universality is to not only try to organize exhibitions in a way that would reflect the "tout-monde," to use the Glissantian concept again, but to think of itself as connected to a web of museum that covers the rest of the world. Yes, that would be the picture that I have in mind.

DG: Then every fragment of the grand encyclopedic museum, or every encyclopedic museum within that field, would have a specific viewpoint on that universal, right?

BSD: Absolutely. Let's use here a philosophical image, which is Leibniz's *Monadology.* Every single monad is, at the same time, totality, because it is a reflection of the totality, but it is also a reflection from its own point of view. Here again, you see the concept of translation.

DG: My last question will be exactly about this. How do you see the concept of translation playing out within that field of museums? You've mentioned it here and there, but we haven't fully grasped onto it.

BSD: I'm glad that your last question is bringing me back to the first element of our conversation, when I was establishing this difference between universalism and the universal. One model of thinking of the universal is to say we go from a plurality of languages. All languages are equivalent, and the nature of human languages, because we are in a post-Babel world—that is, our human condition is to be a post-Babel humanity—we speak many different languages. As Mallarmé said, "Les langues imparfaites en ceci que plusieurs"—"Our languages are imperfect, because there are many of them." At the same time, to overcome the plurality of our languages, we still have translation. Of course, translation is never going to replace the one adamic language.

In other language words, we are not going to have one, through translation, absolute transparency, where everything would be understandable in a transparent and total way. We'll always have misunderstanding. You will have untranslatables, and so on, but that is very important. What it means, then, to be in pursuit of the universal is to understand that one has to be capable of decentering oneself, not just being trapped in your own single monolingualism, but being able to learn another language, and to decenter yourself, to see your own language from the standpoint of a different language.

That is the model I am transferring here. I give that very general understanding of the notion of translation, which means, for me, that the universal is possible. Cultures are not insularities that are only defined within their own context. I believe that they can be translated, and especially in the language of art. In the language of art, you produce forms. You produce sounds. You produce performances in art that are going to speak more directly, probably, to other ways of understanding and other perspectives than what we actually call a language.

To conclude on where I started, the universal, in pursuit of which I think that it is the task of our time to engage, is a universal of translation, universality of translation. Umberto Eco once said, "The language of Europe is translation." But I would rather go toward something Ngugi Wa Thiongo said, which is that "the language of languages is translation," which actually goes much further than what Umberto Eco said. He was talking about under, south of Europe. In this case, we have to generalize it further, as Ngugi Wa Thiongo did when he said that the language of languages is translation. The task of the encyclopedic museum is to manifest this within the experience of art. (2019)

AFTERWORD

Unsettled Thoughts for a Changing Global Encyclopedia

Mary E. Miller
Director, Getty Research Institute, Los Angeles

If you live in Los Angeles in the first quarter of the twenty-first century, you find plenty to think about with respect to the subject of this book, the encyclopedic museum. Our local exemplar, the Los Angeles County Museum of Art (LACMA), has been devoted to the encyclopedia for most of its existence, beginning with its roots in Exposition Park as the Los Angeles Museum of History, Science and Art (LAMHSA) in 1913. LAMHSA's acquisition in 1950 of the collection of William Randolph Hearst, for example, included works from around the world, long before the doors opened to the William Pereira signature building of LACMA on Wilshire Boulevard, in 1965. There were both aficionados and collectors of Pre-Hispanic art in Southern California from the late 1930s onward, my own field of study, and today the two museums both host significant collections. Once established, LACMA grew its own collections in Pre-Hispanic, starting with major donations from Phil Berg in 1968, with exhibitions of the collections of Proctor Stafford following in 1970 and of Berg in 1971, establishing a major presence for the Arts of the Ancient Americas.[1]

In this, LACMA beat America's best-known encyclopedic museum, the Metropolitan Museum of Art, to the punch. Long dedicated to the arts of antiquity, broadly described across the Mediterranean and the Middle East, the arts of Asia, and the European and American traditions in painting and sculpture, the Met absorbed the contents of the Museum of Primitive Art in New York City to open the Rockefeller Wing in 1982, suddenly promoting the arts of Oceania, Africa, and the ancient Americas to the fore, and re-animating the collection purchased from Louis Petich in 1900, which had spent most of the twentieth century out of sight, some pieces on view across Central Park, at the American Museum of Natural History, and others at the Brooklyn Museum, another encyclopedic collection.[2] Of course no museum can be truly encyclopedic: it is outside the realm of possibility to collect all art traditions of all times, and, simultaneously, to stay atop current traditions the way that both the Met and LACMA attempt to do. The two coastal anchors of the American museum, LACMA and the Met, are the two most encyclopedic of the nation's museums.

So let's step back a bit and sketch a quick, subjective picture, for which exceptions can be identified along every dimension. The museum, of course, is a particular artifact of the Enlightenment, and a descendent of the European—generally French, German, Dutch, and British—collections formed in the years after discovery of a world beyond Europe, in which the curiosities, from the shell or fossil or bone of natural history to exotic or ancient, usually three-dimensional, artifact of antiquity were grouped behind glass in a cabinet or gathered together in a room for private viewing; in some cases this is the ancestor to the natural history museum, sites for discovery about the planet, its context, and all of its occupants, from plants to humans. The market for paintings and other bourgeois accoutrements took off in Holland in the seventeenth century; elsewhere, paintings were commissioned by elites more than collected after the fact until the eighteenth century. Public collections and exhibitions of painting and sculpture, national academies, and a wealthy bourgeoisie all contributed to the rise of the art museum, theoretically open to some swath of the public. The truly encyclopedic museum, in which finely executed works invested with meaning, and executed anywhere and ideally everywhere in the world, and including the country where that museum exists, emerged in the twentieth century. The peoples of the world studied primarily through anthropology, rather than history—and in this one hears the echoes of nineteenth-century anthropology itself, the civilized, savage, and barbarian, the Cold War language of the twentieth century, in First, Second, and Third World—were the last to have their works gain entry to the encyclopedia. After 1982, at the Met, the encyclopedia still lacked some entries, especially for Latin America after 1534, but the concept was in full force.

For many museums in the United States and Canada, the move to the encyclopedia came to the fore in the mid-twentieth century, and particularly with the inclusion of African, Oceanic, and ancient American art. This is true for the Art Institute of Chicago; the de Young Museum in San Francisco;

the Museum of Fine Arts, Houston; the Cleveland Museum of Art; the New Orleans Museum of Art; the Saint Louis Art Museum; and many others, although a few objects often entered the doors only because of dedicated donors, and with little curatorial intention. The Cleveland Museum of Art, for example, acquired three Nasca pots in 1930, and then benefited from the great generosity of Mrs. Emery Norweb from 1939 onward, who made extensive gifts of Pre-Columbian and Chinese art, especially after the Second World War.[3] The New Orleans Museum of Art expanded broadly, acquiring first a major African bronze in 1953,[4] and then to include Pre-Hispanic, recognizing its role within the two umbrellas of its collections—one, Mediterranean antiquities, which the museum had acquired early in the twentieth century,[5] and the other, Latin America, where the museum made a major push to build a comprehensive collection of Pre-Hispanic, colonial, and modern works in the mid-1960s.[6] In Canada, the Montreal Museum of Fine Arts built an encyclopedic collection under the guidance of curator F. Cleveland Gordon; he purchased the first African object for the museum in 1940.[7] When the museum closed in 1973 for nearly a decade, the institution prepared the touring exhibition, *Cultures of the Sun and Snow,* Pre-Hispanic and Inuit works drawn principally from museum collections; the show launched at the former Belgian pavilion of Expo '67 and traveled for years, with energetic support from Leo Rosshandler, who had already curated Montreal's first major exhibition of Pre-Hispanic art, *Man-Eaters and Pretty Ladies,* in 1971.[8]

An interesting and important subset of the encyclopedic museum is the university and college encyclopedic museum. Like all museums, the collegiate museum often has idiosyncratic origins, but most such museums have small acquisition budgets and depend on their alumni and alumnae for the shape, contour, and context of the collections. Alumni travelers, missionaries, and diplomats have often contributed to their alma mater. Two of the first university museums, the Ashmolean and the Fitzwilliam, at Oxford and Cambridge, respectively, are repositories of exceptional works. The former is particularly known for its Mediterranean antiquities; the latter features galleries of European pictures and decorative arts, yet juxtaposed with an important collection of Asian and Islamic ceramics. Neither aspires to the encyclopedia.

The collegiate collections in the United States are often very diverse, if not intentionally encyclopedic. In general, classical art was usually foundational to the collegiate collection because of instructional attention to classical language and literature. The desire to provide academic study from casts sometimes prompted the foundation of a museum altogether, along with the spaces for art students to practice drawing from the classical forms. Among the first acquisitions of the Princeton University Art Museum (founded 1882) were antiquities; over the course of the twentieth century it became an encyclopedic museum, particularly after Gillett Griffin became a curator in 1967. Mount Holyoke included African art almost from the beginning (1876) and with the intention of being fully encyclopedic. Founded in 1941, the Indiana Museum of Art (now Eskenazi Museum of Art) had at its founding the ambition to be a collection of the works of all peoples and all times. The Michael C. Carlos Museum of Emory University, a compendium of ancient art broadly construed, as well as art of traditions beyond Europe, acquired collections of nearby ancient Etowah finds in the 1920s, and then added more than 1300 Pre-Hispanic works to its collections from 1988 to 1991, largely the gifts of William C. and Carol Thibadeau, yielding a different and incomplete sort of encyclopedic concept. Although a few Pre-Hispanic objects entered the collection of the Yale University Art Gallery before 1958, that was the year that a substantial collection of New World textiles, ancient and modern, as well as the collection of Fred Olsen (much of which bears a 1973 accession date, the year the Olsen loan converted to university ownership) entered the museum. With the establishment of the department of Indo-Pacific art in 2009, the Yale museum became as encyclopedic in its reach (if not in its depth) as the Metropolitan Museum of Art. The Fogg Art Museum, of Harvard University, was purpose-built for the education of both scholars and museum professionals and held and emphasized study materials, particularly of Europe, in its earliest iteration. In what might have been a move toward filling more volumes of the encyclopedia, the Fogg at Harvard exhibited the Peabody Museum's large seated figure from the Copan Hieroglyphic Staircase for many years, set within what was known as the Maya Room. The Fogg then returned the monumental Maya work to the Peabody in the late 1930s,[9] in order to separate what could be construed to be ethnographic art from fine art, and seemingly rejecting the encyclopedia. As of this writing, a single Moche portrait vessel on loan from the Peabody brings Pre-Hispanic America into the Harvard Art Museums exhibition.

In 2000 the Louvre opened a gallery on its first floor that features 108 objects from the Quai Branly three kilometers west, thus making it technically an encyclopedic museum. But to be clear, these 108 objects from Africa, Oceania, and the Americas belong not to the Louvre itself but rather to the Quai Branly, including a Pre-Hispanic object that has never been exhibited at the Quai Branly itself but is part of that museum's identifying logo. The Louvre may be the only encyclopedic museum in Europe that includes European and modern traditions alongside those of the world, broadly defined, in distinction from European institutions like the British Museum, which eschews modern European art.

The universal and encyclopedic museum began in Europe. But it does seem that in its widespread practice, from the city museum to the collegiate, from museums with only a few thousand objects to the largest institutions in the United States, that the encyclopedic museum has emerged as a particularly American phenomenon.

Why this push to the encyclopedia? There are certainly several motivating factors for the encyclopedic collection, and the case of Pre-Hispanic art is instructive. Before 1940, most Pre-Hispanic objects were acquired in their country of origin, and sometimes by archaeologists and explorers as well as travelers. But by 1940 there were dealers in both Los Angeles and New York with far more material from Mexico and points south than had been offered for sale previously. Earl Stendahl, of the Stendahl Gallery of Hollywood, in operation since 1921 and mainly a purveyor of paintings until 1935, developed a high-volume inventory, and he placed works in museums and collections around the United States, as well with clientele that comprised Hollywood actors, directors, and more.[10] The first motivation for the move to an encyclopedic museum that included Pre-Hispanic art was visibility, in turn suggesting availability, for which Stendahl provided inventory. Additionally, the timing was right: the Stendahl Gallery opened in 1940, just when dealers in the United States saw their access to European sources sharply curtailed, as shipping lanes around the world were closed.

Yet, by 1940 some museums—the Fogg and the Metropolitan among them—had decided *not* to show Pre-Hispanic objects, and to assign works that they might have shown or owned an ethnographic identification. In both Cambridge, Massachusetts, and New York City there were prominent museums of natural history, more typically the preserve of collections of non-European arts and archaeology, as well as geology, botany, and paleontology. There was no single path for the Pre-Hispanic object in the museum, and many cities—New York, Philadelphia, New Haven, among them—developed collections of Pre-Hispanic art in more than one kind of museum. Just as some museums were trimming their encyclopedic displays, others were getting on board.

In the post-World War II period, the number of institutions and the numbers of acquisitions with Pre-Hispanic objects began to grow, from the Des Moines Art Center, which acquired a pair of Nayarit tomb sculptures in 1964,[11] to the Dayton Art Institute, which purchased a Colima dog in 1960.[12]

Both of these works belong to the larger world of West Mexico, shaft tomb works known by their states of origin: Colima, Jalisco, and Nayarit. A new visibility was key: for the 1959 film *North by Northwest*, Ernest Lehman's screenplay spelled out that the microfilm was to be secreted in a Mexican "Tarascan warrior" figure from "Kolemia," won at auction for the price of $1,750.[13] Colima figures were commonly circulating in the United States by then, and so the presence of such an object in highly charged scenes directed by Alfred Hitchcock was not out of place. The scene was staged so as to suggest that the sale price of $1,750 was excessive.

By the end of the 1950s, more dealers had come to the fore, with an expanding business in the 1960s, and especially in New York City. As Elizabeth Benson recounted, by the mid-1960s a group of New York dealers—Alphonse Jax, André Emmerich, Edward Merrin, and John Stokes—were the principal sellers to Dumbarton Oaks (as well as to many other institutions across the United States).[14] Building a base of clients required attentive dealers, who constantly worked to convince curators and directors of the value of the expanding purview of the art museum. Three years before the Munson Williams Proctor Institute (MWP) in Utica, New York, would acquire its first Pre-Hispanic art object, André Emmerich organized an exhibition at the MWP, and the cover of the exhibition catalog was an object that the museum would acquire in 1968.[15] Emmerich wrote regularly to Ed Dwight, director of the MWP, and Emmerich stoked his interest and stroked his ego to build the relationship.[16] The MWP would build a strong, small Pre-Hispanic collection that would be featured in *Before Cortés* and other exhibitions.[17]

The availability and visibility were certainly key to the success of the market. But in the years of Presidents Eisenhower and Kennedy, idealism across the United States may also have played a role in building diverse museum collections. As clearly evidenced by the formation of the United Nations and the establishment of its headquarters in New York City in the postwar period, there was a longing for a global solidarity in the United States, as the nation viewed itself, despite the fallacies now in evidence, to be a land of immigrants, the united states of the world.[18] Nothing exemplified this collective human identity more clearly than the 1955 exhibition of photographs at the Museum of Modern Art, *The Family of Man*, which showed the shared practices of humanity around the world, from birth to celebrations, from harvest to death. The accompanying book would not include the picture of the mushroom cloud of nuclear explosion that was staged near the end of the installation itself, but in the exhibition of 504 photographs (of which 503 were in the book), the giant photomural of the United Nations

General Assembly followed the depiction of nuclear annihilation, along with a caption from the UN Charter.[19] A montage of images of children from around the world closed both exhibition and book (an optimism and sweetness that has long been criticized).[20] This close to both exhibition and book spelled out the hope for a world peace that would take place in a modernist America, embodying liberal idealism. This flurry of optimism could not be fully dampened by the Cold War. Edward Steichen, curator of the exhibition, noted in his preface that the subject matter would range from "primitive peoples to the Councils of the United Nations," drawing a unifying line between non-European cultures and artwork of New York City.

In museums and in sales galleries alike, and across the United States, Pre-Hispanic art of Mexico found its way to glass vitrines in spaces often not far from abstract Modernism. Being a connoisseur of the Pre-Hispanic past spoke to one's international knowledge and prestige, along with the sophistication that characterized cultural knowledge outside the Western tradition.[21] Museums across the nation took steps to diversify their collections at both ends of the spectrum suggested by Steichen's statement, collecting both non-Western and the latest works of the avant-garde. In fact, this range from the Pre-Hispanic to Abstract Expression was the very definition of the inventory of André Emmerich's sales gallery on East 57th Street in Manhattan.

By the end of the twentieth century the term *primitive* would vanish, most clearly exemplified in the absorption of the Museum of Primitive Art by the Metropolitan Museum of Art within the Michael Rockefeller Wing (1982), effacing the word *primitive*. With this monumental addition to the building, the Met was filling out the encyclopedia. Ambitious exhibitions have amplified the permanent collection in the twenty-first century, especially of Latin American more broadly, most recently exemplified by *Golden Kingdoms: Luxury Arts of the Ancient Americas* and *Painted in Mexico, 1700–1790, Pinxit Mexici*. The Met was not alone: by the end of the 1960s and continuing on through the 1980s, museums in the United States, from the collegiate to the municipal, from Kalamazoo to Dallas, from Philadelphia to Los Angeles, had by and large embraced at least a part of the encyclopedia, often as shaped by collectors and donors, and so always with uneven attention to all the possibilities that the encyclopedic would seem to embrace. The Kimbell Art Museum in Fort Worth owns only about 350 works, but they range across most of the world, with the exception of areas and periods collected by museums elsewhere in the city. In many cases it took art history departments longer to catch up with such worldwide embrace than it did museums.

But at the turn of the twenty-first century, something different began to take place in US museums. Some museums began to narrow their brief, actively trimming collections in ways that turned away from the encyclopedic. To be clear, there were always institutions founded with a strict focus, often with attention to a limited chronology, among them the many museums of modern or contemporary art in the United States. In the United States, others had a focus on American art and occasionally a focus on a single artist. In order to pursue the deaccessioning that allows for the sale of entire collections, museums turned to their trustees or boards, developing new frameworks for the works within their walls that would determine future acquisitions and lead to deaccessioning existing collections.

Two museums in New York State have taken on this process of narrowing their purview since the turn of the century. First, the MWP made a decision in 2000 to sell their Pre-Hispanic, Islamic, and Mediterranean antiquities, starting with the Pre-Hispanic.[22] As previously noted in this essay, the MWP had built a significant collection of Pre-Hispanic art in the 1960s and early 1970s. The most famous acquisition of the museum was Chalcatzingo Monument 9, a work sold to the museum by André Emmerich in 1969.[23] The sales in 2000 and shortly thereafter of Pre-Hispanic art resulted in a substantial endowment to be used for new acquisitions, funds that the MWP had not previously had available to them, in a process following the existing guidelines of the American Association of Museum Directors. The MWP director at the time, Paul Schweizer, exacted a commitment from the private purchaser that Chalcatzingo Monument 9 would stay on view in a public setting.[24] Although the famous monumental sculpture was exhibited at the Art Institute of Chicago for about a year, it subsequently vanished from view once again. Although some of the other MWP objects have found permanent homes in public settings, others have simply vanished from view. All the Pre-Columbian objects were purchased from André Emmerich; when, at the time of the sales, authenticity was questioned for both an Olmec ceramic object and for two Cycladic works, Emmerich declined to take them back, even for the modest prices paid thirty years earlier.[25]

A few years later, one of the oldest art museums in the United States, the Albright-Knox Art Gallery of Buffalo, New York, also made a decision to concentrate exclusively on nineteenth century through twenty-first century art, and mainly painting and sculpture. This focus of the museum had, in fact, been in play throughout the twentieth century, but it did not stop the museum from accepting major works outside this framework.[26] The American taxpayer underwrote such donations through the benefits that accrue to those who gift works of art, with the unspoken expectation that such works would enrich a community. Would the theoretical taxpayer have subsidized such acquisition if it were known that acquisitions would subsequently be sold into private collections and out of the country? Does it matter that the Buffalo population of individuals of Asian descent—a broad and undifferentiated category in the United States census—doubled between 2000 and 2010, and that a Buffalo audience with heritage interests will discover sometime in the twenty-first century that the museum had sold twenty Chinese objects in 2007? All told, 196 objects were sold at Sotheby's in seven sales in that year, raising some $75 million to be added to the endowment for acquisitions. Only a single Pre-Hispanic object was in the mix of the Albright-Knox collections, an Aztec sculpture of a water goddess;[27] fortunately for scholarship and education, the purchaser then donated the work to the Minneapolis Institute of Art.[28] Unlike Buffalo, its fellow flour-milling giant, Minneapolis does remain committed to the concept of the encyclopedic museum. So do most museums in the United States.

But it is no longer a given that art museums will remain committed to the encyclopedia. Realism, if not cynicism, has replaced the embracing if sugary liberalism that underpinned the *Family of Man*. And there are financial considerations for the encyclopedic museum, especially for museums without substantial endowments, and they converge with the essential end of buying and selling of antiquities without documentation of circulation before 1970. Fewer objects come to market that museums or collectors can acquire with confidence: provenance brings a market premium, and the $75 million raised by Albright-Knox attests to the value that its long-standing museum ownership conferred. Furthermore, the announcement in 2018 by President Emmanuel Macron that France would return twenty-six objects to Benin has unsettled the future for the past. Some museums may just find the uncertainty about the future of some kinds of antiquities a problem they would simply like to avoid: if you want the global, they may say, why not collect just the world's art of the present? Should you just remove them from your website, without visible explanation?[29] In the university, one could see this as the difference between a department of political science and one of history: the former operates without a foundation if the latter is not present. Without grounding in the past, the present becomes a tiny layer on the complexity of human activity. As the globe's residents increasingly play roles far beyond the lands of their birth, they may benefit in myriad ways from art that attests to their ancestors' achievements. The Aztec goddess who herself traveled from Mexico to Buffalo to Minneapolis has gone to a city where, according to the 2000 and 2010 US Census, the population of self-identified "persons of Hispanic or Latino origin" increased by 38 percent in just a decade. For those who see value in the encyclopedic museum, that museum should comprise not just the globe but also the history of the globe.

1. Megan O'Neil, "Collecting Pre-Hispanic Art in Los Angeles," in *Found in Translation: Design in California and Mexico 1915–1985*, ed. Wendy Kaplan (Los Angeles: Los Angeles County Museum of Art, 2017), 176. See also Suzanne Muchnic, *LACMA So Far: Portrait of a Museum in the Making* (San Marino, CA: Huntington Library, Art Collections, and Botanical Gardens), 2015. Muchnic notes the important donations of Pre-Columbian and their display in the Ahmanson Building after its 1965 opening.
2. Joanne Pillsbury, "The Pan-American: Nelson Rockefeller and the Arts of Ancient Latin America," in "The Nelson A. Rockefeller Vision: Arts of Africa, Oceania, and the Americas," ed. Alisa LaGamma et al., special issue, *The Metropolitan Museum of Art Bulletin* 72, no. 1 (Summer 2014): 18–37.
3. Henry Hawley, "Pre-Columbian Art at Cleveland," *Apollo* 68, no. 22 (1963): 489–93.
4. Prescott Dunbar, *The New Orleans Museum of Art: The First Seventy-Five Years* (Baton Rouge: Louisiana State University Press, 1990). The Benin object is illustrated in the pages following 56, no page numbers.
5. Dunbar, *The New Orleans Museum of Art*, 40–41.
6. Dunbar, *The New Orleans Museum of Art*, 242–47.
7. Georges-Hébert Germain, *Un Musée dans la ville: Une histoire du Musée des Beaux-Arts de Montréal* (Montreal: Musée des Beaux-Arts de Montréal, 2007), 63.
8. Germain, *Un Musée dans la ville*, 144.
9. Pál Kelemen, *Stepchild of the Humanities, Art of the Americas, as Observed in Five Decades* (Tucson: Southwestern Mission Research Center, University of Arizona, 1979), 11.
10. April Dammann, *The Exhibitionist: Earl Stendahl, Art Dealer as Impresario* (Santa Monica, CA: Angel City, 2011). Dammann notes that the gallery itself opened in 1921, selling all sorts of inventory, including handmade chocolates.
11. The Des Moines Art Center acquired their only Pre-Hispanic works, a pair of Nayarit tomb figures, from André Emmerich in 1964. Their online record reads "Purchased with funds from the Coffin Fine Arts Trust; Nathan Emory Coffin Collection of the Des Moines Art Center, 1964.4.1–.2."
12. The online record for Dayton reads: "Colima dog, Terra-cotta with red slip; Height: 9¼ inches; Museum purchase, 1960.15."
13. Ernest Lehman, *North by Northwest: Screenplay* (London: Faber & Faber, 2000), 114–15.
14. "Mr. Bliss had got things from Earl Stendhal and then his son Al Stendhal—we got occasionally something from him. Mr. Bliss had also dealt with John Wise who died shortly after I arrived—but I think we did get something from Wise. I don't even remember from whom we got exactly all these things. But the dealers we dealt with mostly probably were Ed Merrin, Alphonse Jax,

André Emmerich a little bit. Who else? We got a few things from John Stokes." From Elizabeth P. Benson interview, https://www.doaks.org/research/library-archives/dumbarton-oaks-archives/historical-records/oral-history-project/elizabeth-p.-benson.

15. *Art before Columbus*, 10 May–14 June 1964, Museum of Art, Munson-Williams-Proctor Institute, Utica, New York, 1964.
16. For example, as André Emmerich prepared a review of *Before Cortés*, he wrote to MWP director Ed Dwight, comparing the now-Metropolitan Olmec Baby (Museum of Primitive Art, New York, at the time) with an object in the MWP. "I don't know what you think," wrote Emmerich on 5 June 1970, "but it doesn't come close to touching your (and once our) baby!!" flattering the taste of Dwight. Letter Emmerich to Dwight, MWP files examined July 2019. This Olmec baby, sold by Emmerich to Dwight, was later determined to have little evidence of authenticity (report of Ellen Howe, dated 15 June 2001, file examined at MWP July 2019).
17. *Before Cortés: Sculpture of Middle America* was a seminal exhibition at the Metropolitan Museum of Art in 1971, bringing together masterworks from Mexican and US museums, as well as private collections. Josué Saenz of Mexico was the single largest private lender, and a work from his collection graced the cover. Although the planning and execution of the transformation would take a decade, both Nelson Rockefeller and the Metropolitan Museum administration agreed that the Museum of Primitive Art would become part of the Met on the occasion of *Before Cortés*.
18. The "melting pot" concept favored only Europeans, ignoring the Native Americans, African Americans, Latino Americans, and Asian Americans. "Whiteness" studies gained widespread recognition with the publication of Matthew Frye Jacobson's *Whiteness of a Different Color: European Immigrants and the Alchemy of Race* (Cambridge: Harvard University Press, 1999).
19. Edward Steichen, *The Family of Man* (New York: Museum of Modern Art, 1955), 184–85.
20. Eric J. Sandeen, *Picturing an Exhibition: "The Family of Man" and 1950s America* (Albuquerque: University of New Mexico Press, 1955), chap. 2; see also https://fkmagazine.lv/2018/07/02/the-family-of-man-the-photography-exhibition-that-everybody-loves-to-hate/.
21. Megan E. O'Neil and Mary E. Miller, "An Artistic Discovery of America," in Kaplan, *Found in Translation*, 162–67.
22. Press release, Munson Williams Proctor Art Institute, 7 September 2000: "MWPAI Deaccessions Precolumbian Objects to Enhance Permanent Collection." Examined in the files of the MWPAI July 2019.
23. Email from Paul Schweizer to Claudia Giancola, 15 March 2010, detailing the William Spratling drawing that former director Ed Dwight had received from André Emmerich in 1969. The purchase was completed on 12 January 1970.
24. Press release, Munson Williams Proctor Art Institute, 7 September 2000: "MWPAI Deaccessions Precolumbian Objects to Enhance Permanent Collection," 3. Examined in the files of the MWPAI July 2019.
25. Archives of American Art—this is AE declining to take back objects.

26. Some Buffalo citizens fought the sales, to no avail: Randy Kennedy, "Despite Foes, Buffalo Museum Makes $18 Million in Auction," *New York Times*, 21 March 2007.
27. *Highlights of Historic Objects Offered by the Albright-Knox Art Gallery*, sales cat. (New York: Sotheby's, 2007), 112–17.
28. The online text reads, "gift of Curtis Galleries, Minneapolis. 2009.33IS."
29. The Montreal Museum of Fine Arts has previously published an extensive printed catalog of their Pre-Hispanic collection. However, none of their Pre-Hispanic objects can currently be located. Here is the statement they put up on their website regarding collections, without editing (https://www.mbam.qc.ca/en/collections/):

    The Museum's rich collections are divided into six major sections distributed among the five pavilions of the Museum complex. Each of which focusses on a particularly strong aspect of the holdings.

    Today, 158 years after its founding, the Montreal Museum of Fine Arts is more forward-looking than ever! This institution is not a government-run museum, but relies on generous patrons for the expansion of its encyclopedic heritage collection, which has risen to a historic total of 43,000 works.

    The Museum's collections were studied and reinstalled in 2001 and in 2011, prior to the opening of the Claire and Marc Bourgie Pavilion of Quebec and Canadian Art, and in 2016 for the inauguration of the Michal and Renata Hornstein Pavilion for Peace. In the wake of this new expansion, the MMFA will undergo a major transformation. Thousands of works will be moved and reinstalled in the various pavilions, in a domino effect generated by the advent of a fifth pavilion. They will be displayed in spectacular exhibition spaces where visitors will be able to admire the Museum's masterpieces from a new viewpoint.

    This web page was created to provide an overview of the collection. Please note that it is impossible to present the entire collection at once. For that reason, the works shown here are not necessarily on display at the present time.

BIOGRAPHICAL NOTE ON THE EDITOR

Donatien Grau currently serves as head of contemporary programs at the Musée d'Orsay, Paris. He holds doctoral degrees in French and comparative literature from the Sorbonne; in philological and historical sciences from the École des Hautes Études, Paris; and a DPhil from Oxford University. He served as advisor to Azzedine Alaïa for the couturier's not-for-profit exhibition space, the Galerie (2014–17) and curated the inaugural exhibition of the reopening of the Getty Villa, Malibu, *Plato in L.A.* (2018). He has published widely on the arts and culture of the Roman Empire, on nineteenth- and twentieth-century literary and art history, as well as on contemporary art and culture. His most recent publication is *Living Museums* (2020).

INDEX

Getty Research Institute Publications Program
Mary E. Miller, Director, *Getty Research Institute*
Gail Feigenbaum, *Associate Director*

Published by the Getty Research Institute, Los Angeles
Getty Publications
1200 Getty Center Drive, Suite 500
Los Angeles, California 90049-1682
getty.edu/publications

Mary Christian, *Editor*
Laurie Bolewitz, *Editorial Coordinator*
Jeffrey Cohen, *Designer*
Suzanne Watson, *Production*

Distributed in the United States and Canada by the University of Chicago Press
Distributed outside the United States and Canada by Yale University Press, London

Type composed in Macklin Text and Macklin Sans

Printed in the United States of America

Library of Congress Cataloging-in-Publication Data
Names: Grau, Donatien, editor, interviewer (expression) | Fumaroli, Marc, interviewee (expression) | Getty Research Institute, issuing body.
Title: Under discussion : the encyclopedic museum / edited by Donatien Grau.
Description: Los Angeles : Getty Research Institute, [2021] | Includes bibliographical references and index. | Summary: "Are encyclopedic museums still relevant? In almost thirty interviews, Donatien Grau probes some of the world's most prominent thinkers, international arts officials, museum leaders, artists, architects, and arts journalists on the past, present, and future of the encyclopedic museum model"— Provided by publisher.
Identifiers: LCCN 2020039170 (print) | LCCN 2020039171 (ebook) | ISBN 9781606067192 (paperback) | ISBN 9781606067208 (ebook)
Subjects: LCSH: Museums—Philosophy. | Museums—Social aspects. | LCGFT: Interviews.
Classification: LCC AM7 .U495 2021 (print) | LCC AM7 (ebook) | DDC 069—dc23
LC record available at https://lccn.loc.gov/2020039170
LC ebook record available at https://lccn.loc.gov/2020039171